Balancing
Heaven and Earth

Also by Robert A. Johnson

Balancing
Heaven and Earth

A Memoir

Robert A. Johnson
with Jerry M. Ruhl

HarperOne
An Imprint of HarperCollins*Publishers*

This book is dedicated to the many godparents who made life possible for me as I went from one stage to another of my life.

—*Robert A. Johnson*

HarperOne

BALANCING HEAVEN AND EARTH: *A Memoir.* Copyright © 1998 by Robert A. Johnson and Jerry Michael Ruhl. All rights reserved. Printed in the United States of America. No part of this book may be used or reproduced in any manner whatsoever without written permission except in the case of brief quotations embodied in critical articles and reviews. For information, address HarperCollins Publishers, 195 Broadway, New York, NY 10007.

HarperCollins Web site: http://www.harpercollins.com

HarperCollins®, 📖®, and HarperOne™ are trademarks of HarperCollins Publishers.

Book design by Martha Blegen

Library of Congress Cataloging-in-Publication Data

Johnson, Robert A.
    Balancing heaven and earth : a memoir of visions, dreams, and realizations / Robert A. Johnson, Jerry M. Ruhl.
        ISBN 978-0-06-251506-3
        1. Johnson, Robert A. 2. Psychologists—United States—Biography. 3. Spiritual biography—United States. I. Ruhl, Jerry M. II. Title.
    BF109.J64A3   1998
    150'.92
    [B]—DC21   97-22306

15 16 RRDH 20 19 18 17 16

Contents

Preface

This book is about the evolution of consciousness as told through one remarkable life. Robert A. Johnson has always lived close to the collective unconscious, which has been both his curse and his blessing. His story is principally an inner journey guided by powerful dreams, visions, and synchronistic events. Others have written about such things, but it is rare to find someone who maintains an ethical obligation to these powerful and mysterious forces. What is most remarkable to me is Robert's example of how to live with a religious attitude in postmodern times.

By *religious attitude* I am not referring to following a path toward redemption or salvation or even necessarily to being a member of a religious institution. A religious attitude relates to the cultivation of soul—an openness to wonder, awe, fear, and reverence with respect to the "other," those numinous forces that exist outside our conscious control. These powers have been called at various times fate, destiny, the hand of God, or, to use Robert's term, the slender threads.

Robert's life is truly guided by slender threads. While most modern people are preoccupied with getting and spending, constantly fretting and struggling to manipulate external reality so that it goes their way, his process follows a different flow. He waits and watches for the slender threads, listens attentively, dialogues with the unconscious, and acts only when a larger pattern has been revealed.

Robert's life story is not lacking in drama, adventure, and humor; he has crossed paths with a fascinating cast of characters that includes Carl Jung, Jiddu Krishnamurti, and an assortment of sages, saints, and sinners. In countless ways his experiences have anticipated the collective concerns of Western society—struggles with loneliness and alienation, a yearning for community, the search for values and personal meaning in a secular culture, the encounter between Eastern and Western philosophies, hunger to connect with something more enduring and of greater circumference than our individual egos.

But like his mentor, Carl Jung, Robert looks upon the outer aspects of his life as incidental, while inner processes have provided the substance and determining value.

I first met Robert nearly a decade ago at a Jungian conference in Colorado. I was already fascinated by the works of Carl Jung and Joseph Campbell and was contemplating leaving an executive position in corporate America to pursue my real passion. Arriving at the conference early, I walked into a reception room and spied Robert sitting shyly in a corner by himself. I recognized him immediately from the photo on his book jackets. Uncharacteristically (for an introvert), I marched up to introduce myself and welcome him. I felt absolute joy that morning. It was one of those all-too-rare instances when one is totally absorbed in Presence, not yearning to be somewhere else, with anyone else, or doing anything else at all. Robert, with his keen sense of feeling, must have picked up on my happiness (he would later tell me that one of the finest acts of devotion to God is simply to be happy), as he asked if we could share lunch. That day, over a picnic in the park, I experienced a true mentor, someone who seemed not only to read my thoughts but also to care about my soul. Our conversation fortified my resolve to leave a career that I had outgrown, and it also planted a seed in me—a seed of belief that I had something of enduring value in my inner life. Robert made me feel valued, and I know he has that effect on many people.

We corresponded for several months before I took Robert up on his offer to visit his quiet home overlooking a beach in southern California. Words do not capture the experience of simply being with Robert, a calm and gentle man who speaks in conversation with the same flowing, musical quality that makes his lectures so magical. His presence brings a peacefulness and a sense of organic order, like being dropped down into a tranquil Japanese garden in which human creation and the matrix of nature are in harmony.

Over the next several years I indulged in his hospitality during many visits, while also completing a Ph.D. in depth psychology with Robert's encouragement. During this time I listened to hundreds of hours of tapes from Robert's private collection, and time and time again I felt a shock of insight in response to some religious commentary or psychological gem contained in one of Robert's lectures.

In 1995 I learned that Robert had chosen to stop writing, a decision that characteristically was made following a dream. In the dream he had sat down at his desk, only to discover that the fountain pen he was using no longer contained ink but was filled only with water. Despite the encouragement of friends, colleagues, and his publisher, Robert was convinced that the writing stage of his life was over.

A few months later, gazing out at the Pacific and welcoming a new day with the customary Johnson breakfast of fresh carrot juice, I proposed to Robert an idea. Most of his books, starting with the perennial best-seller, *He*, had taken readers on spiritual and psychological journeys by way of myths or folktales—the Parsifal legend, the story of Tristan and Isolde, the myth of Dionysus. Yet what about the myth of Robert Johnson? His life itself, I suggested, was the best example of how to find balance and healing in turbulent times. In his seventy-fifth year he could look back on that life with perspective and recognize the slender threads at work. If he would allow me to tape a series of conversations, I would provide the bulk of the writing, and together we might develop a different sort of book, not strictly a biography or even an autobiography, but a story of the unfolding of consciousness within one individual. Dr. Jung had produced such a work in his *Memories, Dreams, Reflections*, but that was a different life in a different era.

Robert heard me out and said he would have to sit with the idea. A few hours later he emerged from his office with a tiny hand-held tape recorder. It was settled, and our interviews began that day. Over the next several months many hours were spent in conversation, first reviewing Robert's life and later amplifying key themes and issues that readers might find helpful for their own development. In the creation of this book I also drew upon Robert's journals and numerous unpublished lectures, which previously have been available only to a lucky few. While reviewing the manuscript, Robert made many helpful suggestions and, I am delighted to say, even took laptop computer in hand and began writing again.

When Robert's first book was published in 1974, the general public was just beginning to rediscover the power and timeless wisdom of myths and folktales. He was one of the first to present Dr. Jung's rich but complex theories with simple elegance and grace. Anyone who has delved into the twenty volumes of Jung's collected works knows that simple is not easy; it requires an in-depth understanding to make such psychological theory digestible.

For a time, Robert was fond of telling a self-effacing story about being elevated to near sainthood in a small Indian village based upon the villagers' observation that he did not eat very much, say very much, or do very much. He joked that these were his primary credentials for addressing the religious life. Of course, what those intuitive villagers in India perceived in Robert went much deeper. Their understanding went to the very heart of the matter. Robert's example has had lasting influence on my own writing, my therapeutic approach, and my daily life. It is my hope that this book will extend that experience to many others.

I would like to thank my wife, Jordis, for her ongoing support during the gestation of this book, a nine-month period when she also was carrying our new son, Oliver. It was a joyous race to see who would arrive first, and "little Ollie" beat the finished manuscript by two weeks.

Jerry M. Ruhl, Ph.D.
July 17, 1997
Denver, Colorado

Prologue:

Slender Threads

It is an audacious notion to put forth in this age of science and willful determination that one's existence is somehow inspired, guided, and even managed by unseen forces outside our control. Whether called fate, destiny, or the hand of God, slender threads are at work bringing coherence and continuity to our lives. Over time they weave a remarkable tapestry.

What are these slender threads? Being in a particular place at just the right time, meeting someone who steers you in an unforeseen direction, the unexpected appearance of work or money or inspiration just when they are most needed. These are the mysterious forces that guide us and shape who we are. They are the patterns that give meaning to our experiences.

Some people seem to exert more free will over their lives. They make plans, set goals, and proceed with full confidence of being in control. That has never worked for me, despite my best attempts.

Looking back from the vantage point of seventy-six years, it is now clear that my existence has always been managed by some benevolent fate. It has taken the better part of a lifetime to accept this idea, and much of the time I still don't understand it. But I have learned to stop fighting it. In youth, I floundered around and followed the slender threads only when I felt like it or when they seemed to be taking me where I already wanted to go. I often struggled to oppose them. As the fruit of my old age, however, I have finally come to trust the mystery. The mystery is this: there is one right thing and only one right thing to do at every moment. We can either follow or resist the slender threads.

We all have free will, and therefore we can try to force situations in life. Perhaps that struggle is what keeps us bound to this earth. But I have gradually learned to accept that the slender threads possess greater intelligence and wisdom than our scrambling egos can ever attain. In good times and bad, one slender thread after another has seen me through and, together, they have shaped what I know and who I am.

This notion of slender threads is essentially a religious idea. I am not much at home with the old-time religion, at least not as practiced in my own culture. And so I often find myself searching for new terms to say old things. I do know, however, that my life is managed by a coherent and intelligent entity of some sort, a guiding hand or patron saint, if you will.

My loyalty to the heavenly world was won forever after a serious wounding claimed me for an interior life. But I was not removed from the necessity of simultaneously building an earthly life. This became the central challenge for me—learning how to balance two realms.

To side with either of these two great realities—heaven and earth—is an error. Over time I came to appreciate that a middle place in which both realms are honored is not only the safest place, it also is the ecstatic place, the holy place. If one works faithfully and patiently at this task of balancing heaven and earth, eventually one may even realize something more remarkable: that the two worlds are in fact one.

Robert A. Johnson
January 6, 1997
Encinitas, California

~

The Golden World:

Living with Visions of the Divine

It all began with the crash of a car against a brick wall and the small knee of an eleven-year-old boy caught in between.

I had been visiting my father, and I was enjoying the late summer afternoon as I made my way home on roller skates. My parents lived three miles apart in Portland, Oregon. I was midway between these poles of my life, almost exactly between my father's house and my mother's house. Certainly the split between my two parents was a place of danger. I decided to buy a Coca-Cola at the local drugstore and was just going in the door with five pennies clenched in my hand when two cars collided in the street before me. My left leg was through the door, but the right one was still touching the sidewalk when there was a crunch of steel and brick, a rush of adrenaline, and the sickening realization that it was too late, my leg was pinned between brick and chrome, the knee crushed. In that instant everything seemed to move in slow motion. A second earlier would have caught both of my legs as I entered the drugstore, while a second later would have had me safely inside the building. But it was that second, just that second, that everything was aligned to give me a devastating blow but leave me just short of death.

I awoke on the pavement, dazed, feeling no pain but bleeding profusely since the main artery of my leg had been severed. The five pennies that I intended to spend on a soft drink were still clenched tightly in my hand. A circle of people looked down at me. Someone asked where I lived, and I managed to whisper my home telephone number. I was weak and nauseated when an alert nurse who lived nearby came running to provide first aid. She improvised a tourniquet, an ambulance rushed me to the nearby Immanuel Hospital, and a bone specialist was summoned to surgery. When they wheeled me into the emergency room, the hospital gurney bumped the doorjamb, a bump that felt like sheer agony. Then came the oblivion of anesthesia.

I knew nothing more until the middle of the night, when I awoke sweaty and shivering in a metal bed, my leg held down by a heavy cast that ran from my neck to my toes. I felt nauseous and horribly weak. No one knew that the sutured artery in my leg had broken loose and was hemorrhaging again inside the cast. I was slowly bleeding to death, and I began drifting away to another world. I knew precisely what was happening, at least in its psychic dimensions. I set my feet against the downward spiral and determined not to die, resisting it with all my willpower. But at a specific moment I crossed a divide—it felt like that bump against the doorjamb—and suddenly I was in a glorious world.

It was pure light, gold, radiant, luminous, ecstatically happy, perfectly beautiful, purely tranquil, joy beyond bound. I wasn't the least bit interested in anything on the earthly side of the divide; I could only revel at what was before me. We have words for this side of reality but none to describe the other side. It was all that any mystic ever promised of heaven, and I knew then that I was in possession of the greatest treasure known to humankind. Later in life I heard the religious scholar Mircea Eliade refer to this magnificent realm as the Golden World, which is exactly right, and I have called it that ever since.

But I was not to leave this earthly world on that August day in 1932; instead I was only to be teased with a brief preview of the Golden World that would figure so profoundly throughout the rest of my life. An alert night nurse came by and noticed blood leaking through the underside of my cast. She set off an alarm and had me whisked off to surgery, where they quickly tried to transfuse blood. My veins were so badly collapsed that I still have ribbons of white scars down my arms where they made incisions, searching desperately to find a vein.

Inwardly, I was harshly interrupted in my timeless ecstasy of paradise by a summons to go back to the earthly realm. I resisted this as strenuously as I had fought the crossing from earth to heaven, but to no avail. I awoke on the surgery table convulsed with pain, hearing the busy sounds of an emergency room, and looking up into a nightmare of tubes and a circle of masked faces peering down at me. One of these, the surgeon, said, "So, you are alive!"

Yes, I was alive but reluctantly so. No one can look upon even the antechamber of heaven without a lifetime of regret at what has been lost. Seeing through this mundane world to the golden, archetypal world was marvelous beyond description, but at the tender age of eleven it was almost too much. I was so blinded by the golden light of the divine world that I was spoiled for regular life. A curtain separating the two realms was for me forever parted. In the morning of that fateful day I was a giddy kid; by midnight I was a very old man in a boy's body.

The physician initially told my mother it was doubtful I would survive, as this was the age before antibiotics. My mother later said that after being brought back from the lifesaving surgery I emerged out of the stupor of the ether and sat upright in bed, and my first words were that I wanted to be buried in the Lincoln Memorial Cemetery in Portland, bringing terror to her already worried face. Apparently I said very little about my Golden World experience.

My leg began to heal in the next few weeks. The blood system, however, never attained proper function. Gangrene set in, and first one, and then a second, amputation was required. Fortunately, both were below the knee, a lesser degree of handicap than it might have been. I spent two months recovering in the hospital before they sent me home. I philosophize now that I was wounded just enough to set off a deep experience of the inner world but not enough to end my life. Just enough!

~

I LIVED WITH DESPAIR for some time following the auto crash. Managing crutches, getting used to an artificial leg, adapting to the world as a handicapped person—all these were difficult enough, but it was the loss of the Golden World after having seen the pure source of beauty that was the most difficult. It's better to live in oblivion of that world than to be teased by it.

I had no context within which to understand what had taken place. I might have believed that my Golden World experience was just a hallucination brought on by anesthesia or physical shock. But at the age of sixteen I saw the glory of paradise again, and this time it was even more glorious because I was fully conscious. Once again I would experience what a biblical passage describes as the morning stars singing together. William Blake knew that world well and captured it for us as only an inspired poet can do:

> To see the World in a Grain of Sand
> And a heaven in a Wild Flower,
> Hold Infinity in the palm of your hand
> And Eternity in an hour.

This passage is from Blake's "Auguries of Innocence." From his writings I know that this poet had a direct experience of the Golden World, which he called Imaginative Vision. In his preface to "The Jerusalem," Blake speaks of that composition as having been dictated to him, as though it came as a revelation. I know now that many others have shared my experience of heaven and have returned to tell of it, but only the seers, poets, and artists come close to conveying its glory.

At the age of sixteen I was visited with a clumsy urge for independence, to go out and conquer the material world and make my place in it. I was very much like Parsifal, the legendary youth in the medieval story who longed to become a knight. Parsifal set off in search of adventure, hoping to prove his manhood, and instead stumbled into a profoundly religious experience in the Grail Castle. Like Parsifal, I stumbled into the Grail Castle as a youth and could comprehend it no better at sixteen than I had at the age of eleven. Here is how it happened.

I had never worked as a young man, not even on a paper route or any other odd job. It was 1937, and the economy was barely nudging itself out of the Depression. I looked around Portland for something to do, but no one would hire me. An artificial leg was a real limitation for the kinds of menial labor that a sixteen-year-old could do.

After observing several of my false starts, my stepfather decided to intervene. He pulled some strings and arranged to get me a night job at the Del Monte canning factory in Vancouver, Washington, where he worked as a manager. The factory was twenty miles from Portland across the Columbia River. I was to work seven days a week, twelve-hour shifts, on night duty. The pay was fifty cents an hour. I saw this as the perfect opportunity to exercise my independence and demonstrate my manhood.

I arrived a half hour early for my first shift and was swallowed up by a great mechanical beast, the Depression-era factory. Of course I wasn't used to sleeping during the day and arrived primed with excitement at 6 P.M. I was pumped full of adrenaline and ready to take on the world.

It was hot and noisy in the factory, a dark and ugly building that stretched on for more than a block. The tin-roofed cannery employed more than a thousand workers. Rows and rows of women were peeling pears by hand with curved knives; farm boys twice my size were scurrying about loading and unloading carts of fruit. People were shouting and cursing over the din of machinery. It was a chaos of activity, noise, and sheer ugliness, an angry existence, with people snarling at one another and swearing at the tops of their lungs. It had been a warm summer, and tons of pears and peaches had ripened early. The cannery was running twenty-four hours a day to get the ripe fruit canned. My shoes stuck to the floor and made a sucking noise with every step across the concrete. My job was to check the cans of fruit as they came spitting out of the cooker in an unending stream.

I was just getting the hang of my new job when the night foreman decided to pirate labor to help with a bottleneck farther down the production line. My job of inspecting cans was expendable. I knew nothing of fending for myself in the work world, and I soon found myself on one of the most grueling jobs in the factory, hand-trucking four-hundred-pound loads of hot cans from cooker to warehouse. I had never been near a two-wheeled hand truck before, let alone one with cans stacked high above my head that had to be carefully balanced. With my first venture I spilled the entire stack of cans across the floor and was roundly chewed out by the foreman. I wasn't very strong, and the job was far beyond my ability, but I was too determined to admit defeat. I clung to the task at hand and decided that this was a true test of my manhood: either I was going to prove myself or die in the attempt. As the night wore on it was nearly the latter.

I spent the next six hours pushing that hand truck from one end of the building to the other. Sometime after midnight I was given a short break, and I was relieved when the foreman assigned the job to someone else. But after my break he sent me back to the same exhausting task, and again I went to it without saying a word. By this time the junction of my leg and the artificial leg was soaked with blood. The blood had run down into my shoe, and my wool sock was so wet that you could have wrung it out, but I prided myself on not complaining to anyone. This was my test, and I was going to do it or die. I don't know what was worse—the pain from my leg or my first untempered look at the harshness and ugliness of the world. They merged together in my mind into pure misery.

At 4:30 A.M. I punched my time card and walked out into the damp night air. As I started my borrowed car I suddenly realized that if I didn't see something beautiful I would not survive. I needed to get home, soak in a bathtub, and collapse into bed, but another need was even more powerful. I had to have the beauty of life confirmed again, or I felt that I could not continue to live. I drove up into the hills west of Portland, where I knew I would find a view overlooking the valley, reaching to the four snowcapped mountains that surround the city. This was my answer to the compelling need for something to counterbalance the horror of the preceding hours.

I parked the car and hobbled out onto a promontory just in time for the sunrise. The sun began to inch its way over the horizon, and—unbelievably—the Golden World shone forth again with all its glory. The same world I had known at age eleven, the same golden light, the same condensation of pure beauty—it was all there. It was the same world that I had lost and mourned several years before, and I knew it with an intimacy and delight past any other value in human life. At eleven, I had been forced onto the edge of the next world, but by some quirk of fate I had recovered and reentered human existence. This time, at the age of sixteen, it was the same Golden World, but my reception of it was different. There was more consciousness in me. Before, I was a child blundering across a corner of heaven by accident, but I now had the consciousness of a young adult, and my birthright had been restored to me.

I can't really say whether I heard, saw, smelled, tasted, or touched that sunrise. No matter. It was an antechamber of heaven, and it was my native land. It lasted for about thirty minutes of clock time, but it was eternity in the heavenly realm. Language fails me when I try to describe what I experienced, so I must again turn to the words of others.

Even Dante, one of the world's greatest poets, finds it nearly impossible to describe his vision of Paradise: "In the heaven that receives most of its light I have been, and have seen things which he who descends from the above neither knows how nor is able to recount." The great American poet Walt Whitman comes closer in his lines referring to the same or a similar Golden World experience. Whitman writes in *Leaves of Grass*:

> As in a swoon, one instant,
> Another sun, ineffable, full-dazzles me,
> And all the orbs I knew, and brighter, unknown orbs;
> One instant of the future land, Heaven's land.

...ry David Thoreau, that lover of solitude and mystical communion with nature, also surely tasted the Golden World, as indicated by these lines from *Walden:*

> I hearing get who had but ears,
> And sight who had but eyes before,
> I moments live who lived but years,
> And truth discern who knew but learning's lore.
>
> I hear beyond the range of sound,
> I see beyond the range of sight,
> New earths, and skies and seas around,
> And in my day the sun doth pale his light.

When the sun was up, I returned to ordinary consciousness. My physical exhaustion came pouring back in, and my leg began to hurt again. I limped back to my car and was quickly pulled back to mundane realities by a flat tire. The Golden World was entirely gone by the time I changed the flat. I was back in a gray existence, desperately tired and disillusioned, my leg hurting; but at least I had the comfort of knowing that the Golden World was not just a once-in-a-lifetime experience. I had been to that sublime realm a second time, it was real, and this time I would never doubt it again. My life would never, could never, be the same.

I don't believe in chance. India has more insight into these things than we do in the West. We don't have a language for comprehending such irrational experiences. In India they talk about an old soul. This term is used to describe someone who is ripe enough to experience the deepest mysteries. If there is such a condition, then perhaps my soul was ripe—ready to be plucked from this life and introduced to another one. The problem was that those hardworking physicians had brought me back to the old realm. I would have to learn to live on earth with an indelible memory of heaven. Much of the rest of my life would be spent seeking a balance between these two realms.

I FERVENTLY BELIEVE that my "accident" in front of that Portland drugstore was no accident. Later in life one of my spiritual teachers told me, "If you had not been injured in an accident at eleven, you would have experienced this contact with the unconscious as a psychosis." I must admit that I tremble at such a statement. If it is true, it reveals to what extent our lives are controlled by those slender threads of an intelligence far superior to our own.

These openings into another realm can be terribly dangerous; indeed, visions of heaven break some people by interrupting their sense of identity and continuity. For years my life seemed upended by this glimpse of the divine. Nothing on this earth could fill my hunger for more of the ecstatic experience. None of the aspirations or goals that seemed to drive other people could hold my interest for long. History is filled with examples of mad ones, monks, sages, and seers who have undergone numinous encounters, and for such souls it becomes nearly impossible to lead an ordinary human life.

Perhaps if one can absorb some of the experience through the physical body, it helps to reduce the overwhelming impact on one's psyche. That seems to have been the case with me. The timing of that auto accident and the result that I would lose one leg and not two has always been fascinating to me in this respect: It wounded me enough to ground me, but not so much as to knock all the life out of me. The wounding was sufficient to claim me for an interior life and loyalty to the Golden World, but it was not so severe that I was removed from the necessity of simultaneously building a life on earth.

It is particularly dangerous to experience a divine vision at such a young age. It is much more tolerable for a mature personality. After thirty minutes of ecstasy on the mountainside that morning, I spent the next ten years in terrible suffering—not physical suffering, but the subtle hell of loneliness and isolation. I was doing all the standard things in life, but they meant very little to me. My visions came close to destroying the practicality in me, the usual human dimensions of existence. I went into solitude and found what solace I could in music and by surrounding myself with animals: homing

_, an aquarium of tropical fish. I spent hour after hour in my own world, an inner realm. All this time I was getting top grades in school, but my heart was never really in such achievements. My allegiance was elsewhere.

I now believe that many young people experience the Golden World to some degree. The poet Wordsworth aptly wrote that we come into this world trailing clouds of glory. We are born whole, and, God willing, we die whole.

Children come into the world with that sense of celebration and delight in the awesomeness of life. Then we eat of that wonderful, terrible fruit depicted in the story of the Garden of Eden, and our lives become divided. In childhood we have innocent wholeness, which then is transformed into informed separateness. If one is lucky, a second transformation occurs later in life, a transformation into informed wholeness. A proverb puts it this way: in life our task is to go from unconscious perfection to conscious imperfection and then to conscious perfection.

As we grow up, most of us retain an intuition that heavenly wholeness exists somewhere, however harsh our lives may be. The boundary between the two worlds seems to be particularly thin during adolescence, a condition that does not occur again until we reach the age of forty-five or fifty. Then there is a chance to experience the Golden World again. Unfortunately, adults often dismiss such experiences as "only a dream" or "childish talk." We tell our children to grow up and face the realities of life. As a result, many people give up on ever finding wholeness.

For me, the essence of life comes from these experiences of the Golden World. Such encounters with the divine have been called visionary, mystical, manifestations of cosmic consciousness, or, in secular language, peak experiences. Such experiences were the goal of life in the Middle Ages, when they were referred to as the Unitive Vision.

I am fascinated by the word *ecstatic,* which in its original sense means to stand outside oneself. We work so hard to make a personal self, an "I" or ego, with clarity and continuity. This is extremely valuable, but one pays a price for this "I"—we become small, personal, and limited; we are a highly circumscribed entity in our "I-ness."

The ecstatic experience involves escaping from the "I-ness." This requires that we break the boundaries of our separateness to experience a greater realm, a realm that taxes our finest poets and artists to convey. It is the most valuable experience any person can ever have. The beauty of the Golden World is that one sees a vastness, something so much greater than oneself that one is left speechless with awe, admiration, delight, and rapture.

After childhood, in our twenties and thirties, we are called upon to fulfill the cultural tasks of the society in which we live. In India this is called the householder stage, the time for building careers, raising families, paying bills, meeting all of our social obligations. But at midlife many people hunger again for some glimpse of the Golden World. By the time most of us become adults, we have lost all contact with this world. I only have to look carefully to see the spiritual hunger in the eyes of most Westerners. Rarely do you see radiance in the faces of middle-aged people. And so instead of re-connecting to the ecstatic realm as adults, we see the infamous midlife crisis in which one tries to fill the emptiness with all the extravagant things we have around us. This is the tragedy of many modern lives.

Most of our neuroses come from hunger for the divine, a hunger that too often we try to fill in the wrong way. We drink alcohol, take drugs, or seek momentary highs through the accumulation of material possessions. All the manipulations of the outer world carry with them an unconscious hope of redeeming our lonely, isolated existence.

The experience of paradise in the wholeness of youth is our birthright. It is a gift. However, seeing the Golden World again as an adult has to be earned. It requires inner work, a commitment not just to material success but to bringing some sense of meaning and purpose to one's life. There is a paradox involved here. The Golden World cannot be acquired like a possession, and enlightenment cannot be turned into a project. We do not select an ecstatic experience; rather, it is delivered upon us as a state of grace. However, we can do the necessary inner work so that we are open to and prepared for such experiences when they arrive.

I can't tell you how many times after that morning when I tasted heaven that I went to some high place to watch the sunrise again, hoping to hear the morning stars singing together as they had done at that glorious dawn. I yearned desperately to get a glimpse of that world. Everywhere I went I would find myself looking over the horizon or peering into someone's eyes, hoping to find it. Sometimes I would see just enough of it to tease me and make me feel even worse.

It is ironic that often our breakthroughs into consciousness of the divine grow out of breakdowns in ordinary consciousness. Contacts with the divine may at the time feel like pure suffering, and I sometimes wonder if all suffering is a vision of God too great to bear. The Buddhist tradition informs us that enlightenment is often perceived as tragedy or total disaster from the ego's perspective. Very few people have the intelligence to surrender with dignity to forces greater than themselves. Most of us have to be hit in the head, or in my case the leg, and thereby forced into a realization of the Golden World.

I hate it when people say after a tragedy, "Well, it's all for the best" or "It's all in God's plan." It also is said that "Man's tragedy is God's opportunity." These sayings are true, but they are almost always said at the wrong time by the wrong people. Out of mouths that parrot them like verses in a greeting card, they are false.

I recall a Zen story in which a master is sitting in his hut when a student comes to him and asks, "What is Zen?" The master points to the moon. Time passes, and one day the master goes into town. While he is away, the student is charged with minding the monastery. A young stranger comes to visit and asks the student, "What is Zen?" Recalling the action of the master, the student points to the moon. Just at that moment, the master comes home, witnesses the conversation, and goes into a rage. He pulls out a knife and cuts off the student's pointing finger.

This is a harsh lesson but one intended to demonstrate that consciousness that truly knows Zen is different from the consciousness of one who is just quoting, abstracting, or theorizing. Mundane comments about other people's suffering deserve to be cut off. Even if you say the right thing, when it is said at the wrong time it is wrong. Or, worse yet, if a wrong person says the right thing, then it is most certainly wrong.

I also believe that the ache of loneliness relates to knowing there is something more than one can have. If you hadn't known it at first, it would never bother you. I was hungry for the Golden World that I had tasted and then lost, but I could not articulate that hunger. I can tell the moment people walk into a room if they are searching like I was for a taste of heaven; their eyes scan the landscape as if they were hunting, but most probably if you asked what they are hunting for they could not tell you.

When people enter therapy today with such a hunger, many health care professionals try to talk them out of their experiences; too many mainstream therapists pathologize the client's dreams and visions and make every attempt to get this neurotic individual back into the humdrum world of "normality." Alternatively, individuals can be taken aside and given some tools to maintain this process, find their own balance, and live with a foot in both worlds. Of course, to help someone find this balance assumes that the helper knows how to do it.

Nowadays we often don't recognize when someone has been shaken by a view of heaven. Yet, the meaninglessness of the modern world arises from having a taste of something so glorious that the beholder can neither find it again nor settle for anything less. There is an old Christian proverb that says, You would not search for Me if you had not first known Me. This applies to anyone who remembers glimpses of the Golden World. Each of us can become stuck in egotism, which is merely a half-consciousness, suspended between two worlds and continually yearning for something that is scarcely re-membered. How does one continue to live on the face of the earth when he or she is half blinded and spoiled for anything less?

Dr. Carl Jung was one of the few voices in the modern world who even addressed such a thing. Freud said the human personality is nothing but the ego and that the unconscious is essentially a scrap heap of leftover conflicts with your parents and the society around you. Dr. Jung said something very different—that the earthly world and the Golden World are two faces of one reality. He believed that the ego is the master of its own little separate domain but that there is a larger, more encompassing Self. It is a lifetime's work to recon-cile the earthly world and the Golden World, the ego and the Self.

Strange. The automobile accident that morning in Portland nearly ended my life, but I have never regretted it or its outcome. Ironically, one way of constellating the Golden World may be to reach the most desperate situation tolerable, as both my experience in the hospital and again in the steam and din of the canning factory were ugly and terrifying.

When I visit Portland I often make a pilgrimage to the street where my leg was sacrificed. The building is still standing, and I can still see the damaged brick near the door. And although the canning factory has long since been torn down, I also drive into the hills out-side Portland to watch the sun rise and remember that morning when the stars sang to me. If it were not for yet another visitation of the heavenly realm many years later, I would have to finish my story by recounting the perpetual loneliness of a fruitless search for the ever elusive Golden World. But it would come again.

2

Finding My True Family:

The Need for Godparents to Nurture Spiritual Growth

The dilemma of my life has been how to live in two worlds, balancing heaven and earth. After my accident I chose, or perhaps was chosen, to remain in this earthly world. But I could never forget the Golden World, and this led to immense suffering, despair, and loneliness, as nothing else ever compared with the heavenly realm. The accomplishment of my life has been to find some synthesis, to learn that heaven (and hell) is not some other time or place but right here, right now; but it would take decades of struggle for me to understand this.

I came into this world on May 26, 1921, an only child born to Alexius Johnson and Gladys Williamson. It is still amazing to me that I ever made it to adulthood. In thinking back on my adolescence, I am in awe that my life held together at all, given the nature of my inner experiences and the lack of understanding within my own family.

My father was a weak man and a tyrant. One of my earliest memories, probably at about the age of four or five, is of him announcing in a big display that he could take no more and was leaving us forever. The first time he did this it was terrifying. By the ninth or tenth time it had become a weary joke. In the middle of one of these performances I ran upstairs to my room to hide. He followed me up and demanded that I come out so he could say goodbye "for the last time." He dragged me out from under my bed, only to hand me a dollar bill and insist that was his gift to me marking our final farewell. My lifelong disdain for money began at precisely that moment.

Of course, he returned within a few days, and one night at dinner I couldn't help but blurt out, "I thought you were gone forever. Why do you keep coming back?"

He had no answer, and I was quickly dispatched by my mother to my bedroom to learn some manners.

My mother eventually could no longer tolerate my father, so when he started receiving a government pension for war injuries, he moved to a boardinghouse three miles away. Everyone was greatly relieved.

~

ALEXIUS JOHNSON WAS BORN IN SWEDEN and immigrated with his parents to America just before World War I. He was twenty-one at the time and quickly gained his citizenship in the new world by enlisting in the U.S. Army. Apparently there was a shortage of officers at the time, because despite minimal education, he was made an officer and shipped back across the Atlantic Ocean to fight. He was never physically injured, but soon after his release from the service he came down with a severe case of arthritis that eventually turned him into an invalid. His personality was devastated by something I never understood. I don't think it was the war, because he would spin stories about it and pull out his uniform to show me; being in the army may have been the only time he felt really alive. I don't know if he was a hypochondriac before the war, but after he returned to America his arthritis gave him an ideal excuse to hide from life. His fear must have grown out of something from his own childhood. It was a physical fact, however, that the bones of his spine were gradually dissolving and fusing into one another, an extremely painful condition.

Curiously, my father obliterated all ties to his heritage in the old world. As a boy, I never heard a word about his childhood or life back in Sweden. Although he spoke Swedish up to the age of twenty-one, he managed to remove any trace of an accent from his voice. It wasn't until I was sixteen that I heard him speak in his native tongue. We were dining together in a restaurant where we came across a waitress from Sweden who somehow charmed him, and suddenly he began speaking fluent Swedish, which startled me out of my wits, as I had no idea he could speak a foreign language.

The manner in which he cut off all his roots led me to believe that there might have been some painful tragedy in his past. Years later, after his death, I found among his scanty possessions a portrait of his parents. My paternal grandfather appeared to be an unyielding, stern, granitelike figure, with some of my own facial characteristics. I inherited both the Johnson profile and my father's arthritis.

Soon after he was released from the U.S. Army in 1920, my father met my mother, and following a whirlwind courtship they married. Apparently they had a rough time of it from the very beginning, and a little more than a year into the marriage I was born. My father had insisted on an abortion when I was conceived, but my mother would not hear of it. She had difficulty delivering me, but still she managed to pull herself out of bed the next day to apply for a job. As my maternal grandmother told the story, my mother lied to the job interviewer, saying that she could type, secured the job, and began working two days after I was born.

My parents continued to try to make a go of it for some years after my birth, even moving to San Francisco for a year hoping that would improve things, but eventually they divorced.

My father went on to live a miserable, failed life. He sustained himself from a government pension and lived a solitary existence in a dreary upstairs room of a boardinghouse for the remaining twenty years of his life. By his own admission, his life consisted of "killing time," and he insisted on seeing me on Saturdays. After walking the three miles from my mother's household to his boardinghouse, I would ascend the creaky old wooden stairs and invariably find my father in bed staring at the ceiling. The room was dingy, disorderly, gray. He would use my visit as a motivation to get up out of bed, meticulously lacing up his back brace and pulling on some wrinkled clothes. Once he was dressed, we chatted for a few minutes, and then I would leave. It is ironic that my auto accident occurred just halfway between the two houses of my parents as I was returning from a visit with my father. He was hardly an inspiring figure for a young boy, but if I missed more than one visit in a row he would send me a sad, pathetic letter. All of them said essentially the same thing:

> Dear Robert,
> I haven't heard from you in a long time. I'm so-so. Please come visit or write soon.
> *Your Father*

There was nothing to write to him, so eventually I began taking sections out of letters to other people and sending them to him. I couldn't think of a thing to say to my father, he was so miserable. During his final years his time was filled with listening to news broadcasts on the radio, going for short walks around the neighborhood, and puttering around making changes on his back brace.

Later, as an adult, I became aware that I carried two lives on my shoulders, mine and my father's, because he lived out so little of his own potential. To be fair, I must also say that, despite his selfishness, every now and again he would do something exceedingly kind. Before his illness became too debilitating, there were times when he took me down to the harbor in Portland where I could look at the ships, which I loved. He financed my first music lessons and, later, gave me my first car. Although he gave me money and a few material things, he never gave me what I most wanted and needed: a father.

I was in Europe years later in 1949 when word came that my father had died; he was buried by the time I received the telegram. I remember sitting in the street outside the telegraph office trying to comprehend that my father was truly dead. He had been dead to me for such a long time.

AN ONLY CHILD, I was raised by my mother and grandmother. They made sure that I was provided with solid Christian values, a work ethic, and a sound education. What I most wanted, however—feeling and relatedness—they, too, could not provide.

My mother, whose maiden name was Gladys Williamson, was born on a farm in Ontario, Canada, the child of Clara Bell and Robert Williamson. Both the Bell and Williamson families were originally from Scotland, but they had farmed in Canada for several generations. My grandfather, whom I was named after, was a wheelwright who followed his work from Ontario to British Columbia and then on to Spokane, Washington. That is where my parents met and were married. Later, most of the Williamson clan moved to Portland, and that is where I was born.

As thin and sickly as my father was, my mother was just the opposite: strong, sturdy, broad in the shoulders; she had unlimited energy, and she loved to work. She often lamented that there were only eighteen work hours in the day, because the more you worked the faster you would get ahead in life. After teaching herself to type for her first job in Portland, my mother went on to learn accounting, and eventually she climbed the ranks to become the head bookkeeper for a newspaper, the *Oregonian*. She was the breadwinner in our family and the disciplinarian, so in a sense she served as my father.

In many ways my mother was ahead of her time, an extroverted, sensation type, a driven woman with a head for business. She was oriented to the material world and did her best to provide me with material possessions, so I never lacked for food or nice clothes. My mother was always kind to me in terms of what she understood and valued—the physical things of the world—but she had very little feeling sense. As I grew and became more interested in my heritage, I would ask my mother about her life before my birth, and she would reply that the subject was too painful to discuss. My father certainly would have been a trial for anyone, but my mother's solution was to put over her feelings a twenty-foot-thick slab of concrete that no one could penetrate.

One day I asked my mother why I had no brothers or sisters, and she said that she took one look at me and couldn't bear another. The humor of this joke was lost on me, and it wasn't long before I realized that neither of my parents wanted to hear a word about my feelings. And so the only relationship I developed with them was one of courtesy and duty. You can live on a thin diet of courtesy, but it doesn't provide the nourishment that a child requires. My mother's hope was to turn me into a replica of herself, but I refused, so over the years an awkward silence would emerge as soon as we had finished talking about the events of the day. As a result, I was mothered by my maternal grandmother.

After my parents divorced, we went to live in the house of my widowed grandmother, and for me she was the most important figure in our family. An uneducated farm woman, Granny did the cooking and took care of the house while my mother was out working. She was the real feminine presence in our household. She was a strict Baptist, the hellfire-and-damnation variety, so she was quick to punish me if I stepped out of line. I recall a frequent refrain, "You will be sorry. We are near the last days, so you had better shape up now!" Granny didn't like any of the new translations of the Bible, and once said that she "wanted it just the way King James wrote it."

But Granny also was kind, loving, and very protective of me. Within my biological family it was she who was the closest to me temperamentally. Granny taught me to garden and introduced me to music, and she was wonderful at inventing stories. I could always get a story out of her in the evening, but only after my homework and household chores were completed.

Granny had strong opinions about most things, including the proper regimen for maintaining a strong mind and a strong body. Every spring she would roll up a sheet of typing paper and insert a heaping tablespoon of sulfur into the end of it. She then put one end in my mouth and blew in the other end to administer my spring tonic. I would choke and cough from the cloud of sulfur in my nose and throat, which smelled like rotten eggs and tasted like poison. In ancient alchemy sulfur was associated with the devil, and apparently this tonic was designed to blow the devil away with a taste of his own medicine. I tolerated this unwelcome experience for years, but by the time I reached the age of twelve, I was growing pretty tired of it. That year when she prepared to administer her bitter health aid, I surprised her by blowing into the paper first. That was the end of my spring tonic.

The house I grew up in was an old, aristocratic, three-story Victorian structure on a quiet street in Portland. It was a scramble to survive the Depression years, and my mother often juggled two jobs at once. In addition to her work as a bookkeeper, she began redecorating houses. She would collect pictures of show-homes from popular magazines and put them together into incredible hodgepodges that seemed to appeal to people.

When I was eight years of age, my mother decided to remarry. She selected another Swede, a big man named Clifford Lindskoug. Clifford was a foreman in the Del Monte cannery, a hardworking man with solid values. In some ways he was the opposite of my father, but he was not a very clever or inventive person, and I often wondered if my mother chose him because he was so easily dominated. She certainly never gave him any respect. Although he always worked full-time at the cannery, it was she who managed the household finances and doled out allowances both to Clifford and me. I think that after their experience with my father, both my mother and grandmother wanted a man they could rule, and my stepfather filled the bill. He lived like a servant in our house. He was a good man, but docile and very concrete in his thinking.

There was never a quarrel or a raised voice in our household. We were all polite and civil to one another. My stepfather wanted to get to know me and more than once tried to forge a bond by taking me fishing or to a ball game, but I would have very little to do with him. Over time my stepfather and I settled into a truce, and from the time of their marriage until my mother's death twenty-eight years later, we tolerated each other but seldom spoke.

One day many years later when I lived in California, I had an intuition that my mother would die soon. To prepare for her death,

I took the matter into my fantasy life and rehearsed what it would be like to have the phone call telling me she had passed away. I spent many days at this and experienced in advance and in a subtle way what it would be like. I imagined the airplane trip to Portland, the funeral, the worry that they might play some foolish music that would destroy my interior quiet, and on and on. But what would I do with my stepfather? How would we meet when my mother was no longer intermediary between us? Would he usher me out of the house after the funeral and tell me never to bother him again? I did not know and could not even imagine!

When the fantasy became fact some weeks later, I still did not know what reception I would have from my stepfather when I stepped off the airplane in Portland. He was there waiting at the gate, and he took me in his arms, burst into tears, and sought comfort from me. I learned only then that my mother had stood between us and had prevented relatedness between us. She could not stand any feeling quality in the house that she dominated. She was not yet in her grave when I discovered my stepfather for the first time and made friends with him. We had lived in the same house for all those years without any feeling connection between us. We visited occasionally after that, and I was a guest in his home when he later remarried. We corresponded often. I don't remember one letter between us before my mother's death.

So in this odd household in which my mother played the father, my grandmother the mother, and my stepfather the servant, we lived a tolerable existence, but one that never felt like home to me.

The whole meaning of my life at this time was my Golden World experience, that incredible dawn in the hills outside Portland. But I had no way of explaining this or even understanding it myself. Hundreds of times I went hiking in solitude, hoping for a glimpse of heaven again. But I didn't see a scrap of it, which made me more and more lonely and miserable. It was as if for a few brief moments I had viewed the world in color and then had to go back to a black-and-white existence. Maybe once a year or so I would go around a corner and see a bed of flowers or a slant of sunshine, and for just the smallest instant I would recall the Golden World experience, but it was not enough to nurture me. One can die of alienation and meaninglessness, and I very nearly did.

Following the accident, I was out of school for a year, hobbling around the house on crutches. The public school system sent a special tutor to our home to help me complete the second half of seventh grade. She came by streetcar for an hour twice a week, and she was so good at teaching me how to learn that I not only caught up, I soon surpassed my classmates. Prior to the accident I had skidded by in school without much real interest, but after the accident I never received anything less than top grades.

My parents were good to me, but they didn't have the foggiest idea of what I was talking about or what I needed. My mother was such a dominant person that we either had to do things her way or back off and not talk at all. I tried doing what was expected of me, getting good grades in school, but I also rebelled against what didn't belong to me. It was difficult because I couldn't say what did belong to me; it was just a vacancy and an emptiness. If an angel or magic fairy had come along and asked for three wishes, I wouldn't even have known what to ask for to fill that loneliness; I only felt a lack.

PORTLAND WAS A ROUGH AND TUMBLE TOWN of sailors and lumberjacks when I was a youngster, with little talk of spiritual experiences and even less tolerance for sensitive young men lost in their inner world. I took refuge in my pets, which included an aquarium of fish and several homing pigeons, but, most important, I became exceedingly interested in music.

Although my visionary experience had set off all my senses simultaneously (an experience that I later learned has a scientific name—synesthesia), it was the music of the morning stars that seemed to leave an indelible memory in my being. Music was ethereal enough to partake of the nature of heaven yet earthy enough to be demonstrable on the face of this world. Music is curiously free and of the spirit, and it became my link to the Golden World during these teenage years. My grandmother taught me the rudiments of playing the piano, but it was the pipe organ that seemed to echo the immense energy and power of heaven.

My family attended the First Presbyterian Church of Portland, and each Sunday I became enthralled by the beauty of the choir's singing and the grandeur of the church organ. I joined the young people's choir and began practicing with them each week. Eventually I got up the nerve to approach the church organist to inquire about the possibility of organ lessons. I explained to him the difficulty with my artificial leg, but still I wondered if it would ever be possible for me to learn to play the organ.

"No, young man, I regret that with your disability you would be better off pursuing something else," he said flatly.

I moped around for weeks, though I continued to participate in the church choir. Then one week the church organist was out sick and an assistant took his place. Her name was Ethel Rand. We had never met before, and I approached this stranger with my usual awkward shyness, finally sputtering out that I was interested in learning to play the organ and did she think it was possible?

"Well, I don't know why not; at least we could try," she replied.

I began taking lessons with her the following week.

Miss Rand was a spinster who taught piano and organ lessons as well as served as the assistant musical director at the church. She was in her early sixties when we met and still lived with her aging mother. Of English ancestry, she maintained a charming accent that added to her intrigue. She was theatrical and showy. She wore bright colors and dramatic clothing, and when Ethel spoke, she made sweeping, dramatic gestures with her hands; she would come into a room and take control of it. This was just what I needed at that time, and though I did not know any terminology for her type, she was a perfect hetaira woman. This little-known Greek word is the only term I know for that rare woman who can be companion to a man, never a sexual partner, not a wife, but one who provides a grace and charm that men value highly. In the literature of ancient

Greece one hears descriptions of a famous hetaira woman in Athens who had the respect and delight of the highest society of that noble city. We have no word for this quality now—indeed, we hardly recognize that capacity in a woman—so I have had to look to the ancient world to describe Ethel Rand.

In the beginning Miss Rand secured permission for me to practice by coming to church early on weekday mornings before school. It was a cold winter and the church was not heated during the week, so I had to wear gloves with the fingers cut off in order to keep from freezing my hands. I appeared each morning at 6 A.M. to practice, my teeth chattering but my soul warmed by the rich sounds of the pipe organ. One day Miss Rand gave me a composition by Bach, and I loved it so much that the next week I came back with it entirely memorized. Bach quickly became gospel to me, with his wonderful weaving of abstraction and feeling. I acquired 78 rpm phonograph records of Albert Schweitzer playing Bach's masterpieces and did my best to imitate his performances.

From my current perspective, I can see that Miss Rand may have needed me as much as I needed her. She seemed to want a young man to adopt, and each week after my lesson, we would launch into discussions about music, art, and philosophy. She loaned me my first books on India, mysticism, and religion.

Miss Rand quickly became the mother I always wished that I had been born to, the one person who seemed to understand my Golden World experience and who validated my inner world. What I related to her about my visions somewhat frightened her, but she was willing to listen and even seemed to understand something of what I described. It was she who first introduced me to a book by Richard Morris Bucke called *Cosmic Consciousness*. While reading it I realized for the first time that other people, too, had contact with the Golden World. It gave me the first bit of a handhold on what had happened to me.

Lessons were at Miss Rand's home in the late afternoon, and I often stayed for dinner. We would go on talking until 9 P.M., when her dog would courteously insist that it was time for me to go home.

In my own home I was accustomed to retiring to my room immediately after dinner, as there was never anything of interest to say to anyone. Although I didn't know it at the time, I had a great hunger to be parented by someone who understood my inner world.

During this period I didn't know what I wanted or needed, I only felt a great hole in my life. In an unconscious way I began seeking out my true family, not the family into which I was born but the family where I belonged emotionally, the family where I felt at home, the family that could speak my language, nurture me, and bring out the best in me. This is how I discovered the beauty and the necessity of godparents.

Miss Rand was my first godparent, and soon she would introduce me to another one. After a few months, I was told that I was using too much of the church's electrical power, so I lost access to my wonderful pipe organ. My teacher then made arrangements for me to practice at a funeral home, where I could play for a dollar an hour, but my enthusiasm proved to be too much for that venue as well.

It was at this time that Miss Rand heard about an old theater that had an organ dating from the 1920s that hadn't been used in years. Once, the organ had accompanied silent films, and it could produce drum sounds, train whistles, and even the noise of barking dogs. It also had a dozen legitimate stops on it, but they were in terrible repair. Miss Rand had an idea, however. She had heard about an old man who built and maintained organs, and since she could charm anyone, she phoned him up and talked him into repairing the theater organ as a community service. In exchange for repairing the organ, the theater agreed to let Miss Rand's students practice on it.

The organ builder's name was Owen Thomas, and he soon became my first godfather. Mr. Thomas also was in his sixties, and he was overweight and sick much of the time, so I was drafted to assist him. I would meet him at the theater after school and do whatever he told me to do—hold keys, fetch tools, climb into the organ chambers. I was passionately interested in pipe organs and I have good mechanical sensibilities, so I quickly became his apprentice. We got the theater organ working reasonably well, and I was allowed to use it for practice from that point on.

I learned that Mr. Thomas was in charge of maintaining the largest organ in Portland, a four-keyboard instrument in the Municipal Auditorium. This pipe organ was a wonder, with more than 5,000 pipes ranging from three-eighths of an inch for the highest pitch to a pipe that was thirty-two feet long for the deepest resonance. As Owen's new assistant, part of my job was to help tune this organ.

To tune a pipe organ you must transfer the temperament from one chamber of pipes to another. On the flute pipes this is accomplished by tapping a collar up or down to adjust the pitch. Reed pipes, similar to an oboe or bassoon, make their sound with a reed controlled by a wire. It would take as much as twenty hours just to tune this grand organ, and when we were finished Mr. Thomas would fill the huge auditorium with music. At times, while playing, he would become lost in reverie and his mind would drift to other times and other places. I gradually learned that in his glory days he had been the principal organist at Saint Paul's Cathedral in London. His fortunes had shifted, however, and he had immigrated to America and drifted into Portland. Many years later when I was in London I inquired and found the name of Owen Thomas as the cathedral organist for 1920 and 1921. I was profoundly touched by the fate of this miserable old man who had drifted from so fine a position to eke out a bare subsistence in a land so foreign to him. I owe him much, as I feel that he gave me the best of his heritage to carry on as I could. Such is a true godfather.

Mr. Thomas didn't earn enough to live on in America, and his life had dwindled down to very little. He and I grew attached to each other. He saw the glitter in my young eyes, and as his life was fading out, I think he decided to pass along what he had left to me. We took care of each other. I tended to his health and provided physical labor and companionship; he taught me everything he knew about the construction and repair of organs. It was from him that I began to learn the art of building and maintaining keyboard instruments, a skill that would serve me well.

On Sunday afternoons when nothing was scheduled in the Municipal Auditorium, Mr. Thomas would often hand me the keys and tell me to "go down and exercise that musical instrument." As the organist at the First Presbyterian Church had bluntly told me, anyone with an artificial leg is not a good candidate to become a master organist, as this is one instrument that requires the feet as much as the hands. In the organ world there are jokes about a one-legged organist, which were painfully applicable to me. But I developed my own technique and had skill and ability enough to enjoy this touch with the Golden World.

Eventually my dedication to practice got us into trouble, as an official heard about my unscheduled concerts and accused Mr. Thomas of making illegitimate use of the city's organ. They threatened to cancel his maintenance contract, and that was the end of my practicing at the auditorium and working with him. However, it was during my apprenticeship in organ construction and maintenance that I met my third godparent.

While I was still working with him, Mr. Thomas won a contract to move an expensive organ from the home of one of the city's wealthiest families. The organ had been donated to an Episcopal girls' school called Saint Helen's Hall. I helped him reassemble the organ after school and on weekends, earning extra money and learning everything I could in the bargain. We were assisted in the process by the caretaker and handyman at the school, a man named Ambrose Seliger.

Fifteen years my senior, Ambrose became even more of a godfather and mentor to me than Mr. Thomas had been. Ambrose was a tragic figure, an artist who never knew how to make a living in the practical world. He was naturally skilled at many things, including landscape and portrait painting, sculpture, carving, and the art of delicate inlays for musical instruments, but he did not have one practical bone in his body. All his life Ambrose was a ne'er-do-well artist with only a small market for his art in the Pacific Northwest. I don't think he was ever interested in the production of anything; what he liked was to explore.

I soon became attached to this bohemian character, whom I called Andy. He lived with his parents in a barnlike house on a farm they had homesteaded outside Portland. Andy was small, slight, and inordinately sensitive. I wasn't accustomed to the language or sensitivity of a true artist, and I once asked him, "Andy, what would be the worst three colors to put together?"

"Well, let me see, I guess chartreuse, mustard, and . . ." He paused, turned away, and then he threw up. I was shocked, embarrassed, and remorseful all at once. I quickly changed the subject, but I have always wondered what the third color was that so turned his stomach.

A short time after we became friends, Andy was injured in a fall from a ladder at Saint Helen's school. His injury seemed slight at first, a bruise on the shin and knee, but it was a bruise that refused to go away. Over time it became some kind of cancer, eventually requiring that his leg be amputated. The amputation was high above the knee, so an artificial leg never worked for him, and the surgery itself never seemed to heal. The nerve at the point of amputation developed a knot and required several surgeries for repair. From this time on, the poor man was writhing in agony much of the time.

The fact that we both had lost a leg gave us something in common. I spent countless hours talking with Andy about art, travel, and philosophy. He was always kind and patient with me. I'm sure I was a tiresome teenager; things were churning inside me that I didn't know how to express. I brought up my visionary experiences with him one time, and he listened and reassured me that he understood that sublime language. He was the perfect mentor for my experiences that my family understood so little.

Later, after Andy became ill, I tried to return his kindness by spending time with him and taking care of him as best I could. I remember once going out to his old barn/house on a Saturday morning, where I unexpectedly found that he was still in bed. I could see that he had chewed holes in the sheet because the pain in his leg was so great. I've never since seen such physical suffering as that man went through, not even on the many trips to the poorest parts of India that I have taken as an adult.

It was with Andy that I learned the profound art of godparenting, which once was known to the Catholic world but has fallen into disuse as the modern world turns its attention to outer things. A godparent is designated as the teacher of the inner world for a young person while his or her natural parents are the caretakers of the physical and practical aspects of life. Andy knew how to do this to perfection, and he taught me how to relate to the inner world, including the courage and safeguards that are required for this inner journey if one is strongly touched by the Golden World. How fortunate I was to find in Portland, Oregon, a man who could comprehend the splendor of the Golden World and save me from the dangers of it as well!

Andy served as a mediator between myself and my interior world. I saw, by projection (though he also embodied those qualities in his life), my own capacities long before I could live them out myself. My debt to Andy is very great, one I can repay by being godfather to others later in my life. A godson also carries a serious and important role for his godparent. When one is in the later part of life there is a profound need for a younger person to take up the characteristics of one's life, as old age reduces the capacity for work in the world. A godson or goddaughter can stand as a reminder of one's immortality.

OWEN THOMAS, ETHEL RAND, ANDY SELIGER—these three became my godparents, the individuals who somehow were my true family. Ever since, I have believed fervently that we all need mentors to help initiate us and guide us into fulfilling our destinies. We need godparents to finish our emotional and spiritual education. No two parents, however skilled or developed, can do all of that for a young person. Even with the best of intentions, such as my mother had, too often a parent is simply not capable of giving a youngster what is needed for his or her inner development.

I have been a godparent to many young people since I became an adult. If it is a conscious relationship, it is a wonderful thing. For earlier generations there were large extended families, and a child could gravitate to an aunt or an uncle for help. In rural, traditional India, children growing up in village life may be taken in by an artist, a craftsperson, a mystic, or someone who can teach them what they need to learn. It's harder for us now because most of us live in small, nuclear families. Often, to find true mentors, people now do what I was forced to do—search out and find someone to serve as a godparent.

In a Christian tradition that has been practiced for centuries, people were appointed godparents at baptism, but like so many customs this for the most part has become an empty ritual. In most Christian households someone stands at a child's baptism and agrees to be the godfather or godmother, but most people don't know what that means anymore. Being the materialists that we are in Western society, godparenting now means taking over the economic needs of the child in case the parents die. But the true meaning goes much deeper. A true godparent should educate a child in the nonphysical realm. Godparents are essential for our initiation into adulthood, for finding our true place in the world. I often have people come to my consulting room looking for a godparent. In some ways, therapy provides this function for many modern people; it creates a setting in which you can discover your true personality instead of what everyone expects of you, and you can gain encouragement and positive mirroring. One almost always makes a godparent out of one's analyst or therapist.

It also is true that people who have been wounded or dislocated in some serious way, such as I, have special needs that may be beyond the reach of most parents. People who have a great sensitivity to the archetypal world too often are pathologized by modern society and by psychology in particular. These are people who don't have the option of being "normal." In fact, normality may be a great danger to a gifted person, for it is a character structure built upon averages.

Instead of pathologizing people who have a different experience in childhood, it is possible to help them individuate into their own particular genius. I found it interesting to learn that the word *idiot* has nothing to do with level of intelligence; it comes down to us from the Greek and means "outside the canons of one's time." Certainly many people would have looked at my childhood and declared that I was an idiot. My entire life has been unconventional, and as a teenager I was most certainly outside the usual cultural standards. I own to being an idiot in the sense that I was not ordinary. I had to find a path in life that was right for me based upon my particular experiences and needs, and I think that there are many people who simply cannot lead a conventional life.

Some people have asked me how one finds the people who will qualify as godparents, and I have no simple answer. Fate brings us what is important in our lives. I can only suggest that you watch and respect how your energy flows; observe how your natural inclinations gravitate to certain people.

I was a hardworking student in high school, and upon graduation I was accepted to attend Stanford University, leaving my godparents behind in Portland. At the urging of my mother, I tried the traditional path at Stanford and found that it would never work for me. My freshman year was one of the most difficult times of my life. I did well in my classes, but the professors there were teaching a world I didn't want. They were trying to socialize me into a secular world that had nothing to do with my experience of the Golden World. After a year I dropped out.

When I returned to Portland, I tried a semester at Oregon State University, but I soon discovered that bored me, too. I decided to try to make a career out of my passion for music, so I went to Boston to study for the summer under Francis Snow, a renowned organist at Trinity Episcopal Church. An organist with an artificial leg is somewhat ridiculous, but Dr. Snow was astonished at what I was capable of doing, and he cheered me on. After a couple of months I put together a recital and returned to Portland. Immediately I found a job as musical director, choirmaster, and organist at the First Christian Church; they are the second largest congregation in Portland. I thought perhaps I could follow in the footsteps of my godmother. What a disaster!

I had just turned twenty-one, and I didn't have the slightest idea of how to manage a choir so as to keep people happy and motivated. I had no managerial skills and inadvertently offended people through lack of tact and political savvy. I was naive and inept. As church organist I was equally a failure; I selected music that was not entirely appropriate for the congregation, mostly my favorite pieces by Johann Sebastian Bach, and soon the complaints began.

Eventually I found out that the job was 10 percent music and 90 percent public relations, and I was a terrible PR man. At the end of my one-year contract, it was decided by mutual agreement that I would not return. I did manage to fulfill my commitment, but it was one of the most painful failures of my life—my inability to marry a passion for music with the practicalities of the world. I decided that with regard to music I would remain always an amateur, a word that in its original sense means "lover." I happily retreated into amateur status, performing music only because I love it, and I vowed never to be a professional again. I never worked so hard or disciplined myself so much as on music, but I could not will myself to become a professional musician. Music nourished my soul, but trying to make a profession out of it was like butting my head against a rock wall. I was just starting to learn when it is necessary to let go of my will and follow the slender threads. The attitude of "Where there's a will, there's a way" simply did not work for me. I can now see I was not in the right place. I've never tried since to will my way through something as I did with music; I have learned that I don't have to batter myself to exhaustion and fall into defeat.

About this same time my godmother, Ethel Rand, died, and I was inconsolable. I never suffered so much from a death before or since, not even from the deaths of my own parents. And so the most depressing period of my life was about to began. Going to college didn't work, I couldn't make a living with music, one of my guiding lights was gone. I was falling down into a dark abyss, a dangerous, lost, and lonely time.

3

The Red Cross and a Lookout Tower:

Terrors of Loneliness, Pleasures of Solitude

The year was 1944, one of the darkest times of my life. My only real interest was music, but I couldn't find a way to make a living at it. While other young men were going off to fight in the Second World War, I was given the classification of 4F by the government because of my artificial leg. My self-esteem was zero, and there was no one around to draw the best out of me or help with the worst in me. In short, I was lost with nowhere to go.

So at twenty-two years of age I went to the American Red Cross and volunteered. Since I wasn't of much use to myself, I thought that perhaps I could at least make myself useful to others.

This was the height of the war years. Few men were available for work on the domestic front, since any male between eighteen and fifty who could move was in the military. There were about twenty women on the staff at the Portland Red Cross office, and they were delighted to have a man join the team. The office was led by a hard-boiled matron in her midfifties who had worked in World War I and now also in World War II.

The first day I went for a bare bones orientation, and soon I was working six days a week. After a month I felt like a veteran caseworker. At the Red Cross, I saw a river of misery pass by my desk. That service organization did a marvelous thing, filling the gaps in the social fabric that no one else wanted to deal with. We performed every kind of service imaginable, short of handing out money, and a few times I even did that. I remember one fellow who came in, a well-educated man who had been an army officer but who had been sent home after a serious wound. He walked into my office and placed his arms around my neck.

"I'm at the end of my rope," he said. "My disability checks have been stolen, I haven't had a cent for three months. They have discontinued our milk service and cut off the telephone, and my wife and three kids go to sleep at night listening to their stomachs growl."

I heard his tale of woe and was overcome with empathy. It was immediately clear to me that this was no bum. We were supposed to complete many intake forms, write up an evaluation, and wend our way through assorted red tape, but in this case I threw out the regulations and immediately marched down the hall to talk with my supervisor. She agreed that we should pay the man's outstanding bills and get some groceries delivered to his home. That night I found I couldn't sleep a wink, lying in bed and worrying about this fellow. Three weeks after our initial meeting he returned to my office and repaid the money that was loaned to him. He thanked me, shook my hand with renewed dignity, and walked out onto the street. I never saw or heard from him again, but I realized that this experience not only assisted a desperate man, it was somehow healing for me as well.

Another time an elderly man walked into the Red Cross office, sat down before me, and admitted that he hadn't eaten for several days. He wasn't connected to the military, so technically we weren't supposed to help him at this time. I informed him of this, and he responded with silence, looking down at his worn shoes. He then got up to leave, his shoulders slumping. At first I let him go, as I was beginning to acknowledge the advice of my co-workers that it was impossible to save everyone, but when I went back to my paperwork I simply couldn't stand it. I jumped up from my gray metal desk, dashed out the front door, and caught him a block down the street. I pulled out my wallet and gave him all the money I had with me. That got around the Red Cross, and I became suspect as an easy touch. In general, the agency was generous and would stretch a point to help alleviate suffering, but it was an institution and, as in all bureaucracies, there were rules to be followed. That was the most difficult reality for me to accept.

On another occasion the USO called and informed us that they had some "crazy guy" in their lobby who apparently had been subsisting on a diet of Coca-Cola and aspirin. Could we help him? I volunteered for this assignment, and when I went to pick him up at the USO post I could immediately see that the man was psychotic. There was nothing at the Red Cross that would be adequate for his care, so instead I drove to the Veteran's Hospital. We had no proof that the man was a military veteran; in fact, I couldn't even find a wallet with identification, so the hospital refused to take him. The man was caught between bureaucracies and nobody wanted to accept responsibility for him, so I took him home to my small apartment that night and cooked him a hot meal. He said very little, mostly mumbling to himself and staring off into space. That night he slept on my sofa, curling up with a blanket that he accepted with a vacant look but no thanks. The next morning I roused him up and took him with me to the Red Cross, where he sat in a corner of the lobby. It took three days before I could locate a bed for him at a Veteran's Administration mental asylum in the state of Washington. Although he wouldn't talk, he gradually came to trust me, so I was naturally the one to drive him to the asylum. I handed this poor man off to the officials, patted him on the arm, and wished him well. There was not a flicker of recognition in his eyes as I said good-bye, and I felt numb as I drove back to Portland that day to resume my post.

On most days people stood in long lines that often stretched out to the sidewalk and even down the block. Many of the cases revolved around financial problems. A young woman would come in with a child who needed surgery. Or there had been a death in the family and our help was needed to negotiate a leave from the military so a soldier could return home for the funeral. About every third or fourth person was up to a scam of some kind, and we had to weed those people out. I could spot the phonies as soon as they sat down at my desk.

Although this was a time of intense loneliness in my life, working at the Red Cross showed me I could do something and make a difference in the world. It was a relief for my alienation, and it made my own problems seem less overwhelming, pulling my life together and giving it a purpose. If I or someone like me can serve someone else, this is a legitimate way to invest one's energy.

But the demand for help was endless, and by May of 1944 I was burning out and badly in need of a break. I decided to try something entirely different. I got a summer job with the U.S. Forest Service as a lookout in a fire watchtower.

The man at the forest service recruiting office said it didn't matter if I lacked two feet, they would take anyone with two good eyes. I qualified. Again the training was minimal, consisting of a week of classes on techniques for fighting fires and the rudiments of how to run a weather station. The class, which was held in the wilds of Washington midway between Mount Saint Helens and Mount Rainier, consisted of eleven high school kids and myself. On the first day, the old ranger who was the instructor called the roll, looked us over, and announced, "I sure hope we don't have any big fires this summer because we are down to four people on the firefighting crew, and you are without a doubt the sorriest bunch of recruits I have ever seen."

We accepted his abuse, and most everyone agreed that we were a pretty motley group. On the last day there was a "real world" exam. The ranger lit a fire in a contained area a few miles from our training center; our job was to get it under control. The recruits piled into a pickup and sped off to the fire area. It was an impressive test, as by the time we arrived on the scene flames were roaring twenty feet in the air. The ranger had poured gasoline on the fire to enhance the dramatic effect. Unfortunately, the driver of a second truck, which contained all of our firefighting equipment, took a wrong turn somewhere. We stood there helpless, without so much as a shovel to attack the blaze.

"Don't just stand there, you ninnies, do something!" the ranger roared at us.

We looked at one another but had no idea what to do. One fellow went running down the bend hoping to see the truck with the tools. Both the fire and our instructor grew hotter and hotter. Another fellow kicked some dirt over the flames, which accomplished nothing, while the rest of us stood there mesmerized by fear.

"Do something. There is always something you can do," he hollered. "If nothing else, goddamit, then pee on it!"

We didn't know if he was kidding or not. One young lad decided the ranger was serious, ran up to within a few yards of the fire, and started to pee in the general direction of the flames. We all stood there half paralyzed by the emergency of the situation and half laughing at the primitive sight before us. This shocked us out of our immobility, and another boy began throwing dirt on the fire. These measures had not the slightest effect on the fire, but they galvanized us out of our paralysis.

Yes, there is always something you can do in any situation, no matter how small the act. I learned this important fact at that moment and have applied it throughout the rest of my life.

Just then the tool truck arrived, and we managed to get the fire under control. For good or for bad, we all graduated from fire school that summer, and the forest service sent us off to our lookout towers.

That phrase, "There is always something you can do; if nothing else pee on it," often came back to me later in life while sitting in therapy sessions with troubled clients. I would chuckle under my breath, but it always reminded me that introducing something that is the complete opposite of the usual is often useful in helping someone to get unstuck. Jokesters and tricksters play an important role in society this way. They bring in the opposite and break the stalemate.

～

IT WAS A GLORIOUSLY SUNNY DAY when the old ranger took me up into the wilderness with a pack train. We had stopped first at the training center and had loaded up with a month's supply of food.

Most of the kids had no idea how to cook, but I had been camping on my own, so this did not concern me. Our ranger manual included recipes and suggested menus, most containing beans, rice, and canned meats. The assumption was that we would figure it out or lose a lot of weight by the end of summer. In addition to my provisions, I took with me a box of books and my dog, Shep. Shep was a Shetland sheepdog who had been given to me by a friend during my winter at the Red Cross; she was a delightful companion, a city dog who was in seventh heaven to be running loose in the forest. She kept ambling up the trail in front of us, then circling back to bark excitedly and urge us on. The entire way up the mountain Shep bit at the horses' heels and ran in broad circles to make sure that this giant intruder, the horse, was not up to mischief and kidnapping me. We were both in a happy mood. She got so much dust in her lungs on the way up that she coughed for a week afterward.

I was assigned to the top of Burley Mountain, 6,410 feet in elevation, just halfway between Mount Rainier and Mount Saint Helens. The snow glistened on Mount Rainier, while Mount Saint Helens looked like a perfect ice cream cone. It took the better part of a day to get up to the lookout station, which was perched on a rocky edifice near the very top of the peak. When we reached the summit, we had to dig through the snow to find the door of my new home.

The view from the station was incredible. There were windows on every side, and in one direction you could spy the glistening ocean one hundred miles away, while the magnificent Cascade Range stretched out on the other side. After making sure that the key worked, the ranger dumped my boxes on the ground and grunted, "Best of luck."

He was in a hurry to get back down the mountain before dark, and I stood there dumbfounded by the vast silence, watching him wind his way back down the mountainside. It was slowly registering in my mind that I was entirely alone, with infinity stretched out before me in every direction. And for one of many times in my life I stood there thinking, "Robert, what in the name of heaven have you gotten yourself into?"

Neither Shep nor I was very familiar with wild country, and the impact of that endless primitive forest produced a combination of joy and fear in us both. I was unstable on my feet, at best, and all of a sudden my courage was beginning to ebb. I had begun this undertaking with great enthusiasm and energy, but now the realities of my situation began to sink in. I was about to roll into a major panic when something glorious happened to rescue me: the sun began to set into the Pacific Ocean, and as the quality of the light changed a wolf pack began to howl somewhere off in the distance. I was used to the howls of coyotes, but I had never heard a wolf howl before. It was the most eerie, mournful sound I had ever encountered. Shep grew terrified at the sound of the wolves, and she crept in between my legs and shook with fear.

It was not many days before she would sit before the lookout tower and howl back at the wolves. A few days more, and she learned how to run off the black bears that often came by the lookout. Shep instinctively knew that she should stay in back of the bear and bite at his tail until he finally loped off in defeat. A bear can run faster than any dog, but Shep knew to stay in back and frustrate the bear.

Watching the sun set was a magnificent experience in which I felt something akin to what our ancestors must have felt living at the mercy of nature but also close to its grandeur. After a few minutes I shook myself out of my reverie and realized that it was getting very dark and there was no light switch to turn on. I got out the kerosene lantern and my flashlight. I locked the door, and Shep and I curled up together against the window. I slept like a dead man, waking only at sunrise. The next day my hope was renewed, and the dog and I began to establish a daily rhythm that would carry us for the next three months.

For the first few days time weighed very heavy on my hands. I found myself constantly looking at my watch, only to find that the hour hand was moving at a glacier's pace. I was supposed to look for fires fifteen minutes out of every hour and phone in a weather report each day at noon, but otherwise I could do what I wished. By the third day, however, something changed. I took on an animal relationship to time. Time was no longer an entity that pressured me. In a psychological sense, time stopped, a rare experience for modern people. It became like the flow of a river, and gradually I came into accord with the rest of nature. I was never again bored or lonely that summer. In fact, it was one of the happiest periods of my life.

I worked as a fire lookout for two summers, and I noticed both years how it took only three days after I went down to the city to snap back into civilized time again and to become anxious, worried, lonely, and restless. Living in the wilderness frees us from the tyranny of time and reveals how different existence was for our ancestors.

At the lookout tower I had a five-gallon water pack, and it was necessary to walk two miles down the mountain to fill it in a stream. That was about as far as I could walk, and I couldn't completely fill the pack or it would become too heavy for the ascent back up.

I had the luxury most days of investing hours watching the sun set and listening to the performance of the wolf symphony. In the mountains, night doesn't actually fall, it rises. It starts in the lowest valley and slowly rises up until it engulfs the entire world. That was my nightly entertainment, and it always left me feeling full and complete. I never saw a wolf, I only heard them, but bears would venture right up to the lookout tower and drive Shep mad in the night.

I was getting a rapid education in nature. The weather was constantly changing, and when the summer storms came the lightning was amazing. A fire lookout is strategically placed as the highest point on the highest mountain, which also serves as a focal point for lightning. The tower came equipped with a glass stool upon which to sit during a storm. When dark clouds began rolling in, I disconnected the telephone line, which might have been a conduit to bring the lightning flash into the lookout. Then I watched and waited. In a severe storm, the lightning rod attached to the top of the tower would melt at the tip, sometimes as much as a quarter of an inch. As the electrical charge built up from the lightning strikes, there would be a deafening roar and fire devils would dance about.

Fire devils are little arcs of current, sometimes as much as three inches high. They would dance across the stove and other metal objects in the room. The old ranger had described them and had assured me that I would be safe so long as I remained on the glass stool and didn't go outside during a storm. When there was a direct hit of lightning on the tower, it felt as though someone had hit me on the head with a pillow. At the height of a storm, Shep crouched on my lap, shivering. Her fur would stand on end from the static electricity so that every hair stood at a ninety-degree angle from her body. When she tried to lick them back down, she got a shock from the electrical charge.

We survived a half dozen severe storms that first summer, and only once did the lightning start a fire. A tree caught fire about half a mile down the slope from me. I immediately phoned down to the headquarters to report the strike, and the old ranger seemed remarkably calm.

"With any luck, it will burn itself out. Just watch it and let me know if it starts to spread," he said.

The fire never spread beyond the tree, just as he predicted, and I breathed a major sigh of relief. I logged forty-five small fires in my district that summer, but fortunately none of them was major.

Despite hauling a box of books with me up the mountainside, I read very little. For once in my life I felt no compulsion to lose myself; I was totally content just to be. Simply to take part in the natural order of the day, to observe the sunrise, clouds, sky, weather, and sunset, was enough to make a liturgical progression of the day. The sunsets were especially compelling; it took a good four hours to watch the sun begin its decline, drop below the horizon, and give way to the night, which came seeping up from the deep valleys. Full dark was glorious, with its stars, changing of the moon, and the northern lights. At full moon I was so identified with the animal life around me that I could not sleep. The entire forest was awake with its nocturnal energy, and I made my way back in evolution to the time before the disaster of the Garden of Eden. During those nights I was out of time and not subject to the self-conscious suffering of fallen humankind. The animals taught me, and I was made humble and safe.

One day the senior ranger phoned unexpectedly and inquired, "How are you, Robert?"

"Oh, I'm fine, everything is going fine up here."

"Are you talking to yourself yet?"

"Well, yes."

"Are you answering yourself?"

"No."

"Well, you're okay then. Bye."

It was the briefest psychiatric exam I ever experienced. There were eighteen different lookout stations, and I found out later that one of the other lookouts had shot and killed himself that day. The old ranger was checking to make sure the rest of us were okay.

I wasn't completely isolated. Once a month groceries were brought up to me. And I also discovered that down in the valley below me was a shepherd who had five dogs to tend to more than twenty thousand sheep. Shep was the one to point that neighbor out. She would head off in the morning, travel down the mountainside, assist with the herding just for the fun of it, and return totally exhausted to the lookout station before sunset. At first I wasn't sure where her adventures were taking her. One day the herder followed her home and offered to buy my dog. He asked how she learned to herd and said she was better than all five of his dogs put together.

"I have no idea," I replied. "We're both city slickers."

The sheepherder explained to me that he had never been able to train his dogs to gather the herd of sheep into a dense pack and run across their backs to get across the herd to the other side; instead, they always ran a long perimeter around them. Shep had done this one day, and the other dogs had quickly learned it from her. But where had she learned? What kind of Scottish ancestry lived on in her that knew the ways of sheep so well?

We agreed that it was simply in her blood, but I informed him that I would as soon sell my right hand as part with Shep.

It was during our conversation that I learned about the code of ethics in the animal world. The sheepherder informed me that very few animals in the wild would kill more than they can eat, with the exception of bears. They were his major nemesis. They would kill many of the young sheep, by all appearances for the sport of it. He also described how a bear may begin eating the flesh of its prey before the animal is dead.

One night after his visit I heard the terrified screams of a lamb, the sound of two rifle shots, and then silence. I knew that he had caught a bear with the herd. I slept poorly that night, and the next day I decided to venture down the mountain to find out exactly what had happened. Since it was a foggy day and the lookout was isolated in its fog bank, the head ranger gave me permission to leave my lookout tower. As I expected, the old Basque had killed a good-sized black bear. In a fit of enthusiasm, I asked him if I could have the carcass. He said that it was all mine.

Although I had no idea how to skin a bear, I thought I would get a bearskin rug to show off to friends for the rest of my life. I had never even skinned a rabbit, but I did have a large knife that was standard issue from the forest service. The shepherd went off to tend to his herds, and I began the task of skinning the bear. It weighed far more than I could lift by myself, so I rigged up a rope over a tree limb to help me turn the bear over. By late afternoon, I was a bloody mess. I had begun with great bravado and visions of Daniel Boone, but now I was exhausted. I managed to get the bearskin off the carcass, but when I rolled it up I found it was so heavy that I could not even lift it. The day was getting late and I had to return to my lookout tower, a climb that I knew would take me a couple of hours. I had to face facts, so I cut a section out of the back where the bear's coat was the thickest. Still, I couldn't begin to lift it. Finally I cut out a small piece about two feet by two feet and, greatly chagrined, carried it with me back up the mountain along with a pocket full of bear claws. It was nearly dark by the time I got back up the mountain, and before shutting myself in for the night I nailed my prize to the side of the lookout tower so that it could dry in the next day's sun. When I got up the next morning I found that some wild creatures had come and eaten nearly every scrap of the bear hide. For all my trouble I ended up with ten claws.

WHEN FALL CAME AND THE AIR took on a brisk chill, I went back down to civilization and returned to my job at the Red Cross. After my summer in the forest, life in the city seemed to be nothing but a pool of misery, depression, and loneliness. But I made an amazing discovery that year. In the mountains I was totally alone but never lonely; in Portland I felt terribly lonely unless I was throwing myself into alleviating the suffering of others. I couldn't understand how I could be so lonely in a city surrounded by so many other people. I recalled having once stood in the middle of Times Square in Manhattan and felt that it was one of the loneliest places in the world. What was to be learned from the fact that I was not lonely when in solitude but excruciatingly lonely when in a city? Solitude is a joy; relationship is warm and happy; but the proximity of other people without a true relationship produces pure agony. The city and the lookout tower raised this paradox to high intensity, and I was to work at it for some time before any clear understanding came to me.

It was from my experience in alternating work at the Red Cross and the forest service that I began to learn the difference between loneliness and solitude. I knew that loneliness was not just the result of isolation because I was surprisingly happy in my fire lookout station with only Shep to keep me company. I now believe that loneliness occurs when our lives are somehow missing one-half of a pair of opposites—being or doing. We can be very busy and surrounded by people yet still feel intense loneliness because our lives are dominated by "doing"; there is insufficient time for attentive solitude with our thoughts and feelings. I know many people in this situation, surrounded by others and yet suffering from intense loneliness. We often try to address this problem with still more doing, such as calling up a friend, going out on the town—anything to get rid of that painful feeling of separateness—but all to no avail. This is the loneliness of a life filled with doing, and I have found that most intelligent people in the West today have far too much doing with little or no time for being. When your life is filled with too much doing, the only cure for loneliness is a strong dose of solitude.

It sounds ironic to say that the cure for loneliness is aloneness. I don't mean that you should just make yourself more miserable; I am prescribing instead a form of solitude that is meditative and open to your inner self. When I lived in the forest service watch-tower I had hour upon hour of solitude, time to slow down and listen to my inner self, time to reconnect with nature and the environment around me. It was easier on the lookout tower because I didn't have to interact much with the social world; there I lived like a child in the Garden of Eden. You don't have to join the U.S. Forest Service to realize this, but you may need to make room in a busy schedule for walks in nature, meditation, or creating a quiet corner in your home that is set aside for inner work.

Although most people these days suffer the loneliness of being cut off from their deep, inner self, loneliness can also work the other way. You can become too self-absorbed, cut off from the world by being while you neglect doing. I would learn this lesson years later when I joined a monastery, and looking back I can see that by the end of my summers in the forest service I would begin to miss human contact.

A crude balancing of being and doing was all I could muster at the age of twenty-three—spending my winters doing for others and spending my summers being in solitude. Both of these processes helped to soothe my loneliness. Working in the Red Cross took me out of my self-absorption and set me attending to the needs of others, a very fruitful and meaningful form of doing. But when taken too far without a balance of being, my psyche would swing to the opposite pole and I would have to be a hermit for three months in the forest. It took many more years before I would learn to balance the opposites of being and doing in a more effective manner.

A symbol that now reminds me to work each day for this balance is the holy cross. It is part of the genius of the Christian tradition to produce such a powerful symbol. I have come to understand the cross as a symbol of two strong opposing forces that must be balanced, with the balancing point always exactly in the center where the two forces intersect. I must confess that it was not until my sixtieth birthday that I began to comprehend this symbol, but I benefited from it in a clumsy, half-conscious way during those summers when I was still a young man in my twenties. You don't have to fully understand many things in this world to learn from them.

Dr. Jung believed that the crucifixion in Christianity is the prototype of the human being crucified between different levels of consciousness. From Jung's reading of Christianity, the appropriate thing was to stay right in the middle and to stay conscious; Christ refused the sedative that they gave to crucified people. You wait between the two worlds until a reconciliation or transfiguration occurs.

Think for a moment of the horizontal beam of a cross as representing doing, or the earthly realm. We have all kinds of daily activities—going to work, raising our family, paying our bills; these are the necessary and proper business of the earthly realm. Often all this doing just fills up our lives. But when we become focused exclusively on doing, our lives start to feel empty and meaningless; we start to wonder why we work so hard. We may secretly ask: Is it worth it? What's the point? What is the meaning of my life?

This is a sign that we have neglected the opposite of doing, which is being. Now think of a vertical beam of a cross as representing being, or the heavenly realm. We also must have time and place in our lives in which we connect to something that is larger and more enduring. We need at least a taste of the Golden World to make our lives bearable, and this requires time for reflection, for meditation, for inner work and attentive solitude. In short, we need a balance of doing and being.

The word *heresy* was laughable to me for many years; I thought it was just a term for anything that the Church Fathers in Rome didn't like. But then I found out that in the Christian tradition all heresy is a misunderstanding of the nature of Christ. The famous heresies in medieval Christianity invariably were arguments about whether Christ was more human or divine. If you said he was more human than divine, you were wrong. If you said he was more divine than human, again you were wrong. Christ was fully divine and fully human, both of heaven and of earth. Anything that departs from that exact balance is a heresy.

The power of the word *heresy* came when I began to apply it in my own life. You don't have to be a Christian to understand when a heresy is taking place in your psyche. When my life becomes more doing than being, then I am in heresy. Alternatively, if my life becomes more being than doing, then again I am in heresy. Now the word *heresy* is very useful to me. Heresy is a dislocation of the center of gravity of the personality. We often fall into heresy, and it is a wonderful term to describe when we lean too far to one side or the other, the divine side or the earthly side. It is one of the best concepts I have found to describe the paradoxical nature of human life.

I have thrown the word *spirituality* out of my vocabulary because it seems to imply abandoning the earthly dimension. I have little patience with people who say they are on the spiritual path, because almost invariably they are trying to advance the vertical (lofty, unearthly) part of their lives at the expense of the horizontal (earthy, human) dimensions of their being. As such, it is a heresy. Spirituality as something other than that midpoint is a heresy. Anything that has an opposite is inadequate and quickly throws you into heresy.

Along these lines, I once heard a wonderful story about Saint Teresa of Avila. It was told that Saint Teresa was often taken by raptures, another word for visions of the Golden World. People were greatly awed by this capacity in Saint Teresa; it was as if she had some direct connection with God. One day someone observed that Saint Teresa never had a rapture while cooking, and some ancient wag joked that not only could Saint Teresa chat with God, she also never burned dinner!

I love the humanness of this story; it demonstrates that even the most deeply religious people must still maintain sufficient contact with the earthly world and obey its laws. Saint Teresa was not only capable of the highest form of being—communing with God—she also kept up a human life.

Which of these two realities is better, doing or being, fulfilling your earthly duties or serving heaven? If you side with either one you are in heresy. To err on either side is a sure formula for loneliness as well, because it means that you are separating yourself either from the world or from God.

What has been even more remarkable for me has been to learn that the proper balance between these two is different for each person. There is no simple recipe. When I was in my twenties, my parents would say to me, "There's a party tonight, don't you want to go? Robert, why don't you get out and meet some new friends? Surely that will make you feel better." That was heresy for me. I had plenty of doing in my life, and going out to a party was just one more outer activity when my inner self was dying from neglect. I felt terribly lonely because I was so out of balance with my own requirements. Each person must determine where the cross of being and doing should intersect.

Buddhists speak of the middle way and call this balancing act "walking the razor's edge." Throughout my life that middle place, when I can find it, has been an ecstatic place, a holy place. It's like a hurricane: if you can manage to stay in the middle, you will find calm. Most people in the West don't believe that the middle point is the solution; instead we want to do something. On many occasions I have advised a friend or a client: "Don't just do something, stand there!" Our Western heresy is most often an overstatement of doing at the expense of being.

It is a brave and wise person who understands that he or she belongs right in the middle of a dilemma and that the solution is not to avoid it but to sit in the middle of the opposites and work through them. Of course, we all have great difficulty putting these opposites together, so this requires much work on our part.

My family was no aid whatsoever in helping me to find my own proper balance of being and doing. They were committed to stopping the process altogether and getting this mixed-up kid back on a normal track. My mother's solution for everything was to work harder and fill life with more doing. Fortunately, both my godparents served this balancing process well. I spent another winter with the Red Cross followed by another summer with the forest service, which helped me to understand my own needs.

For the second summer up in the fire lookout tower, I took along a battery-operated portable radio that my father had purchased for me as a gift. I could get a daily news broadcast, and so I soon arranged with my colleagues to put the telephone receiver next to the radio; all eighteen of the young lookouts at the different towers could then hear the news broadcast. It was during one of those broadcasts, in August 1945, that we heard the remarkable news that a new kind of bomb had been dropped on a city in Japan called Hiroshima. The entire world was electrified by reports of the devastation. Sitting up there alone on a mountainside I could not take in the enormity of this event. I stared off into the sunset that night and pondered the destructive power that humankind had put into motion. I could not feel triumphant or sad; I was just overwhelmed by a hollow emptiness. A few days later a second bomb was dropped, and by the time I left the mountain, the war was over.

I never lived in Oregon again after the summer of 1945, and despite my reprieves in the forest, I never saw the Golden World during that time. If I were to have an argument with God, I would say, "Do anything to me, but do not throw me into a sea of loneliness without a clue of how to cope with it." I had devised my own makeshift solution, but for much of the time I still lived on the edge of desperation, and I was still searching for answers.

4

First Encounter with the East—Krishnamurti:

Taking Back the Alchemical Gold

While I was working at the Red Cross in Portland, one of my co-workers was a devotee of Krishnamurti, a sage from India who had become something of an American guru. This co-worker would talk on and on about Krishnamurti, how he had taught her the meaning of suffering and had given a real purpose to her life. She praised him to such an extent that eventually I decided to find out for myself. So in September of 1945 I packed up my car and drove to Ojai, California. I would spend the next two years trying to find salvation through my first encounter with the East.

I had been interested in India since boyhood. Perhaps it was the exotic descriptions of elephant-headed gods and colorful rituals that drew me, or maybe it was simply the romanticism of a far-off land. From the time of my Golden World visions, I hungered for a tradition that would contain and help make sense of my experiences. A slender thread was probably already at work leading me to India, two decades before I would gain the courage to go there; Krishnamurti was as close as I could get at the time.

In 1945 Jiddu Krishnamurti was happily surrounded by admirers and was living an Eastern life in the Ojai valley, one hundred miles north of Los Angeles. Ojai was like a little Shangri-La. In fact, the motion picture *Lost Horizon,* which depicted the story of a lost paradise where peace and harmony reigned, was filmed in the Ojai valley by the Hollywood director Frank Capra. It is one of the strange coincidences that I fell in love with the movie *Lost Horizon* in my youth and had seen it at least fifty times, though I never made the connection that it had anything to do with Ojai.

Krishnamurti had a ranch called Aryavihara, which means "home of the Aryans." The word *Aryan* has become associated with the Nazi movement in Germany and white supremacy groups in the United States, but its history goes back for centuries in India. The Aryans were an early people of European origin who invaded India in waves. Alexander the Great and his army were, perhaps, the best known of these invaders, leaving the heritage of their cultural traditions and their light skin color throughout northern India. One can still see the gradation of skin go from light to dark as one travels from northern India southward. India's caste system was originally set up to separate these invaders from the dark-skinned Dravidian people who were already living in India. The Brahmins, who are the highest caste in India, are almost invariably lighter skinned than other castes. Krishnamurti was a Brahmin.

If there is one word to describe Krishnamurti it would be *aristocratic*. He had a refined, well-sculpted face, soulful dark eyes, and a delicate body. At our first appointment in his home, I found him dressed casually like a Westerner in pants, shirt, and sandals. It was said that he was a dandy early in life, and indeed he was a handsome man even at the age of fifty-nine when I met him. He received me in his small office, which opened out onto a porch surrounded by an orange grove, and motioned for me to be seated. After exchanging a few pleasantries, he asked,

"What is your relationship to theosophy?"

"What's that?" I replied.

He smiled, rolled his eyes, and said, "Well, thank God, at least we won't have to go through all that."

He told me a few things about theosophy: that it was founded by H. P. Blavatsky, a Russian woman who I would later learn was part mystic and part charlatan. Blavatsky had arrived penniless in New York in 1873, and within a few years she was leading the American spiritualist movement and had helped found a new organization called the Theosophical Society. Blavatsky traveled to India in the

1880s in search of spiritual masters. She was followed in the next generation by Annie Besant, an Englishwoman who carried on the theosophical tradition and who also made many trips to India. It was Annie Besant who gave forth the information that a new messiah, or incarnation of God, was soon to appear on earth. One day in 1909, one of her associates spotted a young boy in Calcutta. Like many modern-day Brahmins, he was destitute, since the old system of supporting the Brahmins in India has broken down in this century. The handsome young lad was swept up and sent to study in London in 1910, then was taken to America. In southern California the new guru quickly became a darling of Hollywood celebrities and an assortment of spiritual seekers.

By 1929 Krishnamurti was beginning to get disenchanted with being the new messiah. It is told that one day he came out to talk on spirituality at Ojai and surprised everyone by saying, "Look, this is total nonsense. The age of gurus is over. You must be your own guru. You must take responsibility."

This abrupt announcement shocked his devoted followers. Some renounced him and set about looking for a new savior, while others sought to emulate his austere form of self-reliance. Krishnamurti began teaching the refusal of any set creed.

Krishnamurti was very warm and gentlemanly at our first meeting. I was certain that he liked me, which was confirmed when he invited me to return the next day for lunch. I must admit that I was in awe of the great man. Shortly after I arrived the following day, however, I overheard a confrontation that helped me to see him in human dimensions. Krishnamurti became entangled in an argument with Raja Gopal, his confidante, personal assistant, and business manager. They exchanged harsh words, and as Raja Gopal stormed out of the room, he shouted, "Well, you just have a messiah complex." With that he slammed the door and departed.

That was quite a thing to say, because Krishnamurti had been hailed by the Theosophical Society as just that—the new messiah! I sat there waiting for a thunderbolt to fall from heaven and obliterate Raja Gopal. It never happened, and Krishnamurti turned back to me, smiling, and resumed pouring tea as if nothing had happened.

In 1945, many years after he had denounced gurus, Krishnamurti still had a dedicated community of followers in Ojai, and he held regular audiences with students at his house. Soon I was among that audience. He had a high-pitched voice and would begin nearly every dialogue at the very top of his vocal range. For still greater effect his face would go into a contortion and he would raise his right hand above his head and slowly bring it down. "No, no, no, no, no, no, you don't understand at all," he said on more than one occasion. His eyebrows would go up into little peaks as he spoke. "Can't you understand? Is that too much to ask of you? All you have to do is be *aware*. Is that too much for you? Just be *aware!*"

During audiences with the public, he would alternate between being aloof and displaying enormous frustration that people did not understand him. The fact was that I didn't understand most of what he told me over the next several months. In general, he taught that you must set aside all philosophies, all tools, and see through them with a kind of concentrated awareness. It was like putting people up against a vertical stone wall and telling them to climb with no handholds and no help. Neither I nor anyone else that I knew of his followers was able to do this, and the poor man lived in constant frustration that his Western audience was not able to comprehend his simple teachings. I learned that he was not the first great teacher who had failed to educate his followers in a simple doctrine of awareness. Christ taught an equally simple example, *love;* but that proved to be equally elusive for most Westerners. Krishnamurti's *awareness* was just as difficult.

There was a major hole in my life, and I needed more than a fine-tuning of my awareness. It's true, in a sense, that one's awareness determines one's experience of life. But saying this to a young person doesn't help when his or her world is falling apart.

I realize now that different truths are important for different stages of life, and Krishnamurti made the awful mistake of indiscriminately introducing an old person's wisdom to people of all ages and stations in life. Krishnamurti would allow his students no tools to help in climbing the vertical cliff he confronted us with. For example, he said that dreams were only more of the world of illusion and totally useless for a student. I learned that he had a whole cupboard full of journals in which he had written down and studied his dreams earlier in life. At one point I confronted him with this fact, and he exploded back at me that yes, he had done such things as look at dreams, but it was not at all necessary and only a waste of time. All one had to really do was to be *aware,* he insisted.

I had been reading about India since my teen years, and here was an Indian guru right before me. I projected all of my own gold onto this teacher, while my own psyche continued in a downward spiral. The gold I speak of is our capacity to experience the Golden World, which is represented internally as our highest value.

The term *projection* is used by Jungians to mean that each of us places some quality of our own being onto something or someone else. Aspects of reality of which we are unconscious are projected onto the outer world, where we see them in terms of events and people outside of ourselves. This psychological process works like a projector in a movie theater: we take something that is within the projector and blow it up onto a screen or backdrop, where we see it more clearly. Since this process is unconscious, we often think it belongs to the outer object when, in fact, it belongs to us. It is not only a person's negative qualities that are projected outward in this way; in equal measure we project our positive qualities, including our gold.

I had projected my gold onto a number of things previously—church, university, music—but everything I tried to affix ultimate value to couldn't hold it. Krishnamurti was the last major target for this projection. I tried to find a model for my life in Krishnamurti. In many ways he was a good man, but he couldn't provide me with the tools to reclaim this projection and thereby become my own model. I presumed for many months that the fault was mine, that if I could just discipline myself sufficiently I would be on the path to wisdom and happiness. Only slowly did I realize that no one else in the inner circle around the guru seemed to be getting it, either. I saw people in the Ojai community praising Krishnamurti to the skies and adoring him like some God incarnate. But they were essentially projecting their own wisdom onto him. This was exactly the opposite of what he was telling us to do. Krishnamurti was explicit in his teaching that the age of gurus was over and that one had to take the responsibility for one's own life into the self. But few people heard this, and most of his community consisted of people who adored the master. Adoration is a possible way of discovering one's own gold—in India it is called the way of bhakti—but it requires a high consciousness few people are capable of bringing to their inner worlds.

Later I was to hear this same teaching from two other great men who were highly conscious of their inner worlds, Sri Aurobindo in Pondicherry, India, and Dr. Jung in Zurich, Switzerland. The teachings of these three titans of the inner world agree that as modern people we must find a way to take interior responsibility, which is very hard for our Western temperaments; we tend to want someone else to carry the work for us.

Krishnamurti at this time seemed to be trying to recruit me, and on more than one occasion he intimated that I might be chosen as his successor if I was devout in my training. I was stupid enough to be flattered by this and to repeat it to another member of the community. Word of this flew around the valley in a matter of days and caused a great stir, with many people soon clearly resenting me.

I struggled with this situation for months, hoping that I was approaching enlightenment when, in fact, I was simply going down a gigantic whirlpool. At first I was excited to be part of a community of like-minded people, but over time it began to feel like a straitjacket.

In retrospect, I can see what was happening. He was talking from his point of view, which was a very high state of consciousness indeed, but he was either not willing or not able to speak to people on their level of development. Only now—at approximately the age that Krishnamurti was when I knew him—can I begin to see the wisdom of what he was teaching. A good teacher must understand that one should speak on the level of his or her student. Otherwise, the teacher will only have the admiration and awe of the student but will not further the student's development.

Krishnamurti's attempt to blend Eastern thought into Western psyches was like trying to fuse two beehives. Suppose that you have two beehives that you want to bring together. If you take the bottom off one and the top off another and try to force them together, the two colonies of bees will kill each other, as I have learned from experience. However, if you spread a sheet of newsprint between the two hives and then stack the hives together, by the time they chew through the paper they will smell enough alike that they won't be able to tell one colony from the other. Then they will join into one hive.

WHEN EAST AND WEST WERE JOINED in the early decades of this century, my sense is that the filter paper was never adequately applied. For one thing, early editions of the great books of the East were badly translated, but even when the gurus and holy men such as Krishnamurti spoke directly to Western audiences, they seemed to lack the necessary vocabulary. Krishnamurti spoke of concepts for which there was no adequate explanation; by this I don't mean a language barrier so much as a psychic barrier. I am now convinced that the psyches of the Westerners who worshiped him, including myself, were fundamentally different from his own. Even as Krishnamurti was stating his truth as articulately as he could manage, it was not the truth needed by most of his followers. The wisdom of India bends Western language badly out of shape. For example, when a Westerner says "I" and an Easterner says "I," they mean quite different things. The Westerner means a little ego, while the Easterner, particularly if he or she is Hindu, is referring to a larger entity that is inseparably connected to family, community, and nature. To this day, I can't adequately translate this concept *I,* though perhaps Dr. Jung came closest with his concept of the Self. He used this term to express the idea of the center and, simultaneously, the circumference of the personality, embracing both consciousness and the unconscious. The Self has been known as the Atman in India, Christ in Christianity, the Tao in China, the stone in alchemy, and other symbols such as circles and squares.

I now believe that a Western student following an Eastern teacher creates a dangerous situation that is fraught with perils. We can learn much from the East, but time and time again I have seen that Westerners do not understand the guru relationship that is practiced in the East. The vastly different concepts of "I" held by a Westerner and an Easterner often produce very different results for interior work. A Westerner is in grave danger of producing an inflation (a high arrogance) instead of an enlightenment (a finding of the right proportion of life's elements) if he or she uses techniques designed for the Eastern psyche. A Westerner can learn a great deal from Eastern insights but must never consider himself or herself an Easterner.

Since East and West are so different in their psychological structures, a teaching that is pure gold to one may be quite dangerous for the other. This works both ways and leads to a great deal of misunderstanding. If holiness (deriving from the root word *whole*) means to bring one's personality to a state of wholeness, it involves finding the missing parts or the faculties that are lacking in our natures and restoring them to a dignified place in our personality. The missing faculty for a Westerner is quite likely to be the very opposite of what an Easterner needs. If it is the feeling nature and capacity for relatedness that is missing in a Westerner's character (which is often the case), then these are the faculties that the Westerner must nurture and learn to honor. An Easterner's missing qualities are apt to be his or her capacity to cope with the physical world and maintain awareness of ordinary practicality. So, in this way, the teachings needed by one are often just the opposite of those needed for the development of the other. It was often observed that Krishnamurti emphasized stillness and awareness for his Western audiences while he talked about pressure cookers and practicalities to his Indian disciples.

I am impressed that Sanskrit has ninety-six words for love while English has only one. Western culture is highly specialized in technology yet quite primitive in terms of feelings. This points out how differently an Eastern culture prepares its members for life compared to a Western culture. One is not better than the other; each has different strengths. We desperately need to learn from each other, but obviously there is a wide gulf in which misunderstandings inevitably occur.

India labels the outer, physical world nothing but maya, or illusion, and deems it of little importance. The traditional Hindu thinks the inner world of dreams, imagination, and visions is the "real" world. We, in the West, appraise reality in exactly the opposite terms. For us reality is found in the material, physical world of things, while the world of interior images is thought of as "only a dream."

To return to the definition of *I*: to Westerners the "I" is a distinct, separate individual consciousness, alone, unique. We demand vehemently that this consciousness and distinctness persevere into the next world and that it not be extinguished; we would rather risk hell than extinction. We even insist that the physical body with its individual characteristics persevere into eternity, as seen in the Christian dogma of the resurrection of the body in the world to come. A kind of idealization of the body results in the notion that bodies in eternity function well and are not subject to the ills and aging of present mortal existence. Few points of view are so strong as the Westerner's insistence of the continuation of individuality after death even to the point of physical characteristics.

Indians think quite differently on this subject. They are inclined to use the imagery of a dewdrop to describe human existence. Yes, the dewdrop has individuality while it exists as a separate entity, but it is destined quite quickly to flow back into the great primal ocean of existence and to lose all individuality. A Hindu sage delights in asking the perplexing question of his students, "Does the dewdrop cease to exist when it falls back into the sea?" Well, yes and no. Nothing is lost, and the dewdrop continues with its existence as part of the great sea; but its individual form is no more, and one can no longer talk about a unique dewdrop that continues its separate existence.

Indians look upon it as the highest attainment to merge individual existence back into the great primal sea of existence. All efforts are directed to this end, and just the thought of such an accomplishment creates an ecstasy of delight. To be rid of this life of loneliness and isolation is the highest goal. Individuality, the most precious possession of a Westerner, is an intolerable burden to an Easterner, who longs to drop it as soon as possible.

I knew a highly trained and intelligent Westerner who devised a sarcastic appraisal of the Eastern view by saying that it was the ideal of going back into something like a cosmic soup in which everything is merged. Cosmic soup or primal sea? This is the fundamental difference between the two perspectives.

Small wonder, then, that Easterner and Westerner take such fundamentally different views of everyday experience. Westerners cling to everything that defines them as individuals. To threaten or abridge this formation of individuality is the Western nightmare. To be exiled into exactly this individuality is the Eastern hell. When may the dewdrop slip back into the shining sea? That is the cry of the Easterner. When may I have the permanent bliss of a personal heaven? That is the great hope of the Westerner.

A traditional Easterner looks upon the loss of life as incidental. If one's fate brings death, well, that is a welcome turn of events. At the temple of Juggernaut in India there is a great festival each summer in which the god is put in his huge cart and is pulled through the city streets to greet his followers. The British were horrified to see people throwing themselves or their children under the great wheels of the cart so as to accomplish their death under the benediction of the god. To die in this manner was to leave this vale of tears legitimately and be absorbed into the great primal sea. The British took this story back to the West, and the term *juggernaut* came to mean that which rolls over or crushes; this term has since been absorbed into every Western language.

Westerners have taken individuality as the highest value, and we protect it with every means possible. Death is bearable only if it guarantees a life after death containing all the characteristics of one's individual human life.

With this difference in mind, it is not at all difficult to see how differently a Westerner and an Easterner view life and death, mortal experience, and the ordinary events of the day.

In traditional India, learning is passed on from guru to student, and the personality of one's teacher can have an enormous impact. Often the material given to students is just a way of filling in the spaces while the relationship takes place between the two individuals. India has a term for this, *darshan*, where you are simply in the presence of the teacher. My feeling-oriented personality used to luxuriate in being in the presence of Krishnamurti, but after several months I slowly began to realize that my life was getting worse, not better, while living at Ojai. A big and fascinating pile of information was forming in my mind, but Krishnamurti was no help in sorting it out.

I would now agree with Krishnamurti that the age of worshiping others is over, though a different terminology may make this clearer. I believe that the medieval era is over, the era in which people could live their religious life out through a teacher or an external projection of some kind. For most modern people this medieval model just doesn't work at all.

The desire to live out one's religious life through someone else is probably the most common form this projection takes in Westernized society; we glorify it as romantic love. In romantic love, we briefly put all of our gold onto someone else, and of course the projection cannot hold up. The overwhelming joy and beauty that we experience when we first fall in love diminishes fairly quickly and often leaves us disillusioned. Instead of seeing that the problem is our projection, we blame the other person. As I discuss at great length in my book *We*, relationships generally begin with this type of projection, but to be maintained they must evolve into a sustainable human love. The projection of the inner gold must be gradually taken back.

Everyone's psychological process can be likened to an exchange of alchemical gold. Alchemical gold is another term for the soul. Soul work, or inner work, takes place when something moves from the unconscious, where it began, into conscious awareness. The path is never straight and neat inside oneself, as if you could go to a library and do all your inner work there. Instead, when something is ready to move from the unconscious to the conscious, it needs a host or intermediary. Generally this intermediary is some person or thing. Suddenly, it seems as though you must possess a certain person. If it's your gold—your soul—that is coming to consciousness, your first inkling of such a deep internal change will likely be that someone else begins to glow for you. It is your gold, but you see it in someone else; you are putting the alchemical gold on that person.

Some people think that the alchemists of the Middle Ages were somehow greedy, obsessed with making gold from lead so they could be materially rich, but the best and most insightful alchemists were very careful to differentiate in their language, and they made it clear they were not after vulgar gold, that is, the stuff of the marketplace. In their alchemy, they were talking about the creation of soul. In the twentieth century, more and more people are concerned with this interior alchemical gold, the art of meaning. No other hunger is so great in our age.

There are several possibilities for finding the alchemical gold. You could conceivably go to another person and, with all of the dignity and depth that you are capable of, consciously ask that person, "Would you carry my alchemical gold for a time? The meaning of the world somehow glows in your eyes for me, and I would like to talk about it."

Of course, no one does that. Instead we put our gold on someone else without being conscious of it. We are so shy and frightened that we often don't even tell the person, or when we do, it is to announce romantic love.

Other exchanges of gold are possible. At a meeting over coffee or at lunch, two people will banter with each other, kidding, joking, and playing. If you listen to such conversations the content appears to be nothing but nonsense. But if you listen a little closer, you will hear that some alchemical gold is being exchanged. The participants in such a conversation go back to work brightened for the day, and it wasn't the coffee so much as the exchange of alchemical gold. We seem to need someone else to carry that gold for us for a time, even though it is rightfully ours.

The person who carries our gold has enormous power over us. A smile from her or a frown from him can send us to the heights or the depths in an instant.

If the process continues, you grow enough so that eventually you can stand to carry your own gold. You develop the capacity to take your gold back, and you realize that this highest value originated in

you and rightfully belongs to you. It is very good to take your alchemical gold back, to realize that it was brought up out of the unconscious and was awakened by someone else but that it must
return to your own personality. This should in no way diminish the
other person in stature or beauty. The other person also has his or
her own gold. To exchange a love for another person based on one's
own gold for an appreciation of the other's true being is a sublime
evolution. One stops seeing a reflection of oneself and, instead, sees
the reality of the other person. Reality is always far nobler than any
projection.

Several rules apply to this process, which, if understood correctly, can save you a lot of trouble. One rule is that if you put your
gold on someone else, you have no right to pester or smother that
person. If you appoint another person to be the carrier of your gold,
you must protect that person from the distortions that might inadvertently be imposed upon him or her. It is an intolerable burden to
carry another's gold, even though we may be flattered and like the
experience at first. Worst of all, the projection of one's own gold
upon another robs us of the capacity to see the real value of that
person. Making a person into your mirror is no way to find his or
her value. Romantic attachments so often lead to severe disillusionment and suffering. True human love, a far more valuable experience, can be obliterated by romantic attachment. Yet the Western
world persists in basing marriage on romance.

Another rule is that the alchemical gold is an entity in its own
right and should not be mixed with anything else. Other things may
accompany the exchange of gold, such as friendship, companionship, fun, work. But when you mix the alchemical gold with these
activities or think that the gold is to be expressed through one of
these other means, you set up the most intense suffering for both
persons.

You may end up marrying the person who carries the gold for
you, which is entirely legitimate, but don't mix the gold with the
other facets of relationship. Marriage is a sacrament in and of itself,
but when we marry seeking our own gold in someone else, then at

some point in the marriage each partner has to take his or her gold back. This leads to terrible disillusionment and often results in divorce. The wife says, "You are not the knight on the white horse like I thought," and the husband says, "You are not the princess I married." The gold comes clattering down, followed by accusations and incriminations. In fact, this is an opportunity to move beyond the adolescent quality of putting your gold on someone else and to take it back and begin a truly human-sized relationship with your partner. It is at this point that one must find a truly religious attitude toward life so that one will not place that faculty on a base that is too small to support it. Probably the next important evolution of Western humankind is to find a proper container for religious life so that we do not unrealistically expect another mortal human being to carry this high value. In short: don't ask a human to be God for you.

Many different people had projected their gold onto Krishnamurti, and I remember watching him closely one day as we went on a walk together. We ambled along a path near his home in Ojai and eventually came across a small, elderly woman kneeling on the ground. Krishnamurti scarcely acknowledged her, and we walked on. At first I thought this was very cold. Later, he explained to me, "She has put the image of God on me. She knows what she is doing, because all she asks is that I carry this image for her. She never talks or asks anything of me, but whenever I go for a walk she seems to know where I am going and appears. It is all right." This was a very touching moment for me, most particularly Krishnamurti's attitude that if this woman needed to do this, then he would accept it. This presumed that both people concerned understood the levels involved and were able and willing to follow appropriate laws.

Most of us are very clumsy about taking back our alchemical gold. Sometimes it feels just too heavy to carry ourselves, but when someone ceases to glow for us, we are likely to get disillusioned, sarcastic, or even angry at the person. I often suggest making a ceremony when someone is involved in this process. You might get a little piece of gold, or something that is gold colored, give it to the person who has glowed for you, let that person carry it in his or her pocket for a while, and then experience that person giving it back into your hand. By doing something like this, perhaps you can avoid angry recriminations and adolescent door slamming and instead retrieve your projections and walk out the front door gracefully.

When some quality jumps from you onto another person, you have an opportunity; this is one of your best chances for an advance in consciousness. But you must differentiate carefully and not mix the gold with other levels of relationship. Gold is gold and that is enough. The Bible tells us, "Blessed are the pure in heart." *Pure* doesn't mean "good," it means "unmixed." Almost all psychological suffering results from a mixing of levels. I believe that everything in us is good; it is the mixture of things that goes wrong and leads to psychological problems. A possible definition of evil would be to say that evil consists of a right thing in a wrong place. It is not the thing that is wrong; only its placement.

The process of projecting one's gold that occurs in romantic love is essentially the process that goes on with a guru. But gurus have some training and expectation of such projections, so there is more of a chance that the relationship can remain impersonal. No wonder the average person, lacking training or tools, has problems in this arena! However, projections often prove too much even for gurus to hold. I don't need to recount the abuses we have seen in the West in recent decades of the guru-student relationship—gurus buying fleets of cars, going on alcoholic binges, sexually and psychologically abusing their students. Ideally, what should happen is that the guru carries the projection until the student grows out of the need for it and is ready to take back his or her own gold. Unfortunately, many gurus cannot handle the projections of their Western students.

The alchemical gold has been processed differently in other cultures and other eras. In the medieval period, people had a local saint or hero or at least a relic to hang onto. If you couldn't have the saint around to hold your projection of the divine, at least you could have a bone or a piece of his or her clothing.

In today's secular societies, while we are channeling the religious impulse and projection of the highest value into romantic love on the individual level, we are at the same time channeling it into celebrities at the collective level. We worship not only the would-be gurus but also the Sunday afternoon sports heroes, the movie stars, and the latest rock 'n' roll bands. We create Hollywood and Disneyland to carry our projections of greatness. But as a society we are putting ourselves at risk in this process, for a celebrity may not be a true hero. As the great mythologist Joseph Campbell once pointed out, the celebrity lives only for his or her own ego, while the hero acts to redeem society. We have many celebrities but few true heroes these days. Modern Westerners have evolved psychologically to the point where we are placing our gold on living beings rather than dead bones, as was done in medieval times, but it remains to be seen whether we can learn to carry our own gold and find heaven within instead of without.

~

KRISHNAMURTI WAS MY LAST GREAT ATTEMPT to find the gold in someone else. Toward the end of my stay with Krishnamurti I had an important and prophetic dream. The dream appeared as follows:

> I am back in Oregon where I grew up. It is a dreary Sunday, with a drizzling rain filling the sky and not a bit of color. I live in a community of people, and together we decide to go out for a Sunday afternoon walk in the drizzle. I am the leader, and everyone follows me single file. No one says a word. We walk through the scrub brush in our raincoats, following a path for a mile or more. Then we come across a small landslide in the trail. We decide that we should remove the mud so that we can use the trail on the way back.
>
> I get down on my knees and begin shoveling with my hands. As I am plowing through the mud, I suddenly break through to a hole in the ground. The most wonderful golden light is pouring through the hole. The brightness of the golden light is in great contrast to the surface, where everything is a gray drizzle and there is not a scrap of color. It is a glorious shaft of light. As I dig deeper I find that I have discovered an

ancient civilization that no one knew existed. It is all beneath the ground. There is a huge temple giving off the light. I can see that it is a man-made chamber, with sculptures, ornaments, and many giant doorways leading into other rooms. The other people in my group are as amazed as I am, and one fellow runs off to get a ladder so that we might descend into the hole. I am so awed that I am totally speechless. My friend returns with the ladder, and he scrambles down into the underground cavern. He quickly comes running back, however, and exclaims, "Just wait till you see the library." Then he pops back down again. This time he comes back and says, "Just wait till you see the music room." Again he descends, comes running back, and this time he says, "Just wait till you see the treasure room."

When my friend finally comes back up the ladder, he turns to me and says,

"Now, Robert, let's be practical, it was you who discovered this chamber, but it was I, the extrovert, who was the first one to go down it. Let's get the story straight right now, because you are going to be so famous that you will get suntanned from the flashbulbs." End of dream.

This seemed silly at the time and was completely a muddle to me, but I wrote it down anyway. I can see now that it was pointing me to my own alchemical gold and that I would have to retrieve it by going down into the deep cavern. It also was a compensatory dream. I was in the mind-set of unrelenting depression and despair at the time, and the dream suggested that a great treasure was about to be mine. I was down so low that the dream exaggerated the situation by stating that if I did my inner work I would become so famous I would "get suntanned from the flashbulbs"! Dreams often exaggerate to get their point across and generally are not to be taken literally.

One might expect that having such a dream would have been encouraging, but I remember waking up that morning and feeling even more depressed. "Does God have to pour salt in the wounds and make me feel even worse?" I thought at the time. "My life is falling apart, and all I can do is glimpse the Golden World through a silly, meaningless dream." That shows how blind I was to my own inner gold. I had a lot to learn.

~

ONE DAY I WAS OUT WALKING in the orange groves of Ojai, trying to sort things out. I was surrounded by nature's beauty, and yet I was feeling miserable. I stopped suddenly and said to myself, "This isn't working."

At that point I knew I had to try something else, but I had no idea where to turn. Later, I went to talk with a friend, and I burst into tears when I told her that I felt I must leave the Ojai community. I risked telling her my dream, which she listened to patiently. She was wonderfully understanding and responded to me, "Robert, what you should do is go see Fritz Kunkel in Los Angeles." She then explained that Dr. Kunkel was a Jungian analyst, a man who worked with dreams. She was certain that he could help me, she gave me a phone number, and she insisted that I call Dr. Kunkel. That slender thread took me in quite another direction.

Many years later I wanted to find Krishnamurti again to tell him how much I loved him and also what a wretched teacher he had been, but he died before I was able to share these feelings. In the next stage of my life I would begin the hard process of recollecting my own gold, and I would not return to my fascination with the East for many years. True, Krishnamurti had awakened the alchemical gold in me, but he did not know how to teach this clumsy Westerner how to reclaim it for himself. It remained for dreams and the process of Jungian analysis to accomplish this for me.

5

Fritz Kunkel Saves My Life:

Working with Dreams

Dr. Fritz Kunkel was my first analyst, and I found him through one of those slender threads that have guided my life. My friend in the Ojai community was wise enough to see that I was deteriorating badly while studying with Krishnamurti. She intervened just enough—not too much—to point me in the right direction; this is a rare faculty in a friend. She simply put me in touch with Dr. Kunkel, and much of the rest of my life has proceeded on the basis of that simple kindness. Call it luck or fate if you will, this type of synchronicity has occurred so many times that I now take it as a principle that whatever I need will turn up if I am patient and have the awareness to perceive it. These turns of fate have been so unpredictable and yet so wise that they are beyond any intelligence that my ego might claim.

At the time, it seemed as if I simply blundered into Jungian analysis with this elderly German gentleman. Dr. Kunkel was kind, fatherly, gentle, and warm; he was altogether an encouraging and supportive person. When we met he was in his sixties and had unruly white hair. Dr. Kunkel had been badly injured during World War I and had lost an arm. He dressed in a wool suit and tie, even during the heat of summer in Los Angeles, and he would tuck one sleeve of his coat into the side pocket.

Although he was not Jewish, he had fled Nazi Germany in the 1930s when he recognized the horror that was coming to that land.

He traveled all alone on a ship to America to build a new life, his family and children staying in Germany and following only many years later after the end of World War II.

My beginnings in therapy were less than auspicious. Dr. Kunkel agreed to take me on as a patient, but some days after my first interview he wrote a letter saying he was too busy and would not be able to continue with me. That nearly crushed me. It is difficult enough to get up the courage to begin psychotherapy, but then to face rejection from the analyst is really almost too much. I would find out later that Dr. Kunkel, by his own admission, had a serious flaw of never saying no, and he was capable of doing so only through such an indirect method as writing me a letter.

Following his rejection, I went to interview with more than half a dozen other therapists, hoping to find someone to help me. Others agreed to take me on as a client; however, no one but Dr. Kunkel seemed to understand the particular problems that I faced. To my credit, I persisted in contacting him again, and it was that persistence that made it impossible for Dr. Kunkel to turn me away. One day I drove to Los Angeles and parked outside Dr. Kunkel's house, where he had his office. I sat on the doorstep, and when he came out the door I burst out, "Dr. Kunkel, I cannot find anyone else who understands me. You have to take me." We began our analysis later that day.

I had read a bit of Carl Jung's work while I was in the Krishnamurti community, most particularly an essay that discussed Eastern wisdom and psychoanalysis, *The Secret of the Golden Flower*. There wasn't much of Jung's work that was available to me at the time, so I really didn't know what to expect in an analysis.

At our first official session, Dr. Kunkel gathered background information about my life, my current living and financial circumstances, my friends and social supports. He spoke slowly and deliberately, which was precisely my pace. I found out early on that he was fascinated by dreams and believed that they were critically important in finding a balance in one's life. This was a different approach for me.

Dr. Kunkel insisted that I immediately begin writing down my dreams and that I bring them to our sessions. "Pay particular attention to the dream you're going to have tonight," he said.

It was quite amazing to me what happened next. That night I had a remarkable dream:

> I hear that there is going to be a special showing of "reality" at the local cinema. I am very excited by this and can't wait to go. I arrive at the theater and step down into a basement, where there is a small, dark room. "At last I'm going to get to see reality," I think to myself. Then I become aware that my mother is managing the projector! The room darkens, the projector begins to whir, and my excitement continues to build. There is a flicker or two of light on the screen, and then the film breaks. An announcement is made that there will be a five-minute intermission, with an apology for the disruption. The film is repaired, the lights go down again, there is a flicker of light on the screen, and again the film breaks. The houselights come back up. I am getting more and more frustrated by all this, but I think to myself that if I am this close to reality I really shouldn't leave. So they turn the lights off again, and this time when the first flickers of light start to appear, the projector bursts into flames. The film is ruined, and even the screen somehow catches fire. I then realize that behind the screen is a huge, barren, warehouse type of building. It is like an aircraft hanger, with a concrete floor and no decoration. It is a godless place, totally devoid of warmth or feeling. In the middle of the warehouse is a middle-aged woman who is crying and asking for help. End of dream.

While this dream made little sense to me at the time, I can now see that it was telling me that I was going to get my reality but that it would not be as romantic and thrilling as I thought it would be. In the years ahead, after I became a Jungian analyst, I found that the majority of patients who came to see me were middle-aged women; so indeed, I spent a good deal of time listening to the reality of a lonely woman, stuck in an environment devoid of beauty and feeling, crying and asking for help. The feminine aspect of humankind continues to weep over the barrenness of modern life. That dream ushered me into my reality.

After that I began to dream pages and pages of big, elaborate dreams. Dr. Kunkel was fascinated by them, and he told me that many of the images were archetypal, a term that was entirely new to me.

Dr. Kunkel's teacher, Dr. Jung, believed that archetypes are blueprints of the basic human qualities we all share. The archetypes themselves are undefinable natural patterns or forces that shape life in all ages and places. They cannot be known directly, but archetypal themes and images appear in myth, fairy tales, dreams, and fantasies. We tend to think of ourselves as unique individuals, and to a great extent we are. But just as there are shared patterns that shape our physical existence, such as having two arms and legs, two eyes, ten fingers and toes, so there are underlying patterns that shape our psychic existence.

We see the expression of archetypes every day, and we can recognize them by their power to fascinate us and activate our emotions. For example, we may say that a particular woman is a "real earth mother" because she is nurturing, caring, and down-to-earth. Or we may say that an overly macho, aggressive man "thinks he's Rambo." These are archetypal images to describe patterns of behavior that everyone recognizes.

Dr. Kunkel pointed to many such archetypal images in my dreams, and together we began to unravel how they might be influencing my thoughts, feelings, and behavior. Early on in our analysis I had a remarkable dream, which came to me as follows:

I somehow become aware that there is an extremely valuable thing at the top of a mountain. There is a sense of urgency on my part to locate this valued item, and so I jump into my car and drive through the city up to the mountain. The mountain road is filled with many curves, and I continue driving up and up until I am past the timberline. As the elevation increases, my car begins sputtering. The carburetor is no longer working properly in the rarefied mountain air, and eventually my vehicle will go no farther. I park the car along the side of the road, get out, and begin walking. The mountain road continues to wind up higher and higher. When at last I reach the summit I can see that there are a few buildings and a small community living here. A group of highly intelligent, purposeful people resides up here, including Dr. Albert Schweitzer.

Dr. Schweitzer is a hero of mine. An accomplished musician, an author, a noted humanitarian, Schweitzer wrote the best book on J. S. Bach that I have ever read. I totally agree with his approach to performing the music of Bach, that it must be played slowly and deliberately, with ornamentation and great attention to detail. I dislike performers who rush through a Bach composition as though it were a mathematical exercise.

At this point, my dream becomes very specific. There is a small organ, which the dream examines in extraordinary detail. This organ is contained within an eight-foot cube. The upper keyboard is short, and the keys are black and ivory colored but reversed from their normal positions.

After examining this organ, I see Dr. Schweitzer. Then the most extraordinary thing happens—I eat Albert Schweitzer! As I bite into his flesh he quivers a bit, but it does not seem to cause him pain. As though cannibalism is quite natural, I finish devouring him and then walk back down the mountain. End of dream.

This was quite a shocking dream to me, though Dr. Kunkel helped me to sort it out. In dream language, which is vivid and often overexaggerated, I was learning to assimilate my own greatness. Dr. Schweitzer was a hero of mine, and like many young people I was projecting a hero image onto someone else rather than learning to express it through my own life.

A saying from the 1960s comes to mind. Health food advocates used to advise, "You are what you eat." This is also true psychologically. What you consume and emulate psychologically today is what you are capable of becoming tomorrow.

Dr. Kunkel never said much about my dreams, and he thereby taught me that the key is not so much to interpret a dream as to appreciate it and befriend it. The dream has a wisdom that is complete unto itself. What Dr. Kunkel provided, and what I so urgently required, was someone to value my dreams and to back me up as I worked to form a relationship with the dream images. Mostly he acknowledged what I was, no more and no less, warts and all. When I found that I could talk about anything and that he would listen unconditionally, it unleashed a torrent in me.

It is amazing what people can do if they are given the tools to help themselves and the emotional support to do so. That is really the essence of Jungian analysis—providing an environment that supports and encourages self-discovery. If the analyst does too much, it distorts the personality of the patient; if he or she does too little, it leaves the patient high and dry and the process bogs down. There is a middle ground where the therapist must stand and provide courage for the patient, assisting by providing tools and a safe environment in which to experiment by applying those tools. I could have projected my inner gold onto Dr. Kunkel as I had done with Krishnamurti, but he never asked for it; instead he had the wisdom to turn me back to myself via the dreams. Krishnamurti didn't want the projections of his followers, and he would continually tell them that the age of gurus was over, but Dr. Kunkel did something far more powerful: he explained how the mechanism of projection worked and gave me the tools to take my own gold back. For that I will be forever grateful to him.

Different analysts have different ideas about how much advice to dispense to their clients. After Dr. Kunkel I would later participate in analytical sessions with five other people, divided between men and women—Jolande Jacobi, Emma Jung, Carl Jung, Toni Sussman, and John Sanford—and each of them would teach me something unique and important. I think it wise to divide time in therapy between men and women and between different personality types, as they will draw different things out of you.

My dream of Dr. Schweitzer was indicative of the healing process that was taking place in me at this time. I had to learn to become my own Albert Schweitzer. He had a multiplicity of interests and refused to let any one thing dominate him. Throughout my life I had always been in danger of being a jack-of-all-trades and a master of none, so in a lesser way I was like Dr. Schweitzer. He was an accomplished physician, musician, and philosopher when suddenly at midlife he announced he was leaving his practice in Europe to become a missionary in the jungles of Africa. He came back to civilization occasionally to raise funds for his mission or to give an organ recital. Dr. Schweitzer was a great prototype for the heroic aspect of myself, and the genius of the dream was to assimilate those possibilities and suggest that I needed to "swallow" them into my own personality.

I am still in awe of how we grow psychologically. At first we admire a hero, never realizing that he or she only represents what needs to be realized in ourselves. Then, one year or five years later, if we are reasonably intelligent about working with our projections, we wake up to find that we have become someone very much like that hero. We affix our own possibilities by projecting them onto someone else, and then we gradually assimilate them. A fourteen-year-old sees his future in a sixteen-year-old—and in two years those admired qualities have been assimilated. A sixteen-year-old youth admires the qualities of a twenty-year-old, and if things go well she incorporates those qualities into her own personality by the time she is twenty.

This process continues throughout our lives. Our projections of the hero onto others always represent where we are headed. The process generally slows down as we get older and our personality becomes a bit more formed, but the basic mechanism is always at work. Modern people, as I have said, can no longer house their souls in another person or thing; we must learn to house them our-selves and find the highest value within.

⁓

THIS DREAM THAT I HAD early in my analysis with Dr. Kunkel pointed the way for me. Dr. Kunkel helped me to ground the dream in my life by giving me a very practical homework assignment. He told me to make a list of the things that were important to me and then to prioritize them in the order of their importance. I thought that sounded interesting and that it would only take a few minutes. We all know what is important to us, don't we?

I nearly drowned in that process. I worked for weeks on that list, thinking of new things, subtracting old ones, changing the order of what was really important to me. When I finally got them on paper I could see that many items overlapped. In fact, the priori-ties in my life could be condensed into three categories.

Number one was my love of people. Most of my life has always revolved around relationships with a few key people. During my teenage years it was my godparents in Portland. At the time of my analysis with Dr. Kunkel I had a couple of close friends in the Ojai community, and I was such a quiet, shy, and introverted person that the few friends I did have were invaluable to me. Dr. Kunkel pointed out that I demanded too much from any person I got close to. I began to learn that this intensity on my part broke down rela-tionships through the sheer weight of my own expectation.

Number two on my priority list was my love of nature. As a child growing up in Portland the sky was gray and it was raining so much of the time that I felt insulated from nature. But my need to be close to nature became apparent during the two summers that I worked as a fire lookout for the U.S. Forest Service in Washington. Today I even resent layers of clothing that separate me from my en-vironment, which is why I enjoy living near the ocean in southern California. On nearly any day of the year I can walk out my door and interact with nature.

My number three priority was music. Music and nature vied with each for the number two and number three positions. In times of my deepest depression it was always music that carried me through. Making my list and clarifying what was most important helped point me in a direction for my life. Money and power were not important to me; having time with my friends and the solace of nature were as essential to me as air and water.

For a time I was like a desperate monkey clinging to Dr. Kunkel with all four feet. I continued to live in Ojai, where I had purchased some land and had built a small adobe house while studying with Krishnamurti. Twice a month I drove to Los Angeles for my analytical sessions. Typically I would meet Dr. Kunkel for an hour at the end of the day, spend the evening in the city, and then meet again for an hour the next morning before driving back home. The ideal situation for analysis is to meet every week, preferably a couple of times each week, but that was not possible for me. Although I probably would have benefited from the consistency of more frequent sessions, I found that once the growth process began it soon took on a life of its own. I remember later hearing about an analysis conducted by a mentor of mine entirely by mail. This was dictated by the fact that World War II made travel impossible at the time. The analyst, who resided in London, agreed to work with a woman in Norway. The therapy went on for several years, though the analyst and the client never met in person. While far from ideal, even this situation worked.

Our analysis went on for several months, and I grew more and more centered and confident. Dr. Kunkel encouraged me to "leave a place for heaven" in my life, but by working with my dreams and visions he also helped me to become more grounded in the earthly world. We worked from the inside out.

I once asked Dr. Kunkel, "How do you learn psychology?"

He provided a wonderful answer. "There are three ways," he said. "One way is to read all the ancient Greek mythology, because it is all right there. A second way is to read the collected works of Carl Jung. And the third way is to wait and watch—that is really the best way."

For a time Dr. Kunkel carried the alchemical gold for me, and he did a relatively good job of giving it back at the right time. Although he saved my life, in retrospect I fault him for one serious error in our analysis. He should have instructed me about the possibilities and dangers of a large inflation when I took my gold back. Before beginning my analysis, I had been living out such a small percentage of my actual potential that when things began to turn around for me they went too far in the opposite direction.

In an inflation, it is as if a pendulum has been held to one side. When the pendulum is released it doesn't nicely return to the center point; instead it travels almost as far in the other direction. As my analysis progressed I got into a severe inflation, which embarrasses me to this day. I became cocky and arrogant, just the opposite of what I had been for so many years. There is no stopping an inflation like this once it gets going, but with some guidance one can at least put some discipline into moderating it. But Dr. Kunkel apparently was not aware of this psychological mechanism. He seemed proud and delighted at how much better I was doing. I now understand that inflation is an inevitable aspect of the analytical experience and that a good therapist should assist the client not only in pulling out of a downward slide but also in adjusting to the new challenges of feeling good.

I had another important dream toward the end of my analysis with Dr. Kunkel, a dream that was probably trying to warn me about the perils of my coming inflation. Here is the dream:

> I am sitting in the ground floor of a big forty-story building, when suddenly there is a terrible earthquake. I cannot get out of the building in time, and all the floors start to collapse on top of me. Amazingly, when the dust finally settles I am still alive and a shaft of sunlight guides me through the debris. I find my way out of the wreckage by following this beam of light. End of dream.

I didn't know what to make of this dream, and I don't recall doing much with it in my analysis with Dr. Kunkel. As so often happens, the unconscious continued with this theme, increasing the urgency and the drama to get my attention. A short time later I had another similar dream.

> This time I am standing next to a one-hundred-story building. There is no earthquake, but the building begins to collapse of its own weight. The building has been built up far higher than the underlying structure is capable of supporting. I can see the building begin to tremble, and people on the ground floor begin streaming out the front door to escape. Then the second floor collapses downward, becoming the new ground floor. One by one, the floors come crashing down on top of the one below, in each case leaving just enough time for the people to get out safely.

Today I can see that this dream was a clear signal that my overblown psychic structure was in danger of collapsing, though the human element could be saved without much harm to my personality. However, at the time I ignored this dream. Toward the end of my analysis with Dr. Kunkel I was feeling more confident and happy than I had ever been in my life. I would drive back to Ojai and tell everyone about the wisdom of my dreams while playing at being the big, important man.

Under Dr. Kunkel's tutelage, I was beginning to realize that my visions of the Golden World were not a curse but that instead I seemed to have a psyche that was finely tuned to the timeless wisdom of another world, the divine or archetypal world. For some reason, I was an individual who lived with very close contact to the collective unconscious, and Dr. Kunkel had opened up to me the value of reaching this inner world. I was even starting to believe that this somehow made me special instead of an outcast who was unfit for human society. As I have noted, I fault Dr. Kunkel for not spotting the inflation that was growing in me; I only wish that he had warned me that there are dangers in flying too high, but still I credit Dr. Kunkel with turning my life around. He put the tools in my hands that would change my life forever; principally, he showed me the power of dreams.

When a patient comes to my consulting room today, I always begin by reminding myself that I have no idea what is going on in the person and that I have no special wisdom to impart. The wisdom is not in me, it dwells within the patient, and so, like Dr. Kunkel, I begin by asking for a dream. The wisdom is in the dream. Dreams are transformers. Dreams are transformation. I generally don't take dreams literally, but I consider them a mechanism for fine-tuning. If I am doing too much of anything, the dreams will tell me. Some dreams are of the housekeeping variety, and it is only occasionally that I will have a dream that is significant for my entire lifetime. The dream of Albert Schweitzer was a big dream that provided a road map telling me who I was at the time and providing a guide as to the kind of person I was capable of becoming. I lived with that dream for years, puzzling over what it meant to develop the Schweitzer quality in me.

Telling someone else a dream is one of the most powerful things you can do, as this anchors it in consciousness. Even if the other person knows nothing at all about dreams, the act of writing a dream down and discussing it with someone else can be powerful. It is difficult to work on dreams by yourself. I later outlined procedures for working with dreams in my book *Inner Work*.

Some people still think that dreams are meaningless, which means to me that these people have never taken the time to write their dreams down over a period of time and open to the images. My counter to this belief is that dreams are the speech of God and that to refuse them is to refuse God. It's true that sometimes one should argue with them. I don't take dreams as gospel truth, and often they exaggerate something in the same way that the ego is exaggerating the opposite aspect in life. So you can't just follow whatever the dream says. Dreams are, however, highly curative and affirming. It is not that the dream is always right, but it always represents the situation in the unconscious just as it is at a particular point in time. It is dangerous to think you can just go off and live according to instructions in your dreams—but you can dialogue with them and use them to inform your life. Some people want to give up their authority to dreams, which is just as silly as ignoring them. For example, if you dream about the second coming of Christ, it doesn't mean that you should sell all your possessions and begin saving souls.

Often it is more important to pour energy into a dream than to work on its interpretation. The ego wants to pin down a meaning for the dream so that it can hold a prize in its hands, but that is not always essential or even necessary for the evolution of the psyche.

There is a wonderful story from India called "The King and the Corpse" that is relevant to the way in which many modern people dismiss the power of dreams. In the prologue to this story, the king is on his throne holding court. The kingdom is still small enough that the subjects can come to appear before the king and ask for his judgment on different matters. He holds audience each morning, and each day a monkey comes through the window and places a piece of fruit down before the king. This pleases the king, but when the monkey is gone the king always takes the piece of fruit and tosses it back behind the throne. This daily ritual goes on for some time. Finally, one of the king's chambermaids gets around to cleaning behind the throne, and she informs the king that there is a heap of jewels—priceless jewels and dozens of them! It turns out that a jewel had been hidden in each piece of fruit, and the arrogant king had been tossing them all away.

Just like the king, we receive a jewel each morning in our dreams, but we dismiss it because it seems to come from a monkey rather than a wise man or woman.

I once had a series of dreams that repeated the same motif over and over. In each dream I was trying to play the organ and something went wrong. There were endless variations of what went wrong, but the result was always the same. I began working on this dream, listing all my associations with music, hoping to unlock its meaning. But the dreams continued, with things ever happening to thwart my playing. I never did get a handle on that dream series, but in the last one I was sitting down at the organ for a recital and when I looked at the music sheet it was all squares and triangles. I realized in the dream that it was happening again—the same frustrating thing—but I remained lucid enough to stay with the dream. I began playing the organ. Although I had no idea what I was doing with those squares and triangles, the most beautiful music came out. Later I awoke, and I never dreamed of that subject again. I still don't understand what that dream series was about, but some aspect of my psyche was changing.

Eventually, I knew it was time to end my analysis with Dr. Kunkel, and once again the wisdom came to me in a dream.

> Dr. Kunkel is wearing a black suit and carrying a black briefcase. I have to lead the way along a path we are following, and as I can see that he is growing increasingly tired, eventually I also have to carry his briefcase. End of dream.

I realized from this dream that it was time to let go of my teacher and move on to the next stage of my life. I had assimilated most of the projection that I had given over to Dr. Kunkel and was ready to carry my own strength.

6

Unexpected Friendships, Unforeseen Blessings:

Slender Threads at Work

In 1948 I was flying high. Dr. Kunkel had turned my life around by showing me the power of my own dreams, but in moving out of a deep depression and stepping into my potential, I began to rebound too high.

I didn't realize it at the time, but I can now see that my transformation under the guidance of Dr. Kunkel quickly became too much of a good thing. As I have described, I entered a period of inflation. Carl Jung coined the term *inflation* because so many people who are in this state have dreams about being up in the air, like a bubble or a balloon. It's as though the dream is trying to tell us that we are full of hot air. When inflated, we also may have dreams of flying or being carried by a strong wind or being precariously perched in a high place. When one is flying high, it doesn't take long before the bubble bursts and we come crashing down. But at the time I had no notion of this psychological law. I felt great, and for perhaps the first time in my life the world seemed ripe with possibilities.

One of the first things that happens when we begin to carry our inner gold is to inflate. I had stopped projecting my highest value onto music and Krishnamurti, but in reclaiming it for myself, my ego began to identify with the inner gold instead of relating to it. Generally we are so amazed to find that the fount of wisdom comes from within ourselves that the first thing our egos do is to claim it. We start thinking that we are the guru.

I was happy, confident, strutting around like a bantam rooster. I even began telling others what they should do with their lives. One day I was talking with a friend who responded to my rising arrogance by asking, "If you could do anything you wanted, what would it be?"

"I would go to Europe," I blurted out.

I had long yearned to see Europe and to explore the roots of my culture. I was nourished by the music of Bach, photographs of Gothic cathedrals, and the literary pinnacles of Western civilization such as the works of Dante, Blake, and Goethe. But I never had the least notion of actually traveling to Europe. In the height of my new-found inflation, however, it suddenly seemed like exactly the right thing to do.

With that, my friend looked me in the eye, bid me *bon voyage,* and walked away. He had called my bluff.

There was no commercial air travel to Europe in 1948, and most of the ships had been sunk to the bottom of the Atlantic Ocean during World War II. However, I found that I could get a one-way ticket from New York to France on a converted troop transport ship for the princely sum of 168 dollars. So I announced to my dumb-founded friends in Los Angeles that I was off to Europe. It was quite unlike the shy, deeply introverted young man that they all knew, and, in fact, I had no idea what I was getting myself into.

Within a matter of weeks I was in New York checking in at the shipping agency. I soon learned that there was a new war scare. It was the beginning of the Cold War, and the rumor was that the Russians were going to march to the sea and take over all of Europe. As a result, more than 70 percent of the passengers on my ship had canceled their reservations. But with my inflated sense of personal power, no mere Red army was going to stop me. I was determined to follow through with my plans. I was off to Europe.

Upon boarding the ship, I discovered that the converted troop transport was not converted in the slightest sense. There was not so much as a chair on deck, but I was basking in excitement and quite content to sit on a hatch cover. I joyfully watched the gangplank being hoisted up. A whistle blew, and a smoky tug appeared to pull the ship from the wharf.

Then, the inevitable happened: without warning, the bubble of my inflation burst. I was suddenly terrified. What, in the name of God, had I gotten myself into? I began trembling, and my knees quite literally shook. I had no idea of where to go after the ship docked in France; I knew no one in Europe, and I spoke no French. My funds were limited. I was all alone. The shoreline of America was receding in the distance, and it was already too far away to jump overboard. My high-flying inflation swung like a pendulum to the worst sort of pessimism as I crawled below deck to my cabin. Within hours, I could barely hold anything in my stomach, a condition I blamed on seasickness, but it was more than that.

When we allow ourselves to be taken over by an inflation, we set ourselves up for a strong dose of its opposite. A little bit of inflation is inevitable, as our moods come and go, but in this culture we tend to push the opposites to dangerous extremes. Alternatively, a healthy life is like walking: you put your weight on your left foot, then the right foot, then the left foot, and so on. There is a natural rhythm of thinking you are a bit more than you really are, then a bit less, then a bit more, and so on. It is necessary to stop every now and then to regain your equilibrium. We get into trouble when we allow the rhythm to get drastically out of balance (such as charging off to Europe without having thought through the consequences). I did not simply have an inflation. An inflation had me.

The evolution of consciousness is a dangerous process, and it remains to be seen if this experiment in nature will succeed. When we stop projecting the alchemical gold outside ourselves and find it within, we then must go through a stage in which we identify with the highest value rather than trying to serve it. On a collective basis, we are in this stage now. Western society is all ego driven, secular, scientific—operating under the assumption that rational consciousness can determine all things. This is a perilous time in which we live; collective inflation can be seen in the madness of Nazi Germany, the proliferation of nuclear weapons, the poisoning of our planet by pollutants. On an individual basis, one must also suffer this period of arrogance, but then, hopefully, we realize that we are here to serve the Golden World, not to rule it.

In an inflation, we identify with the Golden World, when what is needed is a humble and respectful relationship to it. No one, and no society, can maintain an inflation for long. Just as stock markets crash and artificially stimulated economies must come down, so do people.

As our ship left the harbor, I fell into despair and deflation. It was a ten-day ocean crossing, and the ship was nearly empty. I had my choice of bunks in a dormitory room arranged to house five people. That first night I curled up against a wall, pulled a rough wool blanket over me, and sobbed myself to sleep.

Eventually, however, I had to emerge from my lonely cell. When we come crashing down from an inflationary high, the best prescription is ordinariness and order. I needed to be a nobody again and to be accepted for my ordinariness. I sat on the deck of that ship scribbling in a notebook. I tried drawing a coat of arms for myself with a tiny figure taking one step forward, sliding two step backward, but making it to heaven in the end because he was going the wrong direction in the first place! It seemed like I had to learn everything the hard way.

That was when I met Art. While walking along the deck, I happened upon a young fellow standing at the rail and looking out to sea. He was at least a foot shorter than my lanky six-foot-three frame, with dark curly hair, a hawk's nose, and intense brown eyes. I edged up and introduced myself.

"Good morning. I'm Robert."

He appeared to be slightly startled.

"Yeah?" After glancing in my direction, he returned his gaze to the horizon. "Big ocean out there, isn't it?"

I felt awkward and clumsy. My loneliness pushed me out of my shell, but I didn't know what to say next. I put one arm over the rail and stood as he stood, looking out at the water.

He turned again to size me up. Then he held out a hand.

"Good to know ya. I'm Art. Art Meyer."

Art was a native New Yorker. He spoke with a clipped cadence and was as outgoing and confident as I was shy and frightened. Having recently turned twenty-one, Art was a few years my junior, but he seemed much more worldly. I soon learned that he was totally materialistic. For Art life was an extended arm wrestling match in which there were winners and there were losers. Art had no patience with losing.

"New York is nuts," Art said. "I've had enough of that town to last a lifetime." He was headed to Paris to "see what's left over there."

Art carried the conversation, and I made a sympathetic audience. We managed to find a common interest, however. We both played chess. From our first chess match I quickly learned that Art took no prisoners.

There was little to do on the ship, so our daily battle of wits at the chessboard soon drew an audience. Word got around that there was a duel to the death taking place on deck. We took long deliberations between moves. As Art became increasingly intense, I realized I had two choices. If I beat him at chess, our friendship would end as quickly as it had begun, and if I let him win he would lord it over me for the entire voyage. Neither alternative seemed attractive. I don't like winning or being won over, but I couldn't think of a graceful exit. I began looking for a way out. Three days into the chess match, a storm began brewing up at sea and the ship started rolling with increased vigor. When a good-sized wave sent the ship lurching, our chessboard slid off the table and the pieces tumbled to the deck floor. Art and I both looked up and almost simultaneously announced that we couldn't possibly remember where the chess pieces had been. The match could only end as a draw. Both of us had determined to value our newfound friendship more than the competition. To this day, I remember exactly where every piece on that chessboard was positioned.

I gradually came to suspect that Art's bravura and self-importance were a cover for a deep sense of insecurity. But I knew he would scoff at any discussion of feelings, so I kept my speculations to myself. Our conversation remained safely restricted to the world of things, where Art was comfortable. I was glad to have a friend for the balance of the ocean crossing, even though we planned to go our separate ways once the ship docked in Le Havre. Our chance meeting was a slender thread that would become a major influence in my life.

During my voyage across the Atlantic I did manage to make one other friend, a young Frenchman named Michel. We became acquainted when he got entangled in his life jacket during an "abandon ship" safety drill. I was the one to extricate him. I gradually learned that Michel had been in New York only six months. He had traveled to America after the war to make his success in the new world, but he had not found the streets to be paved with gold. He had become homesick.

Michel called himself "the last remnant of the bourgeoisie." He wore a black beret much of the time, which added a touch of the bohemian to his pale, delicate appearance. Possessing a sweet disposition, Michel was, like me, driven by feeling. He was the polar opposite of Art. Michel was never cut out for the world of business and commerce, and there was no way for him to survive in the sharp-edged, hard-charging pace of New York. The new world was a deep disappointment to Michel, and I could immediately empathize with his anguish at not fitting in with the American temperament.

One day we were talking about his disappointment with New York, and Michel confided in me. "Robert, it was not beautiful. I saw trash everywhere, even in the water. I thought it would be so rich, so beautiful."

My heart sank. It was such a childish thing to say. He held a glorified, romantic view of the new world. I could see that Michel's fantasy of America had been based upon a projection of the Heavenly Jerusalem. No reality could ever match his expectation, and now Michel was returning home with his tail tucked between his legs. I felt like saying to him, "Well, what did you expect?"

My conversation with Michel immediately reminded me of a dream I had experienced just a few weeks before boarding the ship and departing for Europe. Here is the dream:

> I have somehow found out where the Heavenly Jerusalem is located. With great excitement, I hop into my 1936 Ford and speed away. I am in a great hurry because I know that the gates to the Heavenly Jerusalem close at 5 P.M. I zoom past the gate and enter just in time. In fact, the closing gate nicks the back bumper of my Ford as I race through. I drive up a winding road and come to a gatekeeper. He waves me away, saying, "You can't drive a car in here. Get out! Get out!" Crestfallen, I drive my car back down the winding road and park it at the bottom of the hill. The gate is open anytime for those who walk. Leaving the car, I walk up the road again and find myself before a gatekeeper at the top of the hill. I walk into the Heavenly Jerusalem, and the gatekeeper accompanies me as a guide. This magic land contains all my projections about Europe. There are narrow, winding streets and half-timbered houses. I am walking down an ancient cobblestoned street when a cat runs in front of me with a dog chasing on its heels. I am dumbfounded.
>
> I turn to my heavenly guide and say, "Don't tell me that dogs chase cats here."
>
> "Of course. Well, what did you expect?" he replies.
>
> We continue down the road, until I see a man and woman standing on a second-floor balcony. Clearly they are quarreling, as they are screeching at the top of their lungs.
>
> I turn to my guide again and say, "Don't tell me that people fight in heaven."
>
> "Of course. What did you expect?" he says.
>
> That was the end of my dream.

That expression, "Well, what did you expect?" has been in my vocabulary ever since. When I hear someone talking about their projections I almost automatically want to respond, "Well, what did you expect?"

Michel was too fragile for such a remark, so I held my tongue, but I could quickly see how this young Frenchman was subject to the same psychological patterns that took place in me.

With my two newfound friends, Art and Michel, I gradually overcame my deflation and made it through my first ocean crossing. With the sight of French soil, I was again flush with enthusiasm. As the ship pulled into port, Art and I said our good-byes.

"Have a grand adventure, Robert. Europe is ours for the taking," Art declared.

After the ship was safely docked in Le Havre, I accompanied Michel across the corrugated steel gangplank and down into the busy customs area. As we stepped into a whirl of strangers, fear again began to darken my excitement, and I quickly confessed to Michel that I had no idea where I was going. Michel smiled and took me by the arm, for now he had the home-court advantage. He escorted me through customs and even handled the purchase of my train ticket to Paris. I was thankful for his help and thought that would be the end of it, but in Paris Michel continued to take me in tow. At the Paris train station we were met by his parents and a sizable group of friends. We were swept up into a welcome-home party, in which Michel showed me off like a souvenir from the distant shores of America. Michel's warmhearted clan insisted on including me in a wonderful meal, and before the evening was over, they had me installed in a room a couple of buildings away from the family's apartment. Who could have predicted such good luck?

It was a small room, filled with worn furniture. The floral wallpaper was well past its prime and was curling at the edges. Paris was still bruised and battered from the war. Food was being rationed, and there were shortages of basic commodities. Goodwill was in abundance, however, and over the next several days various people came to my apartment to arrange meals and to take me on guided tours of Paris. They seemed to appear regularly in four-hour shifts. We visited the Eiffel Tower, the Arche de Triomphe, the many museums. Eventually my knees stopped shaking and I began to feel safe in Paris. It was a gift of friendship I will never forget.

One day, while walking alone on the street, I recognized a familiar face. It was Art. What a chance meeting in a city of more than three million inhabitants! We greeted each other and quickly compared notes on where we had been and what we had seen and done in Paris.

Although Art smiled and declared that everything was fine, I instinctively sensed that there was more to the story.

"Art, are you really okay?"

"Yes, I am wonderful." His mouth smiled, but his face was drawn.

"I'm not so sure. What is the trouble?"

"Nothing, I'm fine."

"Why don't I believe you?"

"I don't know, Robert, everything is great."

"Well, where did you sleep last night?"

Eventually he stammered out his sad story. He had been sleeping under a bridge. Art had determined to be a success at an early age. He swore to everyone he knew in New York that he would be a millionaire by the age of twenty-one. He worked numerous jobs, accumulated a savings, and made some investments. But it had all collapsed, and he had lost everything. He had turned twenty-one just before leaving New York, and he was too ashamed to face his family and friends with the reality of his poverty.

Art had managed to scrape together just enough for a one-way passage, but upon arriving in France he was virtually penniless.

I took him off for a good meal and labored for the next several hours to convince him it was not the end of the world. He was in tears and inconsolable. I talked and talked until eventually he looked up and said, "I think I understand what you are saying. I should fight the problem, not myself."

"Yes, Art, that is what you must do."

When we parted company that day I loaned him some money, though I was on a thin budget myself. I presumed I would never see my donation again, but I had an affection for Art, deepened by our secret, unspoken pact to end the chess game. We agreed to meet the next day for another meal, and together we visited the Louvre. It was paradise walking from one long room to another. The glory of ancient Greece touched my heart through marble statues that seemed to breathe. Delicately detailed illuminated manuscripts spoke to me of the spiritual purity of the monks who had labored over them. And wall after wall of paintings from the masters: El Greco, Rembrandt, Titian, Leonardo da Vinci. I was filled with the passion, melancholy, desire, and joy that generations of artists had poured forth into their work.

Art, on the other hand, had little appreciation for art. We stopped before a nineteenth-century romantic sculpture in which a lion was attacking a man, the claws tearing into the victim's tender flesh. Art commented that it was such a silly image. "Why do they call this art?"

I responded that art was about feeling. "Isn't this how you felt yesterday, like claws were tearing apart your flesh?"

He seemed to understand.

Shortly after that day I left Paris. Art and I exchanged addresses and promised to correspond with each other after we returned home. I was still worried for Art's future, but adventure called and so we went our separate ways.

～

WITHIN A FEW SHORT MONTHS, in the fall of 1948, I was enrolled at the C. G. Jung Institute in Zurich, studying to become an analyst (a story I will tell in the following chapter). I was just beginning my studies when one day Art unexpectedly appeared at the door of the institute. I was surprised and delighted to see him in Zurich, but what was most astonishing was his appearance. Art appeared to be the model aristocratic gentleman, from his black homburg hat down to his white spats and finely polished shoes. I immediately noticed the sizable diamond in the ring that graced his hand. Art's luck had clearly undergone a transformation.

Later that evening when we met at one of Zurich's finest restaurants, I refrained from asking Art about his good fortune, thinking that the story would eventually pour forth. We enjoyed a sumptuous feast, ordering a variety of dishes that in combination cost more than my weekly allowance for meals. Art ordered a fine bottle of French wine, which he made a great show of tasting and then granting his approval. When the bill came, Art insisted on paying, and what is more, he plopped down a stack of currency before me.

"That is the money you loaned me in Paris," he declared.

I thanked him, rejoicing inwardly at my unexpected good fortune. I never thought that I would see that money again. Even as we walked to the train station to say good-bye, Art avoided discussing the source of his newfound wealth, and I was too polite to ask. It was months before I would see Art again. He returned to Paris, while I set about the business of training to become a Jungian analyst.

Living in Zurich was extremely expensive. In addition to the small room that I rented by the month and tuition at the institute, I was obliged to pay for analysis as part of my training program. By Christmastime, even with the unexpected boost in my savings from Art's visit, I was running out of money, and the handwriting was on the wall. I did not have enough funds left to pay for the spring semester, and, reluctantly, I faced the fact that I would have to leave my studies and return to America while I could still afford a ticket home.

Late in 1948 I informed the institute of my plight and purchased a ticket for a January crossing of the Atlantic. I had not a single friend in Zurich. The Swiss, by and large, are wonderfully efficient, thinking-type people, well suited to watchmaking, banking, and business, but not warm or outgoing with strangers, particularly a shy and awkward American. I assumed that no one would even notice my absence when the new semester began.

And so it was that I boarded a train from Zurich to Paris, bound for a brief farewell visit with Michel and his family prior to my departure for America. But something quite unexpected changed my plans.

I was walking through the streets of Paris with a melancholy heart, taking in the sights and sounds. Shopkeepers scrubbed their floors preparing for a new business day, the smell of fresh bread and strong coffee floated out from sidewalk cafés, motorbikes sputtered by, and barges whistled as they surged up the Seine. The light in Paris is most extraordinary, soft and subtle like an Impressionist painting. It contributes to the feeling that Paris is a feminine city, even in the midst of her hustle and bustle. And at night, when the streetlights come on, it is as though she has donned a sparkling necklace. I was brokenhearted to leave, and had no idea what I would do when I returned home to the United States. In this state of mind I wandered through antique shops, admiring the beautiful craftsmanship displayed in furniture, clocks, and musical instruments. As I wandered about without direction, who should appear before me but Art.

We marveled at the remote chance of bumping into each other again in this gigantic city. I had assumed that by this time Art was back in New York. He figured I was studying away in Zurich.

Unlike Art, I did not try to disguise my circumstances. I quickly told him my plight and of the impending voyage back home. My voice began to complain as I went on and on. I told Art that matters had been made still worse because that very day I had come across a Blanché harpsichord for sale.

During our ocean voyage Art had learned of my great love for the arts and my craving for the culture of Europe, but he did not know that my love for baroque music had been my lifeline to the Golden World for more than a decade and that I had a passion for harpsichords. I explained that a Blanché harpsichord was one of the finest instruments ever built. That very morning, while wandering through the shops of Paris, I had come across just such an instrument. Handcrafted in the seventeenth century, its surface was as sumptuous as its tone. It was ornately painted with pastoral scenes of mountains and valleys filled with flowers. The strings were plucked with little bits of quill, which produced a heavenly sound. Finding such an instrument was like falling in love. The shopkeeper allowed me to return three times that day just to sit at its double keyboard in wonder and awe. Times were still hard in Paris during these postwar years, and the harpsichord was priced at 1 million francs (about 2,000 dollars in U.S. currency), an incredible bargain. But it could just as well have been priced at 1 million dollars as far as my finances were concerned.

Art listened to my caterwauling with the patience I had once afforded him. When I was through complaining, he replied with a smile, "Robert, I don't know a thing about harpsichords, but it seems to me that you cannot go home from Europe empty-handed. I intend to buy you this harpsichord and have it shipped back to New York. I trust that you will repay me someday."

My heart went from despair to joy. This was beyond my wildest expectations. Art further advised me that he was late for an appointment, but we agreed to meet at the antique shop at ten o'clock the following morning. Off he went.

I could scarcely sleep that night, tossing and turning in my hotel bed. I awoke early, shaved, dressed, and charged past the front desk, scarcely noticing when the concierge told me that I had received some mail. I arrived at the antique store an hour early, savoring the thought that this Blanché harpsichord would soon be mine. Ten o'clock passed, and by ten-thirty I began to get nervous. It became eleven, and still I waited. When noon came and went, my heart plunged. Reluctantly, I realized that Art must have had second thoughts about his offer. I couldn't blame him, but that did not lessen the sting I felt trudging back to the hotel.

At the front desk I stopped for my room key and was also handed my mail. It suddenly occurred to me that it might contain some message from Art. I hurried up the stairs, sat down on my bed, and tore open the parcel. It was filled with a pile of money and a note from Art saying that I should return to Zurich and finishing my education.

What a roller-coaster ride! I was exhausted, relieved, delighted, and anguished—all at the same time. I could return to the institute, and my friend Art had come through after all. But I would not get the harpsichord of my dreams. Perhaps that was why Art didn't show up that morning at the antique store—it was too difficult for him to see the look of disappointment in my eyes. Still, I thought, it was a beautiful thing to do, and I had no way of thanking him since I lacked his Paris address. I hoped that our paths would someday cross again.

And so I stashed my newfound wealth in a suitcase, cashed in my ticket for passage back to New York, and returned to the C. G. Jung Institute in Zurich. I reenrolled and began the spring semester.

"We thought you were returning to America," said a fellow student.

"Oh, I was going to, but you see a man stopped me on the streets of Paris and gave me a suitcase full of money," I replied with only half a smile.

No one knew whether to believe me or not.

~

THE SLENDER THREAD THAT BROUGHT ART and me together would have been remarkable enough if it had ended there, but it did not.

The thread picks up some months later after I had completed my analytical studies in Zurich and finally returned to the United States after stops in Germany and England. My summer vacation had turned into a year and a half. I had lived a modest but comfortable existence during the remainder of my stay in Switzerland, thanks to Art's generosity, but my pockets were again nearly empty when I arrived in New York. My father had died while I was abroad, and my plan was to fly from New York to Portland to settle his humble estate and pick up the automobile he had left me. But before leaving New York I pulled out the one-thousand-franc note on which Art had once scribbled his home address and phone number. I called the number and heard a harsh male voice on the other end. I was told that there was no one named Art at that number. Just to be sure, I dialed the number again with considerable care, only to get the same voice, which barked, "Look, there's no Art here, now don't bother me again."

I left New York.

Despite my lack of success in reaching Art, for the next several years I sent a holiday card each December to the New York address he had provided me, hoping to find him one day. Five years passed. By this time I was becoming established in my analytical practice in Los Angeles. One day, out of the blue, I received a letter from Art. It was brief but to the point:

> Dear Robert,
>
> I am sorry that I did not meet you that morning in Paris to buy your harpsichord. I intended to, but shortly after I sent that school money over to your hotel I was arrested. You see, I had taken the money you loaned me and set up a very effective system to forge American Express travelers checks. That is where your money came from. I am sorry to say, however, that the FBI caught up with me at 6 A.M. that morning we were supposed to meet. I have just been released from a five-year prison term in Sing Sing.
>
> Sincerely,
> *Art*

I was absolutely astonished. It wasn't just hearing about Art's fate, it was the realization that I had attended the C. G. Jung Institute on the proceeds from forged American Express traveler's checks. What an ironic twist of fate! I couldn't help thinking that if only the FBI had been one day slower I might also have been the proud owner of a Blanché harpsichord!

I wrote back to Art and told him that I could now afford to pay him back the loan for my schooling, and a cashier's check for the full amount was enclosed. A few months later Art sent me an urgent telegram with thanks for paying back the loan and asking if I could lend him the same amount to help him out of a jam. It strained my finances to the limit, but I scraped together the money and wired it back to Art. I never heard from him again.

And so it was that I boarded a troop ship bound for France, met an innocent lad over a chess match, stumbled through Europe without knowing a soul, wandered into the first training classes offered at the C. G. Jung Institute, was handed a suitcase full of money, became a Jungian analyst, and paid 100 percent interest on my unofficial student loan.

This was just one of the many slender threads that have guided my life. Who could have predicted the friendships I made, the doors that would open, or the directions these contacts would lead me? It was all beyond my wildest imagination. Yet, as I look back on it now, there was a coherent pattern at work. My fate was being guided in ways that I still did not understand.

I continue to grapple to find new terminology for talking about the religious life. Each age needs its own language for understanding enduring truths, and while many people feel uncomfortable talking about religion, our ego-centered, so-called real life is disintegrating at this point in history. The ancient world didn't have much of what we call reality; they lived, instead, by the slender threads. We have gained ego reality but have lost the mystical and religious functions that should guide our lives.

The concept of listening to the will of God is difficult for many modern people to follow, as it collides with our love of freedom and our insistence on free will. However, I must declare that, with respect to the most important aspects of my life, I am not free. I am safest when I let go of trying to control my life and instead follow the slender threads. This is a religious perspective in the sense that the human ego must surrender to something more powerful than itself.

Freedom insists that the ego can do anything it wishes. I do not mean to toss the concept of freedom out entirely. Of course we have free will, but I am insisting that in every moment there is one right thing to do: we can choose to follow the will of God or not follow the will of God, and only in this way can we live meaningful lives.

I have learned to trust the slender threads for the big decisions in my life while using my ego to take care of the small details. I thought I was free when I willed my way onto a ship to Europe, but my plan soon broke under me. The concept of freedom can become an inflation. When my inflationary bubble burst, the slender threads in all their power continued to function and guide me in a particular way, connecting me with Art Meyer and ultimately taking me to Dr. Jung's study.

Humankind has struggled with the dilemma of how to balance fate versus free will since time began. There have been many rules of thumb for how to achieve such a balance. My personal approach is that the big events of my life follow a slender thread while the details are my business. Nobody but me will balance my checkbook or shave me or keep my house tidy. Those are the appropriate tasks for the ego. The little decisions belong to us, while the great things are like the weather sweeping us along. Yet most modern people spend a majority of their waking hours worrying about larger issues that the ego cannot really control. The small and limited ego is not the proper human faculty for such issues. The ego does not belong in the driver's seat. In fact, the ego often gets in the way of being attentive to the slender threads. We must learn to humble and quiet our egos so that we may follow the slender threads.

After many years of struggling with this, I feel that the ego is properly used as the organ of awareness, not the organ of decision. Almost everyone in our society tries to use the ego as an organ of decision. For example, we may say to ourselves, "I am going to Europe. I will buy the air tickets for this date, and I will stay at this hotel when I arrive." The ego is useful for collecting information about ticket fares and accommodations and things to see and do when you arrive. But the ego does not determine the experience you will have on your trip. People get so preoccupied with trying to control things that are not in the ego's province that they neglect what is the ego's business—heightened awareness. The ego should be collecting data and watching. The ego serves as the eyes and ears of God. It gathers the facts, but it does not make the ultimate decisions. The decisions come from the Self, Dr. Jung's term for a center of intelligence that is not limited to the ego but contains all of the faculties— conscious and unconscious—of the personality. Obviously, this is but a new attempt to describe the old concept of a personal relationship with God.

How do we know if we are truly following the will of God? One knows instinctively; there is a sense of peace, balance, and fullness, an unhurriedness. One of my favorite authors, the French philosopher Hubert Benoit, writes that there is one, and only one, appropriate action in any given moment of time. If you are in that action, then you are happy and peaceful. I am still trying to grow up to this notion of Benoit's. He suggests that if you think you have a choice, you are not seeing the reality of things correctly. The will of God is always singular. I believe this, but I can't always stand the truth of this statement. Certainly, it runs counter to our sense of free will and self-determination. We want the maximum number of choices and the freedom to choose among them. Madison Avenue is the purveyor of discontent; virtually all advertising is designed to create discontent so as to create a market for a product.

When you are following the will of God, there is no choice whatsoever. Here I am not talking about following scripture to the letter. That is one way of being happy, but for most modern people this is not a viable solution. Looking for a manual to tell you what to do, whether that manual is the Bible or the latest psychological theory, is not useful. Listening to the will of God as it manifests within your own psyche, hearing what has been called the still, small voice within—this is the religious life. This cannot be reduced to a tidy formula, but one general guideline is to ask yourself what is needed for wholeness in any situation. Instead of asking what is good or what coincides with our personal interest, ask what is whole-making. Sainthood is the result of wholeness, not goodness. What is required for more wholeness will be different for each person, and it changes moment by moment. This requires realigning yourself each day, each hour, and each moment. When one can live in this fashion, aligning the ego with the inner Self, it has a profound effect on the quality of our lives. Abiding by the will of God gives life—including its misfortunes—meaning, purpose, and dignity. It also removes a great deal of the anxiety of modern life.

I must also caution the reader that following the slender threads does not mean manipulating things so that the ego can get its way. Egocentric spirituality just gets one into more intense suffering. Going after the splendor of heaven as an ego project is very different from having heaven open itself up to you. Many so-called spiritual people set about the task of increasing the amount of goodness in their life or the amount of lightness or brightness or happiness. I disagree with that approach entirely. It is an egocentric journey with no nobility in it. More often than not, seeking more goodness or happiness just leads to their exact opposite. I sometimes think that exhaustion is the best tool for enlightenment, as it gets the ego out of the way. It finally just wears down so that the divine can pour through.

If I don't know how to make a certain decision, I should use the ego to get all the information I can and then wait. Eventually the will of God will be revealed to me. It is deceiving to say, "I will know," and more correct to say, "It will be revealed to me." A friend of mine jokes about this. I asked him, "What are you going to do with your car while you're off in India?" and he replied, "Robert, it has not been revealed to me yet."

The way to approach this manner of living is to start with extremely small things. Don't think about it too much or you will end up in contradiction. Just start by attending to how you make decisions in small things. Instead of weighing all the pros and cons and forcing a decision with your ego, simply try to keep your ego alert, and slap its hand gently when it tries to do too much. For example: I have to get groceries this afternoon. Should I go to the small market near my house or the larger one with a greater selection several miles away? Instead of trying to decide, I will just wait until I know where to go. This is in some ways a ridiculous example, but if you practice you will find that there is a difference when the ego says something and when the Self says something; I know from experience that the impetus comes from different places in me. That other center is capable of decisions, and you can almost feel in your body the difference between a Self decision and an ego decision. The ego decision seems to come from your head, while the Self decision seems to come from your heart or your stomach (we sometimes call it a "gut feeling").

How do we know when to exert our will and when to let go and surrender to the will of God? There are times when we need to exert our wills. For most young people, the focus must be on strengthening the ego, passing the necessary exams, graduating from school, staying with the marriage, and so on. The focus must be on learning to direct the will to accomplish the cultural tasks of life. I don't advise everyone to sit and wait for a miracle to save them or for someone to rescue them. Following the will of God isn't about resignation or sipping a can of beer and watching television or passively "going with the flow." Rather, it means applying the ego to gather as much information as possible to serve as the eyes and ears of God. But for the major decisions of life, it must learn to listen to the heart to hear what is the right thing to do.

THE POSSIBILITY OF THE SLENDER THREADS operating at all times is so staggering that most of us can't bear it. Dr. Jung used his word *synchronicity* to designate a meaningful coincidence. A synchronistic phenomenon occurs when an inwardly perceived event such as a dream or vision seems to correspond in a meaningful way to an external reality. Neither the inner nor the outer event can be explained by causality, yet they seem to be connected. Most people have examples of this, such as when you are thinking of some person you haven't talked to in years and suddenly a letter shows up in the mail from that very person or you bump into the person on the street. Causality is inadequate to explain such phenomena, so we may dismiss them as just coincidence or chance. Dr. Jung speculated that the two events are acausal but are linked by meaning, and this may relate to some archetypal processes at work in the unconscious.

I think that the slender threads are continually present, it is just our ability to accept them that varies. It may be impossible for us to realize this because it would result in our seeing meaning everywhere in all things. This is the perspective of a saint, but for most of us it is unbearable. It is probably true that we live in a universe with more meaning in it than we can comprehend or even tolerate. Life is not meaningless; it is overflowing with meaning, pattern, and connections.

7

A Love of Music, a Call to Psychology:

We Choose a Career, a Vocation Chooses Us

It has been said that when memory and pride are fighting, pride almost always wins out. So it was with me for many years. I used to imply to people that I had crossed the Atlantic in 1948 with the specific intent of studying psychology with Carl Jung. That made the trajectory of my life seem a bit more coherent. But the truth is that a slender thread, not any rational plan, led me to Jung's door. It is highly irrational on our part to presume that God is rational or to think that divine guidance follows a linear path. Often I have felt more like soft putty in the hands of fate. About the only virtue I can claim is that I didn't get in the way when destiny called.

After gaining my bearings in Paris, thanks in no small part to the generosity of my French friend Michel and his clan, I decided to travel to Strasbourg to attend a month-long music festival. It was one of the first cultural festivals to be held in Europe following the devastation of the war, and it was generating great excitement among music lovers across the continent. I took a train from Paris to Strasbourg, and from my window seat I watched the French countryside rolling by: first the suburbs of Paris, then fields of mustard flowering bright yellow in the spring sunlight, followed by picturesque French villages.

When I arrived in Strasbourg and began finding my way around the city, I soon learned to use the towering medieval cathedral as my northern star. The Strasbourg Cathedral is one of the most beautiful Gothic structures ever crafted by human hands. Though delicate and lacelike in its detail, this cathedral climbs to the heavens with soaring power. The stonemasons who labored for decades over this masterpiece surely made stone withstand more stress than any stone should have to withstand. Parts of the cathedral defy gravity, and erosion over the centuries has increased the risk that the whole structure may some day come toppling down. But for now, the Gothic spirit lives on.

I sometimes believe that I am a Gothic person at heart, that I was born in the wrong century. I often ask the earthy elements of my life to support more than is reasonable while I grasp for the heavenly realm. The term *Gothic* was coined for architecture, to describe structures with an abundance of light and interiors that are amazingly airy and weightless with ceilings that rocket up to the stars. The high Gothic cathedrals of France and Germany represent a concentrated focus of energy such as has rarely been seen before or since, an attempt to reach through this world and to touch a world beyond.

The psyche of Europe could not maintain the soaring spirit of the Gothic age, but the cathedrals have somehow held together over the centuries. Even when it was shaken by the bombs of World War II, the Strasbourg Cathedral still held together. Bombs went through the roof, obliterating stained glass that was hundreds of years old. One window was put back together piece by broken piece by the citizens of Strasbourg. This window is eloquent testimony to the destructive power of war, with a disembodied saintly head placed in one section, a lost hand in another corner, pieces of animals stuck together at disturbing angles.

The tower bells also are rich with history. In the sixteenth century, Strasbourg was caught up in the Protestant Reformation, and the cathedral was for a time held by the Protestants. When it was won back by the Catholic Church, the pope decreed that although the cathedral had been a passive participant in the Protestant heresy, the bells had actively proclaimed false beliefs! The pope insisted that the bells be taken down, melted, and recast. Before his orders could be carried out, however, good sense and economy prevailed. It was determined that it would be too costly to remake the bells, so instead it was ordered that the bells be flogged for their heresy. Accordingly, the bells were brought down from the high tower, a gigantic task that was accomplished using primitive squirrel-cage leverage staffed by a dozen workers rotating a cylinder high in the platform of the bell tower. The bells were publicly flogged to induce repentance for their loud sins. Then the bells were brought back up to the high tower and rotated an eighth of a turn so that the hammers would strike a different part of the bell.

When the Germans captured Strasbourg during World War II, some imbecile determined that the tower bells had virtually the same essential ingredients as war machinery—89 percent copper, 10 percent tin, and 1 percent antimony—and should be sacrificed to the war effort. Accordingly, the bells were taken down and shipped to Germany, where they were to be recycled as scrap, but once again fate intervened to save them. The war ended before the bells could be melted in a Third Reich blast furnace. During the occupation by Allied troops, a soldier from Strasbourg found the historic bells covered in dust in the yard of a German foundry. They were shipped back to Strasbourg, where they have remained ever since. These Gothic marvels persist in giving voice to the yearning for God.

Each morning I made my way to the cathedral, and my afternoons and evenings were filled with joyous exultation at the music festival. The Strasbourg festival offered two concerts each day featuring many of the very best musicians who had survived the war.

I will never forget the opening night's concert, which was held in the cathedral itself. I arrived early, but soon every seat was filled and a collective energy was welling up and filling the air with excited anticipation. The performance was Berlioz's *Requiem*, which featured the cathedral's Silberman organ, one of the few such instruments remaining in the world. Silberman was J. S. Bach's organ builder, and he brought organ construction to its very apex.

Other than small lights on the stands of the musicians, the cathedral was illumined only by flickering candlelight, and as the first notes of the requiem began in the darkened cathedral, you could feel a collective sigh of rapture. To survive the daily trials and tribulations of life, each of us must find at least an occasional thread of the divine, some ray of meaning to moisten the soul. For me, this has come again and again through music. It serves as a reminder that there is something enduring, some essence that is only hinted at in ordinary life. If life is not touched by at least some small experience of the divine world, then our existence grows so small and gnarled that it is unendurable. Many people live in that kind of dry, desolate existence where there is nothing but the small empire of ego.

I spent an entire month in Strasbourg luxuriating in the genius of French music.

When the festival drew to a close after four marvelous weeks, I had no idea what was next. I felt a little like one of those cartoon characters who walks out across a canyon not noticing that the land has ended until he is surrounded by clouds and is walking only on thin air. It is only when these little animated buffoons look down that they fall. I managed not to look down.

While in Strasbourg I also tracked down the Saint Aurelie Church, which is the church in which Albert Schweitzer had made his famous recordings of Bach organ works. I was surprised to find that it was a small, diminutive structure. Dr. Schweitzer was such a towering figure in Europe at the time that he could have recorded anywhere he liked, but he chose this small church with a two-keyboard organ. I made friends with the concierge at the church, and soon he let me come to play whenever I liked. The pipe organ at Saint Aurelie was also built by Silberman.

Other afternoons of ecstatic joy were spent playing the Grand Orgue at Saint Thomas Kirke, which houses the largest Silberman organ in the world. It was here that I heard a polyphony of inner voices in Bach's organ works that I had never known before. The muddy, thick voice of twentieth-century organs had always obscured these complex interior voices in Bach's work. But Silberman organs were made in the days when the wind pressure for the pipes was created by stout men wielding bellows. The air pressure available by hand pumping, as opposed to using a modern electric blower, is limited, so the wind pressure of baroque organs is very light and the resulting tone is clear and precise. For the first time, I heard Bach's music as it was meant to be heard. These were wonderful days.

Strasbourg is only a few hours from Switzerland. It seemed criminal to be so close to the Alps and not visit Switzerland. I had attended several concerts in Strasbourg with a newfound friend named Will, a would-be poet who was trying with little success to follow in the footsteps of a famous grandfather of his. I don't recall much about Will. He was an American like me, wandering in Europe in search of something that could not quite be defined. Will had a friend in Zurich, so he agreed to accompany me up to Switzerland. Why not? Neither of us had an agenda or a destination. We were travelers in the truest sense, open to whatever fate might bring our way. So we boarded a train that followed the winding path of the Rhine River, and upon our arrival in Zurich we met his friend for lunch. Somehow the conversation turned to psychology. I described my analysis with Fritz Kunkel back in Los Angeles and launched off into a discussion of dreams.

"Well, if you are interested in dreams, then you most certainly must meet Jolande Jacobi," I was told. "Frau Jacobi is a friend of our family."

It happened just that fast. A phone call was made, and later that afternoon I found myself walking through the streets of Zurich to the apartment where Dr. Jacobi had her practice.

Jolande Jacobi was at that time already a well-known student of Carl Jung. She was a rare type in Jungian circles, an extrovert with wonderful vitality and practicality. Many of Jung's followers have traditionally been more the introverted type, fascinated by the inner world of dreams, fantasy, and myth. Jolande Jacobi was the prime mover in setting up a new school of Jungian psychology in Zurich. Apparently Jung had considered such an idea before World War II, but later he had cooled on it. Dr. Jung regularly gave lectures and even offered an English seminar at the Psychological Club of Zurich, but he disdained the stagnancy of imitation and feared that institutionalizing his creative process would lead others to imitate rather than follow their own unique path to individuation. It was Dr. Jacobi's enthusiasm and organizational skills that were key to the establishment of the C. G. Jung Institute in 1948. By this time Dr. Jung was no longer presenting regular seminars, and he had become much less accessible to interested students. Although Dr. Jung had long opposed such a formalized teaching program, he apparently decided that it was inevitable and that he might at least steer the organizing committee in a direction that was agreeable to him. The institute's original mission was to support research into religion, mythology, dreams, and symbols. As fate would have it, I arrived in Zurich just as the institute's first classes were being offered, and Dr. Jacobi was recruiting students.

So it was that I found myself sitting in Dr. Jacobi's tidy little apartment. Dressed with simple good taste, she wore her hair pulled straight back in a rather severe fashion. She spoke excellent English seasoned with a charming Hungarian accent. She asked about my interest in psychology, and I described my analysis with Fritz Kunkel. After a brief conversation, she abruptly invited me to enroll in the new school. It all happened so fast that I didn't know what to say. I was swept up by her enthusiasm. I was flattered and thrilled at the prospect of being part of a community. I dumbly nodded yes. It was almost as if she had kidnapped me. She made a phone call to a colleague and the head of the new institute, Dr. Meier, provided him with my name, handed me the school's address, and that was that—I was enrolled in the first classes ever offered at the C. G. Jung Institute.

After my poet friend Will went home, I rented a small apartment and settled down to study. There was one section for English-speaking students and another section in which classes were offered in German. I was grateful for the English section since my German is inadequate for complicated discussions.

The school began with just twenty-eight students. Classes were held at 27 Gemeinde Strasse in an old house in a residential neighborhood. The living room served as the lecture hall. I soon learned that despite the institute's name and mission of extending the reach of Jungian analytical techniques, Dr. Jung would not be teaching. He was seventy-three years of age by this time, and although he had already published a great literary opus, he was still to write some of his most important works on alchemy and the psychology of religion. He had suffered a recent heart attack, but I learned this was not the chief reason that Dr. Jung distanced himself from the institute. He simply questioned whether sitting in a classroom was the proper way to learn about psychology.

After medical school, Jung had apprenticed himself to great masters of psychiatry such as Eugen Bleuler, Pierre Janet, and Sigmund Freud. He was much more comfortable with the medieval system of apprenticeship than he was with the classroom. As a result, Dr. Jung did not set foot in the institute.

I was the youngest person in the institute. Worse, as a dropout from Stanford University, I was one of the few people there who did not possess either a Ph.D. or a medical degree. It was a very aristocratic place in many ways. The medical doctors would arch an eyebrow when mentioning a fellow student who "had only a Ph.D." So you can imagine how low I was in the social order. In retrospect, I think that Dr. Jacobi accepted me into the school for all the wrong reasons. They were desperate to get enough students for the new institute, and Dr. Jacobi also was looking for psychotherapy patients. My admission to the institute certainly wasn't based on my achievements or psychological insights at the time.

School was taxing, emotionally as well as intellectually. There was a lecture each morning, time off for lunch, and then a second lecture in the afternoon. My instructors comprised a remarkable cast of strong personalities: Dr. Jacobi, Dr. Meier, Mrs. Emma Jung, Barbara Hannah, Toni Wolff, and Marie-Louise von Franz.

We were discouraged from bringing into class our own dreams or examples from our lives. That was essentially all I had, as I was not a practicing physician or psychologist like many of my colleagues. So I tended to sit in the back and keep very quiet. Many afternoons following the lecture a group of students would reassemble at a small restaurant to continue discussions. The talk would grow heated, and townspeople would eavesdrop on our conversations. Someone would be telling of a dream in which a black snake turned to white or in which the fantastic symbolism of an obscure alchemical text appeared. Listeners would move away from our table and look at us as if we were mad people escaped from the lunatic asylum.

In its first year, the institute had not yet set up exams, papers, or certificates. Each of us was free to explore whatever topics most interested us.

Mrs. Jung lectured on the myth of the Holy Grail, which I found wonderfully fascinating. The story of Parsifal seemed akin to my own life, and it touched me deeply (I would later use this myth in my own first book, *He*). Mrs. Jung tried hard to be scholarly like the other intellectuals, but though she was highly dignified she was essentially a quiet and simple woman. Some students quickly became sarcastic and complained to one another that she assigned topics for us to research only because she did not have enough material to fill out her course. I felt sympathy for her, as she had worked for years in the shadow of her famous husband. The more she tried to appease the intellectuals in the institute, the more labored her presentations became.

Another instructor, Barbara Hannah, was a delight—polite, down-to-earth, and warm. Hannah was English, but after discovering Jungian psychology, she settled in Zurich and devoted her entire life to Dr. Jung. She was one of the half dozen women who surrounded Jung and who were affectionately known as the "Vestal Virgins." She lectured to us on active imagination, and I owe most of what I know about that subject to her insights. Active imagination is a dialogue that you enter into with the different parts of yourself that live in the unconscious. In some ways it is similar to dreaming, except that you are fully awake and conscious during the experience. This, in fact, is what gives this technique its distinctive quality. Instead of going into a dream, you go into your imagination while you are awake. A concise definition for this active imagination process is dreaming out loud. You allow the images to arise, and then in your imagination you begin to talk to these images and interact with them—that is the active part. They often answer back, and you may be startled to find that they express radically different viewpoints from those of your conscious mind. Often this dialogue will tell you things you never consciously knew and will express thoughts that you never consciously thought.

When we participate in this process over time it becomes more and more clear that the images appearing in the imagination are symbols representing deep interior parts of ourselves. However, most people find a hundred and one excuses not to sit down and actually do active imagination. On an egocentric level, giving up control to the unconscious may feel like suicide; the ego gives up its dominance, and in this sense it is a sacrificial act.

I must admit that at first I had strong resistances to doing active imagination, but when I would discipline myself to sit down and do such work, the results were pure gold. As Barbara Hannah explained to us, active imagination does require time, concentration, an open mind, and a willingness to sacrifice the conscious viewpoint. In short, it is very hard work.

When active imagination is done correctly, it pulls together the different parts of you that have been fragmented or in conflict. An important aspect of this work is that the dialogue should be between equals; it is not lucid dreaming where you go in and make your dream go the way the ego would like. Lucid dreaming is an egocentric form of active imagination and not something that I would ever recommend. You must be courteous and give dignity to the images that arise, but you don't simply buckle under to what an imaginative figure says. If some overwhelming figure comes to you in active imagination, you must be able to stand up against it. It must remain a dialogue of equals. When I began experimenting with active imagination I also soon learned that a ceremonial act is an important part of the process. Extending the material derived imaginatively into a physical act of some kind helps to ground it in the world. Without such a ritual there is a danger that fantasy material becomes lost in abstraction.

Here is an example of how powerful active imagination can be in one's psychological process. One day my old electric alarm clock fell off the nightstand one time too many and refused to run anymore. I tossed it into the wastebasket and bought another one. Several days later, for no apparent reason, this action began to bother me. I had the recurring thought: "I cannot dispose of that alarm clock in such an ignominious way." I began thinking of some of the events that alarm clock had awakened me to, such as the time it got me up to see a glorious sunrise and the time it got me going for a meeting with Dr. Jung and on and on. So I retrieved my old alarm clock from the wastebasket and put it in the back of my cupboard. I still didn't know what to do with it, so it remained in the back of my cupboard for weeks. One day I decided to go on a camping trip, and I thought I would take the alarm with me and give it a proper burial. So I put it in the bottom of my bag, and during the camping trip I dug a hole, placed the clock in its shallow grave, and began to talk to it as if I were conducting a memorial service. "I remember the day that we . . ." I recalled probably a dozen different vivid days in my life, and soon I began to weep. It was as if I was recapitulating the previous decade of my life and bringing it to some kind of close with the burial of that alarm clock. Soon I found myself standing there crying my heart out. Finally, my tears dried up and I proceeded to bury the alarm clock. When I walked back to camp, a friend saw me all red eyed and asked what was the matter. I replied that it must be some kind of pollen in the air. That incident brought home to me the power of active imagination, and I felt fortunate to have such a fine instructor as Barbara Hannah. A more complete description of this process is described in my book *Inner Work*.

⁓

AT THE INSTITUTE I ALSO ENCOUNTERED Toni Wolff. In 1948 Wolff was so contorted by arthritis that she would enter the classroom bent over a cane and frowning at anyone or anything that got in her way. I felt that she must have carried Dr. Jung's shadow and that this was part of her physical pain. I never felt enough rapport with her to know her outside of class, but I believe that the intrigues and politics of the Jungian inner circle weighed heavily on her.

Dr. Meier served as president of the institute. Like Jung, he had served as an assistant physician at the Burgholzli Clinic in Zurich. He was affectionately known by the students as Dr. Ya Ya because that was his recurrent response. In analysis he would not ask questions; instead he made himself available and responded to whatever was said with the refrain, "Ya, ya." Dr. Meier was a cool, thinking type, a dry intellectual man, and I was intensely afraid of him. Just his presence in the room would make me uncomfortable. To make matters worse, he lectured to us on complex theory.

Dr. Jung's psychology was originally called complex psychology based upon the research he conducted, and the term *complex* has since become part of our psychological language. Most of us use the term but do not know that it was Dr. Jung who originated it. We often misuse it, for its scientific meaning is a sum of psychic energy that carries a particular character. It is, so to speak, a psychic organ and carries no hint of pathology. Everyone has a mother complex, a father complex, and so on. It is only when a complex becomes overcharged and begins to overwhelm its neighbor complexes that it is viewed as a problem.

Dr. Jung had applied the word-association test to identify those complexes that disturb people and thereby reveal neurotic weaknesses. This test drew Dr. Jung's attention to complexes that exist in all of us. A complex consists of a string of associations that are unconscious, or only partly conscious, with an emotional tone. When the emotion involved is a strong one, the complex can lead to neurotic behavior.

To my horror, one of the first assignments in Dr. Meier's class was to take the word-association test with another student. We were told to look around the room and choose a partner (or more precisely, I thought, a victim). After administering the test, each student was to present a two-hour lecture on the results.

My heart sank. I still hadn't made any real friends. There was a coldness about the school that one often finds among accomplished, highly specialized people. Now my dark soul would be revealed for all to see. Who could I trust with my innermost secrets? As I looked apprehensively around the classroom, I came across an equally terrified pair of eyes attached to someone I had never spoken to. Her name was Helen Luke.

After class was dismissed, I walked over to this small English woman with a kindly round face and asked if we could do the test together. Helen was an introverted, feeling, intuitive type, my own typology. She was intensely polite and proper. Although she had attended the finest schools and had a master's degree from Oxford, she seemed quite unsure of herself.

"My preference would be to take the test as quickly as possible and then burn the results," I said.

"Yes, that sounds perfect. Let's do that," she replied.

Those words initiated a friendship that would last a lifetime.

Helen was an English lady of the first order with a titled husband. She bore all the best aspects of English aristocracy. However, I soon found out it was a bad time for Helen. Her marriage had collapsed, and her two adopted boys were staying with a housekeeper back in London. She had been in therapy with an analyst in London named Toni Sussman, and it was she who suggested that Helen come to Zurich to study.

Helen and I went off to give each other the word-association test, and of course all sorts of aberrations and neurotic tendencies emerged. The test consisted of one hundred words that had been carefully chosen to evoke emotional responses. The person taking the test is asked to respond to each word with the first word that comes into his or her head. The theory is that if one of the words triggers a charged complex, the subject will stutter, take extra time, or produce a bizarre answer. The word-association test has since been superseded by other types of testing instruments, but it pioneered the work of discovering the contents of the unconscious.

Helen and I had a good laugh about our personal idiosyncrasies, which showed up so vividly in the word-association test, and then we quickly scrapped our answer sheets. We found two unsuspecting

Swiss and convinced them it would be great fun to play this new game. We went through the test with them, and the results came out reasonably normal. Those were the test results that we later presented to the class.

~

I SURVIVED DR. MEIER'S CLASS on complex theory, and I managed to keep up with my studies during the first term, challenging as they were. For the most part I was a diligent student. However, one morning I awoke to find a beautiful, shining day and I simply could not drive myself to go to the institute. It was the one day during my year in Zurich that I chose to cut class, and fifty years later, this lovely, peaceful day is still vivid in my memory.

I got on a train and went to the little town of Fleuland, on the east coast of Lake Lucerne. The lake winds through the Alpine valleys, and at Fleuland I boarded a steamboat (*dampfship*) that slowly traveled the length of the lake. Along the way, we stopped at quaint little towns with gingerbread roofs. It was a peaceful, leisurely voyage. When we arrived at Lucerne at about 5 P.M. on the western end of the lake, I disembarked and spotted a sign advertising a symphony concert scheduled for that evening. The program included Mahler and Wagner, and though I had little money and it was a huge extravagance, I could not resist buying a ticket.

The performance was magnificent, led by the conductor of the Berlin Philharmonic, a man named Felix Furtwangler. He was a tall, ungainly fellow who seemed all arms and legs as he clumsily ascended the podium. But when he began to conduct Mahler's fourth symphony, it was as if a marionette master in the ceiling pulled him together. He became something extraordinary to behold. An impulse would arise from somewhere in his center and radiate out to his extremities. It was as much a dance performance as a concert, and I was transfixed by his dark figure. It was jokingly observed in the music circles of Europe that it was difficult to play under the direction of Felix Furtwangler until you learned that the beat might be hidden in his left kneecap. He was beloved of his home orchestra, the Berlin Philharmonic, and it was said those musicians never played their best for any other conductor as long as he lived. When the music stopped, the conductor fell back into his awkward mortal shell, received the thunderous applause, and stumbled backstage. There was much intellectual discussion at the institute about archetypes (enduring patterns in nature) and archetypal energy, but here I had seen a living example of a person serving as a conduit for archetypal energy.

With the usual Swiss efficiency, trains were waiting at the station following the performance, ready to speed the concertgoers back home to all the major cities in Switzerland. Within twenty minutes I was on my way back to Zurich and was safely tucked into my bed before midnight. The next day my classmates asked if I had been ill and I responded, "No, I was just doing some research on Huck Finn."

Sometimes I couldn't bear going back to my solitary room, so at night I would walk and walk through the streets of Zurich until my legs were worn out. Then I would sleep and return to class again the next morning.

I have already related the tale of how my funds dwindled by the end of the first semester and how Art Meyer came to my rescue. When I returned to school after the Christmas vacation, I was surprised to find that Helen was not in class. She was as shy as I was, and none of my fellow classmates seemed to notice that she was missing. I immediately went to her apartment and found that she was sick in bed and under the care of a doctor. She had some vague illness that no one could name, but it resulted in a high fever and total exhaustion. She was all alone in Zurich, so I began making daily trips to serve her tea and companionship. That is how our friendship grew.

Helen gradually regained her strength and returned to London, while I finished out my term in Zurich. As my knowledge of the process of Jungian analysis grew, I came to believe that I might become an analyst. Here was a profession that was focused on the inner world, a world where I felt comfortable and competent. I had been a caseworker with the Red Cross in my younger days, and I knew that I had a certain amount of skill for working in a helping profession. I also found that such work was healing for me as well as for my clients.

My education in Zurich came not just from attending classes. As part of the training at the Jung Institute students were required to undergo intense therapy with a Jungian analyst, and I entered an analysis with Jolande Jacobi.

Dr. Jacobi (who was later the author of many popular books on Jungian psychology) had been my sponsor in getting accepted at the institute, and I was very fond of her. But I soon found that she was not at all the right therapist for me. She would tell me funny stories that were amusing, but she took to giving me unwelcome advice. Her intent apparently was to pull me out of my extreme introversion and get me going on the road of life. I soon came to resent her pushiness. She conducted analytical hours pacing the floor, while I sat in a large chair in the corner watching her. It was said that Dr. Jacobi paced with such ferocious intensity that her neighbors in the apartment below had once brought a legal action against her for disturbing the peace. Dr. Jacobi came to court and informed the judge that she was an analyst, a Hungarian, an extrovert, and that pacing was an essential aspect of her work. The judge listened patiently, took Dr. Jacobi at her word, and then ruled that she could pace only between the hours of 8 A.M. and 10 P.M. so as not to disturb the neighbors.

Several months into my analysis with Dr. Jacobi, I had a remarkable dream. The dream was beyond my comprehension, and when I brought it to her she was less than encouraging.

"That is an old man's dream, and I can tell you right now that we won't touch it," Dr. Jacobi said.

My heart sank. Perhaps it was an old man's dream, but I experienced it at the age of twenty-six. I couldn't put the genie back in the bottle once it was out. I discuss this dream in detail in the next chapter.

What was I to do with my dream? I felt certain that the dream had frightened Dr. Jacobi, so I informed her that I was ending our analysis. Dr. Jacobi never forgave me. From that day forward she refused to look at me in class, and for years afterward she did her best to discredit me in Jungian circles. She told people that I had quit analysis, when in fact I only quit analysis *with her*.

⁓

AS MY PSYCHOLOGICAL WORLD BEGAN to function, music no longer had to carry so much weight in my life. I had another set of tools; working with dreams and inquiring into the nature of the unconscious took more and more of my energy; and my need for music diminished accordingly. Dreams and active imagination provided me with a different means of staying in touch with the Golden World. Perhaps music could never have carried the weight that I placed upon it, as I tried to make it carry the divine realm as well as my need to earn a living. I now see that it served as a stand-in, an interim solution until I could find my true vocation.

A career is not the same as a vocation. Nearly every modern person is required to forge some kind of a career, but a vocation involves a calling or a summoning. We may choose a career, but a vocation chooses us. To choose and manage a career most modern people use rational, logical thinking: you may take standardized tests to explore your aptitudes, a guidance counselor may help you to review your life goals, and many people research trends in the job market to find out where the good (well-paying) jobs will be in the future. None of these things ever worked for me. My high school guidance counselor suggested that I was best suited to become a bank teller, advice that, if followed, would have been disastrous.

I believe that finding work that is meaningful and fulfilling is not an intellectual task but rather an emotional, intuitive, and cognitive process that involves the whole person. In fact, while we may rationally choose a career, a vocation often irrationally chooses us. This means that it is essential to listen to information that comes to you from outside the realm of your ego consciousness. You can become aware of your true vocation only by listening to those aspects of your being that are often devalued in our culture.

Of course, even after a vocation has chosen us, we still have to do the work of balancing the requirements of the two worlds—the earthly world and the divine world. A major obstacle for me was learning to charge money for something that I love doing. I sincerely believe that there are some things in this world that cannot be bought and sold, and for me music was always one of these things. I could never figure out how to make a living without somehow tarnishing the divine aspect of music. At first, I encountered the same problem with analytical psychology. I was absolutely no good at marketing myself, and I found it difficult to charge people for my time. This dilemma continued to haunt me for years until sufficient income from my books and lectures allowed me to stop charging fees for therapy work. Instead, I would simply ask people to pay me what they thought the session was worth. One fellow once paid me fifty cents, but another time a man wrote me a check for five thousand dollars for a one-hour session.

I have never had much interest in money, though I have always managed to keep my checkbook balanced and to pay my bills on time. To me, money is like gravity: everyone knows what it is except the experts, but if you look at it carefully, what is its real meaning? Money is a strange convention. I am appalled that money is often the tail that wags the dog when people choose how to spend the majority of their waking hours, but I also am aware that we live in a money-driven culture. Almost any consideration in people's lives today ultimately comes around to questions like: How much will it cost? How much money will it bring me? Can I really afford to do it? That is a vast error, but as long as we stay in this society we must obey its laws. I couldn't stand to turn music into an economic activity, but somehow after my vocation in analytical psychology found me, I eventually learned to keep a precarious balance between the requirements of the Golden World and the earthly world. "Render unto Caesar what is Caesar's and unto God what is God's" has great meaning for me now.

8

Encounter with Dr. Carl Jung:

Birth and Rebirth of the Hero/Savior Within

I never expected to become a therapist, but some slender threads were leading me to Carl Jung's door. At the age of twenty-six I had no great insight into how the slender threads operated in my life, but I was beginning to understand that if I waited attentively, the will of God would eventually make itself known to me.

After ending analysis with Jolande Jacobi, I approached Mrs. Jung about working with her. As I have noted, Emma Jung was lecturing at the newly founded C. G. Jung Institute on the medieval Grail myth, which fascinated me, and she seemed to me a kind and sensitive soul. She agreed to take me on as a client. Analysis with her was totally different from my experience with Dr. Jacobi. Where Jolande would lecture and bully me, Mrs. Jung would sit quietly and say very little. She encouraged and supported me but seldom offered advice and always threw me back on my own resources. I would bring my dreams to Mrs. Jung and tell her my interpretations. I recall her saying once in a small voice, "Mr. Johnson, I'm afraid that is not satisfactory to me. You must dig deeper."

For several weeks I ruminated over the big dream that I had told to Dr. Jacobi before I mustered up the courage to share it again. When I finally did tell it to Mrs. Jung, she didn't have much to say about it either, but she listened patiently and at least did not cut me off. That evening she took my dream to her husband, and my life changed forever.

Before relating my encounter with Dr. Jung, I must tell you the content of this "big" dream. It came to me as follows:

Every thousand years a Buddha is born. In my dream the Buddha is born in the middle of the night. A star shines in the sky to herald the birth of the Buddha. I am there, and I am the same age throughout the dream.

I watch the birth of the Buddha, and I see him grow up before my eyes until he is a young man, like me, and we are constant companions. We are good pals (the temerity of such an idea). We are happy with each other, and there is much companionship and brightness.

One day we come to a river, which flows in two directions at once. Half the river flows one way, and half flows the other way; where the two streams touch in the center of the river there are very large whirlpools. I swim across, but the Buddha is caught in a whirlpool and drowns.

I am inconsolable; my companion is gone. So I wait a thousand years, a star shines in the night sky again, and again the Buddha is born in the middle of the night. I spend another long period as the companion of the Buddha.

Here the details are lost, but for some reason I have to wait another thousand years for the birth of the third Buddha. Again a star shines, and the Buddha is born in the middle of the night, and I am his companion as he grows up. We're friends and I'm happy. Then I have to wait a thousand years again, till modern times, for the Buddha to be born a fourth time.

This time, however, the circumstances are different and more specific. The star will shine in the sky announcing the birth of the Buddha, but the Buddha is to be born at dawn this time. And he's to be born from the knothole of a tree when the first rays of sunlight fall upon it from the sunrise. I'm overcome with joy and anticipation, because I've waited a thousand years for my beloved companion to be reborn.

The first rays of the sun come. They touch the top of the tree first, descending it as the sun rises (something that wouldn't

happen in waking life). As the rays of the sun touch the knothole, an enormous snake comes out. The snake is huge, a hundred feet long, and he comes straight at me!

I'm so terrified that I fall over backward. Then I get to my
feet and run with all the strength that I have. When I think I've
gone far enough I look around, only to find that the snake is
running in back of me and keeping his flattened head exactly
over my head!

So I run twice as hard in terror. But when I turn around and
look, there's the snake's head—still exactly over my head! I run
still harder and look and the snake is still there, and I know
there's no hope. Then, by some intuition, I make a circle by
touching my right hip with my right arm. I'm still running, and
the snake pokes what he can of his head through the circle, and
I know the danger is over.

When the dream ends we are still running through the forest, but now the snake and I are talking and the danger has diminished.

This was a very difficult dream to assimilate, especially for a
twenty-six-year-old. Such dreams are worthy of a later stage in life,
as Dr. Jacobi believed, and it is difficult when such a dream comes
so early. It was many years before I could stand to face the direct
implications and impact of this dream.

I was startled when the day after presenting my dream to Mrs.
Jung I received a telephone call at the institute. Who would be calling
me? I was told it was Dr. Jung. "Get out here at once, I want to talk at
you," Dr. Jung said. I distinctly remember his use of the word *at*.

I was accustomed to taking the train to Kûsnacht and then
trudging for more than a mile to my hourly sessions with Mrs.
Jung, but I felt considerable trepidation on this particular trip out
to the Jung house. When I arrived, a housekeeper took me to a
waiting room.

Soon I was confronted by a noisy little dog. I had heard the local
legend that this Schnauzer could spot a schizophrenic faster than Dr.
Jung. It was known that Joggi, for that was the old dog's name,

would begin barking and growling when a patient with psychotic tendencies entered the house. When he came scurrying into the room, I felt as though I was being confronted by a temple guardian. Would he sound the alarm and send me packing? By the time Dr. Jung came in from his study, the fierce interrogator was rolling on his back, moaning with delight as I rubbed his fuzzy little tummy.

Dr. Jung looked very fit and alert. I knew that he had slipped on the snow and had suffered a broken leg in 1944 followed by a thrombosis of the heart. He had experienced a second heart attack in 1946. He was seventy-three at the time of our first meeting; his hair was gray, and he looked out at me over small wire-rimmed glasses. He was warm but direct, and I was not prepared for what happened next: he did not ask about school or my analysis with Dr. Jacobi or anything in my past. Instead, he began to lecture me within an inch of my life.

He had in his hand a copy of the dream that I had written down for Mrs. Jung, and he motioned for me to sit.

"You have been claimed for an inner life," Dr. Jung declared. "If you will remain loyal to the inner world, it will take care of you. This is what you are good for in this life. I must tell you at the outset that you should never join anything."

I sat there in shock.

I had been in this man's presence for only a few moments, and he was telling me how to live my life. Dr. Jung continued to talk, and there was no chance to ask a question. He made it clear that he did not want to be interrupted.

"You must learn to accept that whatever you need will turn up for you," he continued. "Even if you never produce anything of social value, your relationship with the collective unconscious will justify your reason for being on the face of this earth."

My dream of the Buddha and the snake, Dr. Jung insisted, was a clear sign that I must live my life with an inner focus. It would take all the resources I could muster just to deal with the forces of the unconscious, which were extremely powerful. Dr. Jung seemed to read my mind. He said that I had always hungered for community and probably would always continue with this yearning, but this was not the proper path for me. His advice then became specific beyond all reason. He said that I should never marry or join any organizations and that I must be content to spend most of my life alone.

"You are one of the solitaries of this world," he said. "Do not join anything. This will just be poison for you. Devote your energies to the collective unconscious. Keep the outer dimensions of your life as modest as possible."

Although some of what he said terrified me, he also was hopeful. I had heard that he possessed a bad temper and would even shout at people, but he was very gentle with me. He seemed to care about my well-being, and I did not resent his lecturing as I had done with that of Dr. Jacobi. He said more than once, "Please remember, it is what you *are* that heals, not what you *know.* In the beginning of my career I knew nothing, actually less than nothing. But still it worked. And do you know why? It was because of who I was."

I was struck by his insistence on this point about healing because I had never discussed with anyone my fantasies of becoming an analyst. When Dr. Jung motioned to me to stand, I did so without speaking and followed him outside to his large garden.

Dr. Jung pointed out a detail at the end of my dream. "When you make a circle with your arm, the snake begins to talk with you," he said. "Do you see this? It is a mandala, a magic circle. This means that you can survive an otherwise overwhelming experience if you will give it form. Do you see? You must focus on containing these energies, or they will destroy you."

Dr. Jung saw the potential in me as well as the dangers ahead. I remember sitting there thinking, "This man is just like me, except infinitely wiser. He understands me completely. He understands."

But I can see now that was part of his genius. He was not like me at all, but he was capable of making me feel as if we were of one mind. Later, when I saw him in other circumstances and realized that our personalities were quite different, I thought, "This man has deceived me. He tricked and manipulated me." But as I reflected on that day in Kûsnacht, I realized that he had given me a very special gift.

Not only did he know how to speak English to me, he knew how to speak in the typology I could best relate to. He chose examples and even figures of speech that were consistent with my introverted-feeling type of personality.

This, it seems to me, is pure genius. Many brilliant people display their knowledge by talking in big words and mighty concepts that serve the dual purpose of inflating the speaker and confusing the listener. They sit like Olympian gods and expect other people to learn their language. But Jung could adjust his discourse in a way that would best serve the needs of the other person. He was a great intuitive thinker, but he did not speak to me in abstract intellectual language; he addressed me in the feeling language that I could relate to.

Dr. Jung was fascinated by the fact that in my dream the Buddha must be reborn four times. The fourth time takes a very different form. In the fourth incarnation the Buddha is born at dawn from the knothole of a tree.

"Your dream foretells the coming of the fourth psychological function," Dr. Jung said. "You have swallowed the three functions, and the dream indicates that in your life the fourth will come to the fore. It will be difficult, but you will be all right." He then began talking about specifics of the dream in a manner that I could not entirely comprehend at the time, going on about number symbolism and "the three trying to accomplish the fourth."

Dr. Jung was at this time deeply involved in research on trinitarian consciousness and its evolution into a quaternity. He saw my dream as a classic statement from the unconscious that a fourth element in the psyche was to be assimilated, a change that I would find very difficult to integrate.

In Jungian psychology, there are two personality attitudes and four different functions, which combine to determine each person's personality type. The ideal is to have conscious access to all four functions—thinking, feeling, intuition, and sensing—and to apply them appropriately in the particular circumstances facing us. In reality, however, two of the functions tend to be more highly developed and relied upon for most decision making. Some people spend their adult years developing a third function, and with considerable inner work they may reach the emergence of the fourth function late in life.

When the fourth function arises, Dr. Jung said, the other three aspects of the personality often collapse into the unconscious (which is where the transformation takes place). This makes such transformation highly dangerous. It is experienced as if all one's usual competencies for dealing with the world have suddenly fallen apart.

Dr. Jung believed that my dream had to do with these four psychological functions. The fourth function in me—the least developed aspect of my personality—was my thinking capacity. He told me it was unusual for the fourth function to emerge in one so young, though the timing of events depicted in dreams is often not clear. I didn't have a chance to tell him anything about my Golden World experiences, but he seemed to know intuitively that I had been through something of that nature. He said that I lived close to the collective unconscious and that this would be both a curse and a blessing for me.

"But Dr. Jacobi told me that this is an old man's dream and that I shouldn't be having it," I stammered out.

"Yes, but it doesn't help to tell a young girl that she shouldn't have gotten pregnant," Dr. Jung said. "If it happens, it happens, and one must cope with it. I don't care how old you are, you must take the dream now and not wait. You do not have a choice."

Dr. Jung knew how skinless and vulnerable an individual is when he or she is going through this kind of psychological upheaval. He recognized that I was close to drowning in the collective unconscious, but unlike Dr. Jacobi, who tried to steer me away from it, he took me directly into that world. He gave me encouragement and advice for surviving a life outside the mainstream of humanity. In our short time together, he tried to teach me how to live close to the archetypal powers of the collective unconscious.

He said many other things, and knowing what I now know about dreams, I can understand how he came to many of his conclusions. In this dream of the Buddha and the snake, the thing that saved me was that I made a circle to contain the terrifying energy of the snake and give it form. That took the venom out of it.

Dr. Jung told me that it may take a lifetime to realize my dream of the three Buddhas and the snake. I think that he knew what I was in for and how difficult my life would be. He found a variety of ways to say the same thing over and over—that I belonged to the inner world. "If you never amount to anything in ordinary cultural terms, it doesn't matter," he told me. "Simply to have taken part in this event of the collective unconscious is your contribution."

But even with his assurances, I was overwhelmed. Just as the dream showed me running from the snake, so I ran for the next three decades of my life. I ran and ran until I became increasingly exhausted.

It was many years after my meeting with Dr. Jung that I came across a story from the life of the Buddha. In this story from the East, the Buddha is sitting in meditation and all the demons in the universe come to him in an effort to stop his impending enlightenment. Fierce storms rage about him, lightning strikes at his feet, but still the Buddha will not be moved. All the dark forces come to put out the light, which is beginning to glow within the Buddha. They storm and they storm, until Naga, the great world cobra, comes and stretches his hood over the Buddha's head to protect him. It dawned on me with a rush of understanding that the snake in my dream had been protecting me, not trying to harm me.

For years I felt that I must run at full speed to avoid being killed by the snake. Eventually I came to realize that all the running was just making it harder on me. All my desperate efforts to control my life and make things go according to my will only made it harder for the serpent to protect and guide me. The snake was another aspect of the Buddha seen in terrifying form.

When I read this story many years after discussing my dream with Dr. Jung, I nearly cried with joy, for I then understood that many psychic experiences that at first appear terrifying are actually the protection of divine grace. All of our egocentric striving only gets in the way of this protection.

I had my "big" dream of the three Buddhas and the snake in 1948. Fortunately, I had Dr. Jung to help me with it. His response to my dream was not the product of any rational analysis. He was amazingly intuitive or perhaps clairvoyant. He had descended deeply into the unconscious himself and had lived to tell the tale, and as a result he had returned with a gift for sensing things. To ordinary human consciousness, it often seemed like he was a magician pulling things out of the air.

My life, in many ways, has been a realization of that one dream and the fulfillment of all that Dr. Jung told me that day. I did not always follow the advice he gave me, but all he said turned out to be quite true. Dr. Jung tried to prepare me for a major transformation of consciousness, which is what my dream of the snake and the Buddha is about.

Transformation may be represented by symbols such as snakes, the Buddha, kings, heroes, and saviors. Closely associated with these figures is the story of a journey and a promised return. Dr. Jung was the first to teach me about such figures and their corresponding journeys. As is usually the case with such things, those people who are most involved in such a pattern are likely to be the most blind to it. But I have since become more familiar with these archetypal symbols and motifs.

The story of the Buddha is an unfamiliar one to many Westerners, but we can examine the archetypal motif of birth and rebirth of the hero/savior through other stories that are more familiar, such as the legend of King Arthur and his court of Camelot. Arthur was known as the noble and heroic king because he had drawn his land into a unity. He was a kind of savior of England, and when he went away it was never believed that he died; rather, the legend tells us that he was spirited off to Avalon. This is a curious name—Avalon—because it means the place of apples. It also has been associated with healing. The story informs us that Arthur will rise again and return when he is most urgently needed.

So many of the saviors and hero figures share this important characteristic: they are the once and future kings. The avatars of India are said to incarnate once every thousand years. Closer to home, the Aztec ruler and hero Quetzalcoatl promised that he would return again in a radiant form. When Cortés arrived in the Americas with only a handful of Spanish soldiers, it was believed by the Aztecs that Quetzalcoatl had returned as promised in a light-skinned form; this is what allowed Cortés to take control despite the fact that his small guard of Spanish soldiers was vastly outnumbered. These examples not only demonstrate the recurrence of the hero/savior's return, they show the great power of a legend. When one hears enough of these stories with similar motifs, one begins to suspect that there is some archetypal structure at work.

The return of the hero/savior is not just a historical, outer event; it is even more true as an inner experience, an experience that each of us must go through in our life's journey. First comes the simple and happy stage of innocent childhood. Then we lose our naïveté and happiness and fall into a difficult second stage in which we worry and become anxious; life becomes a difficult process. Finally, if all goes well, we may enter a third stage in which we regain happiness and simplicity.

In a modern psychological sense, these three stages can be seen as three steps of consciousness: (1) simple consciousness, (2) complex consciousness, and (3) divine or illumined consciousness.

There are many other proverbs and stories from different cultures referring to these stages in the development of consciousness, and they all seem to describe a similar progression. In Buddhism there is the proverb: When I was a child the mountains were the mountains, the rivers were the rivers, and the sky was the sky. Then I lost my way, and the mountains were no longer mountains, the rivers were no longer rivers, and the sky was no longer the sky. But after much self-work, I experienced satori, and once again the mountains were mountains, the rivers were rivers, and the sky was simply sky.

In a similar vein, the Danish philosopher and theologian Søren Kierkegaard made the observation that the simple man on his way home after work is wondering what's for dinner. The complex man on his way home is debating the complexities and the imponderables of life. The enlightened man on his way home from work is wondering what's for dinner. Again, we see three progressions, each quite different from the other.

One of the richest symbol systems for understanding this transformation of consciousness comes to us from the early Christian tradition in the idea of the second coming. I must define how I choose to interpret this ancient prophecy. I am greatly indebted to a British philosopher, Owen Barfield, who told us that all "literalism is idolatry." Along these lines, I choose to understand the second coming not literally but symbolically; I believe that it refers to an inner experience. For centuries some people have been carrying placards that declare: "Repent, for the second coming is upon us." When it doesn't occur in a literal sense, cynics dismiss this promised return as silly superstition or prescientific fantasy. But this is where Barfield's admonition is so valuable: "literalism is idolatry." We must not take this motif of the second coming so literally, or we lose our way.

After getting angry in my early twenties with many of the contradictions of Christianity as I saw it practiced, the power of the symbols in that tradition were restored to me through Jungian psychology. I began to see that the story of Christ could be understood as a process that takes place within each and every one of us—an inner journey. Read in this way, we can see that Christ is constantly being immaculately conceived and born, is confounding the elders, teaching, being betrayed, being crucified, dying, resurrecting, and is making an ascension. All of these are occurring in every moment;

they are mystical facts that exist outside of time. When I began to understand this, Christianity became possible for me again.

What does it mean to interpret the second coming in a non-literal sense? The early Christians expected Christ to return immediately. They anticipated his resurrection in a day or two or at least within the week, and when it occurred time would stop and a new millennium would begin. The world of suffering, persecution, and strife—all the time-bound elements that are so painful to humans—would be brought to a halt. People waited for seven days, and on the eighth day they celebrated. Every mass or service is intended to be a celebration of the second coming of Christ, a stopping of time. Then, after the day of celebration, time begins again. It is the Jewish custom to celebrate the Sabbath on Saturday or Saturn's day or the seventh day (all of these names derive from the number seven as a symbol of completion). After the seventh day (Sabbath) time goes back to one again and the cycle is repeated. The first Christians decided to honor the eighth day of the week as being eternity, ending the cycle of time indicated by the Sabbath or seventh. This eighth day of the week is Sunday and it is still honored by Christianity as the beginning of eternity and the end of time. It was first thought to be the eighth day after the resurrection of Christ but has been continued now as each Christian Sunday, a waiting for the second coming of Christ. It is a cycle that occurs over and over, an intersection of time and eternity. Mystically speaking, this second coming is now—not just on Sunday morning, not at the stroke of midnight in the year 2000, not at some time in the future, but at this instant, in every moment, it is available to anyone who is prepared for it.

It is difficult not to think of these images with a literal mind. A time/space orientation is so ingrained in our thinking that often we can conceive of the Christian symbols only in concrete terms, as events that occurred in the past or that are yet to occur in the future. But as Owen Barfield reminded us, literalism is idolatry. Christ is constantly being born, dying, and fulfilling the promised return. Our society has become so spiritually impoverished today that even when people have great visions it never occurs to them that this might be a second coming or a kind of sainthood fallen upon them.

A helpful way to think of the second coming is as a heightened state of consciousness.

This evolution of consciousness occurs at both a personal and a collective level. At a collective level, the archetypal return of the hero/savior implies that the current age is coming to a close. Again, if we abstain from literalism, the power foretold for the new age is already here. The once and future king is present among us, but humankind is not yet prepared to take him into their hearts.

After Dr. Jung helped me to understand my dream of the snake and the Buddha who is reborn every thousand years, it still took me decades to realize this evolution of consciousness within myself. Over and over again I was clumsy about learning how it applied to my daily life. Similarly, our culture may be in the first awkward stages of rebirth. The big question, a question that should confront every modern person is: how can we make this second coming conscious? How can we participate in this evolution of consciousness? If we can understand this, then our lives can be less painful and we can contribute something meaningful. This task is so important because archetypal patterns such as the return of the hero/savior do not necessarily go in a positive direction. The emergence of the Third Reich, touted in the 1930s as the salvation of Europe and the beginning of a new thousand-year reign, shows how this archetypal power can turn our world into a living hell when not dealt with consciously.

People used to ask Dr. Jung, "Do you think we will make it? Will civilization survive?" He invariably answered, "If enough people will be conscious." This is our task, not only individually, but collectively—to become more conscious. We cannot wait for heaven to save us; each of us must be responsible for the birth and rebirth of the hero/savior within and realize the Golden World through our acts in the earthly world. I finished out my year at the Jung Institute and returned to California. It was extremely difficult to detach myself from the community of school or church or club, but I understood Dr. Jung's insistence on the solitary path for someone of my nature. I understood, but was far from having the courage or strength to follow such a way of life. I would fail to follow this insight many times. It was many years before I could even begin to honor the serpent which held terror over my head and begin to bring the very difficult fourth function into consciousness in my life.

9

Householder Days:

Lessons of One/Two Man

I had changed a great deal in Europe. I had grown in maturity, and after returning to California I soon found that most of my old friends from Ojai now distrusted me. One fellow phoned me up in the middle of the night while he was dead drunk.

"You know, don't you, Johnson, that no one can stand you," he informed me. "When I knew you before you were a small chick who needed to take refuge. Now you stand on your own feet. I don't want to be around you anymore."

I put on a brave front, but my feelings were hurt, and once again I found myself lonely and isolated. Despite Dr. Jung's clear warning that I should never try to be part of any organization, I tried again and again over the next several years to create some sense of community. Much of what Dr. Jung had told me I accepted as unquestioned truth, but I continually ignored his instruction not to join organizations simply because I could not stand the loneliness of a solitary life. Of course, every time I did try to be part of a group it eventually failed my expectations.

While struggling to get a psychotherapy practice going in Los Angeles, I supported myself through a part-time job as secretary to a blind and surly musician named Andre DeSegurola. Maestro DeSegurola—he always insisted on being called Maestro—was Spanish born, and he had made a name for himself singing basso at New York's Metropolitan Opera during its golden days. Caruso was the tenor and Andre was the basso, and my new employer re-lived those golden days of the Metropolitan fondly, grasping them like a prized possession.

The Maestro had been in an auto accident while riding in a taxi years earlier, and a terrible head injury had left him totally blind. By the time I answered his classified ad in the *Los Angeles Times,* the Maestro was eking out a miserable existence teaching voice lessons. His name was so famous that just to have a lesson with him was a valuable commodity. However, he was not easy to work with; in fact, Maestro DeSegurola was difficult in all his dealings with me. He would become so frustrated by his blindness that his rages would shake his entire Hollywood house. I served as his personal secretary, answering the phone, showing his students in and out, taking care of him, and handling his financial matters. He quickly came to trust me, but he never treated me well. He had his own box at the Hollywood Bowl, and one of my duties was to drive the Mae-stro and his guests to performances there. He never once allowed me to sit with him in the box, but he would buy me a cheap seat up in the bleachers so that after the performances I could chauffeur him and his guests back home.

My time with the Maestro lasted only a few months. By that time I could no longer stand his wrath, and a new slender thread rescued me from this difficult situation. I renewed my contact with Dr. Kunkel, who at this time decided to begin a new enterprise called the We Psychology School. Dr. Kunkel's idea was that we all arrive with a primordial sense of "we," of community, but as we grow this sense of belonging breaks down. As a result, we become individualistic, neurotic, and lonely. In therapy, a mature sense of "we" must be reestablished. The idea was appealing to me, hungry as I had always been for community, though I could recognize even then that it did not really constitute a new school of psychology.

In the fall of 1949, I found myself teaching at Fritz Kunkel's school, a turn of fate that not only provided me with much-needed income, it also got me started lecturing about Jungian topics. The We Psychology School, located at the First Congregational Church in Los Angeles, was, unfortunately, short-lived. The school had no financial backing, and no one involved in the program possessed a good sense of management. When I went to the church to teach my first class, I found that there was no room available for me. Fortunately, I lived only two blocks from the church, so I gathered up my twenty students and took them to meet in the living room of my house. The school disintegrated after one quarter, but several people in my class wanted to continue, so I organized a weekly discussion group. I also started to provide individual therapy sessions for several of the students, and slowly my career as a Jungian analyst was launched.

Other patients found me in the most unusual ways, many of them coming to me as the result of one of my own physical ailments. Ever since I had arrived in Los Angeles I had been feeling tired. At first I thought it was just settling into a new city, but when my exhaustion persisted I decided to see an endocrinologist to find out if anything was seriously wrong with me. I searched out the top man I could find; his fee was fifty dollars for thirty minutes, which was a small fortune in the currency of the time, 1950. I went in to see him and mentioned that I had to talk fast because I had enough money for only thirty minutes. He asked about my background, and I soon learned that he was interested in psychology.

"So you have met the famous Dr. Jung." My physician was becoming increasingly animated. "Tell me about him. How is he different from Freud?"

I began explaining the basics of Jungian psychology, and before I knew it my thirty minutes were up and we hadn't even talked about my ailment. About this time his nurse came to the door and said it was time for the next patient.

"Oh, tell them to wait," my physician said. Then he turned to me and said, "This is most fascinating, please continue."

Another half an hour went by, and again the nurse came in and chided him about his waiting patients, but he waved her off and continued chatting with me intently.

When we entered the third half hour I was getting nervous because I didn't have 150 dollars. He apparently could see my restlessness, as he said, "Well, Mr. Johnson, we had better get around to you."

After listening to my physical complaints, he said that he had some samples of drugs that I could try, and they wouldn't cost me anything. Then he informed me that he was only going to charge me ten dollars for the appointment. I was delighted. Then, just as I was about to go out the door, he said, "One more thing, Mr. Johnson—would it be all right if I sent you a patient or two?"

"Of course."

Over the next few years he sent me dozens of patients and became one of my best sources of referrals.

It also was about this time that a Fuller Brush man came to my door. We began talking, and he became so fascinated by what I told him that he, too, began coming to therapy sessions with me. After that, my friends joked that in my own shy way I was a better salesman than the Fuller Brush man.

While my practice was growing, I started making repairs on keyboard instruments to supplement my income. Word got around that there was a harpsichord expert in town, and people began to seek me out. One day I heard a somewhat-familiar voice on the phone inquiring about harpsichords.

"Robert, did you ever find the harpsichord you were looking for?"

It was an old friend from Los Angeles to whom I hadn't talked for years. We caught up on each other's lives, and I learned that he had done well in business. A few days later we got together for dinner, one thing led to another, and before I knew what was happening he agreed to put up some money to help me start a business importing and repairing antique harpsichords from Europe. The first one we ordered came from what was left of a bombed-out factory in Nuremberg, Germany. The seller had scraped together parts from several different harpsichords, and the instrument I received was in terrible condition. But I loved researching the exact construction of these old instruments and restoring them to good working order. My friend took care of the business details while I focused on the repairs, and soon we were receiving all sorts of old wrecks from the sixteenth and seventeenth centuries and restoring them. A harpsichord renaissance was just beginning then, and the instruments were suddenly popular in the recording industry in Los Angeles. They were used for movie scores and an occasional Bach festival. Harpsichords are very touchy instruments and easily fall out of tune. No one else in Los Angeles seemed to understand their temperamental ways as well as I did, and this provided a convenient source of income. I found it extremely valuable to work with material things with my hands while doing analytical work; at least with my repair business I could see tangible results at the end of each day.

While I was starting my therapy practice, Dr. Kunkel supervised my cases and conducted what is called a control analysis. I soon realized, however, that I yearned for a professional colleague. I immediately thought of Helen Luke, my soul mate at the C. G. Jung Institute who had been forced by ill health to leave Zurich. On my way back from Europe to the United States I had made a brief stop in London to visit her home. I stayed for a few days in her beautiful aristocratic house, where I met her two adopted boys. The younger one, Robert, took to me immediately. He was eight years old when we met, while Helen's older boy, Nicholas, was more reserved at the "grown-up" age of ten. He kept a civil distance from me and watched me with some suspicion.

The Luke household seemed to be held together by a delightfully cheery Irish housekeeper, Mrs. Sadie Mitchell, who was always bustling around trying to make everyone comfortable. She was warm and simple, a truly good-hearted person. One day Mrs. Mitchell came home from shopping, out of breath, speechless with excitement. "I saw the king! I saw the king!" She was so totally overwhelmed by this awesome event that she was incapable of making the evening meal or tending to her duties. I secretly wished that I could become so excited from seeing anyone on the face of the earth.

Helen and I had corresponded since my return to the United States. Of course, I wrote her about my growing practice in Los

Angeles, and at some point, with a maximum of intuition but a minimum of conscious thought, I invited her to come and join me in Los Angeles so that we might establish a practice together. Within a few months, she was standing on my doorstep, and, to my total delight, in another year she had decided to stay. We would work together doing Jungian analytical therapy.

Soon after Helen's arrival, I rented a house that was large enough for my living quarters and both our offices. We worked together for a year before Helen felt established enough to send for her two boys and Mrs. Mitchell. I'll never forget the day they arrived. Robert was father hungry and immediately dived under my wing, but Nicholas was distant for many weeks. I seemed to bear the brunt of his anger at his father, and he resented my friendship with Helen. Over time, however, he consented to a relationship with me, and soon both the boys were calling me "Bobsie." For the next decade I would serve as a godfather to them.

Dr. Kunkel supervised all our cases. Helen, two other trainees, and I would meet weekly with Dr. Kunkel, but I undoubtedly learned the most from talking with Helen. Dr. Jung often advised his students to work in pairs at their analytical practices. This provides a means of supporting each other emotionally while helping to bring some objectivity to each patient's therapy material.

In many ways, Helen and I trained each other. I learned so very much about myself that I would never have been able to see by working on my own. For example, Helen pointed out that I would invariably try to do too much for my patients; I had to learn that I couldn't solve anyone's problems and that my proper role as analyst was to help bring out the solution that was already there within each patient. Like me, Helen was an introverted, feeling, intuitive person, so we spoke the same language. We were alike in many ways, including our preference for the inner world over the social world of power and status.

One issue that both of us had to deal with was becoming overworked and overtaxed. Analytical work is highly draining on the analyst, and since both of us were shy and highly introverted to begin with, it was easy for us to be overcome by taking on too much work. We made a pact that each of us was to take one day off each week in which we unplugged the telephone, insulated ourselves from the outside world, and did inner work to nourish ourselves. We tried to support this practice in each other, to honor a sabbath in the deepest sense of the word. To be quiet when you are churned up inside requires great discipline, and it is very difficult to do by yourself. But I found that taking a vow to someone else helped me to maintain my self-discipline. Helen would phone me on my scheduled day off just to see if I would answer. If I did, she would soundly chastise me and remind me that this was supposed to be a day devoted exclusively to my own inner needs.

Helen quickly became more than a business partner, and we established a relationship best described by the alchemical term *soror*. It was the custom for alchemists to work in pairs, most often a man and a woman, who together brought both masculine and feminine insights to the opus, or work. Helen and I supported each other during the lonely and heavy times of learning the analytical art.

Analysis is a very difficult profession and, when done properly, inevitably puts a severe strain on the analyst as well as the patient. One must work very carefully to keep one's own psychic equilibrium. Many analysts find themselves contaminated by the illnesses in their patients; having a companion and/or supervisor to help deal with this is critically important. The psychic material of a patient comes flooding in to the therapist, almost like an infection of the physical variety. Jung once said that after seeing schizophrenic patients, it was his practice to schedule a half hour for his own active imagination to "disinfect" his psyche of the patient's illness.

In the analytical hour, I had no established way of proceeding— it always depended upon the particular situation and needs of each patient—but I did invariably rely upon dreams to inform me of what was going on in the unconscious. I quickly realized that the analyst does not have sufficient wisdom to solve a patient's problems, but the dream does. When a patient would turn to me and ask, "What should I do?," I learned to reply, "I have no idea. We must consult with the dreams that come out of you. The answer resides within you; it doesn't come from me."

I found that many people were greatly reassured by this, as they thought that I was going to lecture or manipulate them. It's almost always true that when people come for counseling, regardless of their intentions, they immediately put up every resistance available. There is fear that the therapist is going to invade the unconscious and try to manipulate it. Most people find it reassuring to learn that the solution to their problems resides within themselves and needs only to be listened to.

To reach the unconscious I would sometimes ask patients to go home and draw or paint whatever came to them. I will never forget one young man, in his early twenties at the time, who replied that he could not draw and that he would feel foolish attempting such an exercise. I explained that the goal was not to produce a piece of art—that he should forget about anything his parents or teachers told him about his artistic talent and just allow himself to be playful. I insisted that he try the exercise without any expectation or judgment of the final product. Reluctantly, he agreed. When he returned to my office the following week, he brought with him a wonderful self-portrait, which is one of the hardest things in the world to draw. We talked about his experience while drawing, which was highly enjoyable to him. I encouraged him to continue with this exercise, and within a few weeks he had purchased canvas and oils and was on fire with a new passion for art. I cheered him on and asked questions about what he was doing. After five sessions, he missed an appointment. When I tried to telephone him, I found that his phone had been disconnected. He never called again, and it was only several years later when I was passing an art gallery that I recognized his work in the window. He had become an accomplished portrait painter! Something erupted inside that young man that was very powerful, something that had been there all along but lying dormant.

Dr. Jung once said that, in essence, there are two problems in therapy: the problem of the twenty-one-year-old and the problem of the forty-five-year-old, regardless of the actual chronological age of the patient. The twenty-one-year-old's problem has to do with getting into life, while the forty-five-year-old's problem is how to get back out of life. Most young people struggle with problems of getting fully into life, such as how to gain an education, earn a living, conduct relationships, and raise children and maintain a family. These are all problems relating to social requirements and the earthly realm. After an individual reaches midlife, however, he or she is faced with preparing for old age, the death of one's parents, and the realities of one's own mortality.

I often reflected on Dr. Jung's distinction while I was building my own practice, and I found it to be generally true, but I also encountered a dilemma that seemed to grow to epidemic proportions in America in the 1960s and 1970s—the individual who is facing both problems at the same time. Such people manage to avoid growing up, taking responsibility, and truly engaging life, thus extending their adolescence into their twenties, thirties, forties, and even fifties. Like Peter Pan, they don't want to grow up and insist on keeping all their options open by never committing to anything. American culture actually seems to celebrate such individuals with its insistence on freedom and self-determination. The media noticed this trend and even came up with a name for that time period in the 1980s—the "me decade." While it's true that social expectations regarding the contour of one's lifespan have changed, still nothing is sadder than an individual who has reached the age of fifty and still has not engaged life, for then he or she must face both dilemmas at once. Such a person must prepare for the second stage of life without ever having completed the first stage. The only way to deal with this is through an accelerated growing-up process.

I would like to share a story that is a veritable gold mine of information about psychological development. All people in all ages and in all parts of the world speak an astonishingly similar inner language, as can be seen in the myths, the epics, and the folktales that are handed down. From Eskimo culture to Aboriginal traditions in Australia, from the Far East to the American West, we find in myth a universal language. In a world that is fragmenting as badly as ours is today, it's wonderfully reassuring to find a common denominator among us, a basis from which we might be able to put our world back together again. We also can find in such stories the wisdom needed to help pull our own personal worlds back together again.

This is the story of One / Two Man, a tale in which a young hero pulls himself together. I am indebted to Dr. Gerald Nelson for this story. The tale comes to us from the Paiute tribe in the southwestern United States, a dry and arid land not far from where I now live.

In my years of conducting analysis I observed that most people seem to dream four or five major themes that recur throughout their lifetimes. The details may change and display endless variety, but if you track your dreams over time, you will begin to see patterns and basic themes will emerge. Similarly, the myths and folktales of the world seem to rely upon a handful of basic themes, and one of the primary themes is the individuation or redemption of a human soul. Be it Snow White, the Apu trilogy from India, or the story of One/Two Man from America—in each of these stories an individual struggles to become whole.

ONE/TWO MAN IS A YOUNG LAD, an orphan, who is being raised by his grandmother. Granny is very good to the boy, so good that his childhood is reasonably happy despite his orphan status. But one day the boy approaches Granny and declares, "Granny, I am bored. Give me something new to do."

Granny always has good ideas. "Why don't you go out and collect some roots?" she suggests. "Go dig, collect all those things that you find under the ground, and make a big pile of them."

This pleases One/Two Man greatly. Like many children, he loves to be out in nature and to get dirty, and he spends the rest of that summer digging roots. He goes out to the woods in the morning and digs until sundown. Several times each day he goes back to the village, leads Granny by the hand, and proudly shows her his accomplishment. Granny responds as a good Granny should: she praises him and comments favorably on how high the pile of roots is growing.

Now, if a person is an orphan and raised by a Granny, someone two generations ahead, then that person has the opportunity to learn some very special things. One's parents are occupied keeping the household going, earning a living, bringing home food, struggling with the daily tasks of life. Someone who is two generations ahead, like Granny, is past this householder stage. These elders are the keepers of the culture, the tellers of the tales, the ones who maintain the tribal history. The reader may recall that I was raised by my grandmother and by godparents, so this story has a special resonance for me, and it concerns issues with which I have firsthand experience.

People who are raised by grandparents almost always have a particular difficulty in life. They have not been nurtured or informed of the next generation of skills which their parents would represent—household, marriage, social graces, and so forth—but have been catapulted into the skills of two generations ahead which their grandparents represent—stories, folklore, history, and approaching views of eternity. This difficulty confronts them with the very serious choice of becoming an artist, healer, or teacher—or, God forbid, a derelict or neurotic failure. Such cruel choices produce some of the best of our culture but also contain the ominous possibility of a failed life.

In our story, old Granny knows exactly what to do with a One/Two Man: she sets him to digging roots—that is, working in the unconscious. What does digging roots have to do with a modern life? You go out with a special kind of shovel—a notebook, a typewriter, paints, or some other tools of the imagination—and you dig. You dig material up from "down there" and you make a big pile of it.

One/Two Man gets very enthusiastic about digging up his roots, and he continues this activity throughout the summer and into the fall. Then, one crisp fall morning, he goes out to his ever-growing pile and is astonished to find that it has disappeared. All of the roots are gone. He goes dashing into the village in a panic, shouting, "Granny, Granny, all my summer's work is gone; the roots are gone!" The boy takes Granny out to the forest, but when they get there he can see that she is not surprised.

"Yes, I know," Granny says, "There is something I must tell you. I have been delaying this for as long as I could, but I must tell you now."

Granny sits the boy down on a nearby log and proceeds to tell his history. It is a story he has never heard before, and the boy is held in rapt attention. She explains that One/Two Man is the son of her son, a great warrior who was murdered by Old Stone Shirt, a medicine man who went wrong. Old Stone Shirt used his shamanic powers in a dark way. He became so selfish that he grew a stone shirt around his body, a shirt that cannot be pierced by any arrow, hatchet, or weapon known to humanity. "Nothing can penetrate Old Stone Shirt," Granny says.

Old Stone Shirt became depraved by his misuse of shamanic powers, and one day he decided to take a wife. He killed the father of One/Two Man, kidnapped his mother, and was about to kill the small boy when Granny intervened and begged that his life be spared. Granny got permission to raise the boy, who grew up as the orphan, One/Two Man.

"Last night," Granny continued, "your father came to me in his spirit form. He said that you should no longer dig roots, for that is the work of a boy. It is time now that you become a man and do a man's work. It was he who took all the roots away, and it was he who gave instructions on what you must do now."

Here we must pause for a moment, for this is a wonderful time in the life of a hero (and we are all potentially a hero), a crossroads in his or her development. The story informs us that at some point in the development of every hero it becomes essential to stop the mechanical collecting of things. These things may be material possessions, books, even therapy hours. These are your roots, and they are important, but there also comes a moment when Granny—whoever that might be, whether inside or out—informs you that it is time for a transformation. This is a major shift in the hero's journey. The pile of roots collected from digging into the unconscious must be put aside so that you can engage the world. And so, our story continues.

Granny addresses the boy, "Your father says that you are to go to his grave, which is under that great oak tree out in the clearing. You are to go to the north side of that tree, where you must dig until you find the bones of your father. You must then take these bones and set them aside. Under the bones you will find a stone ax, a weapon that your father's father gave to him, and his father gave to him, and his father gave to him, and his father gave to him, as far back as anyone can remember. You must take that stone ax, lie down on the top of your father's bones with the ax in your hand, and sleep for four days. During this time, your father's spirit will come to instruct you in all the things required for the special destiny that lies before you."

One/Two Man could not fail to thrill at the promise that all the power and intelligence of his male ancestors for countless generations would come down to him in the gift of a stone ax. Here would be the accumulation of all the best of maleness—the power of all the preceding generations of men, all their experiments and accumulated wisdom, bestowed as one ancestral gift. For a man this is identified as the specific male qualities which our culture has evolved in the hundreds of generations preceding one's own personal life. For a woman it is the same masculine power which is more and more her heritage as women take a place of equality in our patriarchal society. Also, there is much wisdom to be learned by examining the feminine parallel as a woman sets her mother aside to take the woman's accumulated wisdom. Few experiences in life bring such a surge of power and vitality as this moment of taking one's place in the lineage of human consciousness, a man in his specific way, a woman in her equally specific way.

The boy is so awed by what Granny has told him that he forgets all about his roots. Then, suddenly, he grows very frightened, and he finds that his hands are shaking.

It is right to be afraid at this moment. When one must confront the deep parts of one's nature, fear is an appropriate response. To make the transition from a collective mentality to one's own individual journey in which the spirit of the father comes to direct you is an essential moment in the hero's journey. This transformation may take place so automatically that you don't recognize it, but it is better to do it consciously and not trip over your roots. What is being described here is the individuation process: stepping into your own fate or destiny, learning to listen to the slender threads. Dr. Jung coined the term *individuation* to denote the process by which a person becomes whole.

After his encounter with Granny, One/Two Man sits thinking for a couple of days. He no longer has roots to dig, so he cannot go backward, but he is afraid to go forward to his father's grave and to meet his destiny. This is a very vulnerable and dangerous time in the life of any person. Those two days in mythic time may stretch out to months or even years in clock time. Finally, at sunset on the second day, One/Two Man, his courage completely exhausted, goes to the old oak tree and throws stones at his father's grave; despite this, the father does not throw any stones back at his son.

This is such a pathetic moment in our story that it nearly brings tears to my eyes. The boy has lost courage, has fallen off the hero's path, and wants to give up the whole adventure. He wants the spirit of his father to go away, so he throws stones at it. But the story tells us, in such a plain but poignant sentence, that the boy's father does not throw any stones back. It is a wise person who does not throw stones back at a son or daughter on those terrible days when the young person has lost courage. That courage has been lost only for a day or two. If you don't throw stones back, you allow the young hero to gather his or her courage again.

By the next day, One/Two Man has gathered his courage. He goes to the grave, gingerly brushes the soil away, and in a wonderful and terrible moment finds the bones of his father.

It is a wonderful moment because One/Two Man is on the way to connecting up with a long male lineage that is his birthright. But, at the same time, it is a terrible moment because he must set his father aside, must displace the very bones of his father. No youth anywhere under any circumstances escapes this task. If you don't do this, you will never have a journey of your own. After One/Two Man sets aside the bones, he finds the stone ax that belonged to his father, and his father, and his father, and his father, and his father, far back into the mists of time.

This is the moment when One/Two Man finds his masculinity, the legacy of the thousand male forebears preceding him. He now is backed by all the strength of generations of people of his own gender. It is a lineage that comes by way of his father, but only at the cost of going past his father. This is why the hero, whether a young man or woman, must not be deterred by the bones of the biological father or mother, the dry bones of the parent's unlived life. If a person gets stuck at this place, he or she never finds the birthright or connects to a deeper heritage. (We can understand the ax to be a certain male energy, a power that allows a young man to stand tall and be strong in the face of a great challenge, but for a young woman the process is the same, of getting past her mother to claim her own birthright as a woman.) Many people get stuck where their parents were stuck and sit with dry bones, throwing stones at the father or the mother.

So One/Two Man takes the ax. Granny has instructed him that the next thing is to lie down in the pit that was the grave of his father and to sleep for four days. The number four turns up throughout history in stories of heroic transformation. Sometimes it is forty, as when Christ had to go into the desert for forty days and forty nights. Similarly, the great flood was forty days and forty nights. One's occupation with the deep unconscious, a deep sleep, often relates to a cycle of four, with four representing a unity and a completeness.

During those four days, the spirit of One/Two Man's father comes and instructs him in all the wisdom of his tribe. His body grows strong, and when he wakes up four days later, he is full grown, with all the muscles and all the strength required of an adult man. He has gained instruction on how to track animals, how to find water, how to foretell the weather—all the things that he needs to survive in the harsh climate of the American Southwest.

At this point One/Two Man is no longer asking questions or putting up arguments. He is totally immersed in the hero's journey. So he goes to Granny and puts the ax into her hands.

"Granny," our young hero says, "please take all your courage and all your energy, and with one blow cleave me down the middle from the top of my head to the bottom of my feet."

Granny bursts into tears and declares that this is the one thing she cannot do. "You are the only thing I have left," she says. "I already have lost my son who was your father. This request I cannot fulfill."

One/Two Man calmly but resolutely replies, "Granny, it is my father, your son, who told me that this must be done."

Granny cannot argue with this, so she takes the ax, gathers all her energy and courage, and with one mighty blow cleaves One/Two Man from the top of his head right down to the bottom of his feet. He is instantly transformed into two people: Number One Man and Number Two Man. This is how he got his name—One/Two Man.

This sounds violent and raw to a modern ear, but in truth everyone of us must experience just such a cleaving. Though it does not occur in one mighty ax blow from Granny, it does take place as the result of thousands of tiny blows. This is how we are adapted to the society in which we live. Certain behaviors are accepted and others are not tolerated. In the process of growing up, we are divided into ego and shadow. Shadow consists of all the psychic elements that, because of their incompatibility with conscious attitudes, are denied expression in life. Consciousness comes at a price, and that price is a split into duality. As another famous story informs us, when we eat of the fruit in the Garden of Eden we suffer a fall and move from the innocence of childhood into the world of contradiction and suffering.

I know that Dr. Jung never heard this American Indian tale, yet he wrote of this same theme in his autobiography, *Memories, Dreams, Reflections*:

The play and counter play between personalities No. 1 and No. 2, which has run through my whole life, has nothing to do with a split or dissociation in the ordinary medical sense. On the contrary, it is played out in every individual. In my life, number two has been of prime importance and I have always tried to make room for anything that wanted to come to me from within. It is a typical figure, but perceived only by the very few. Most people's conscious understanding is not sufficient to realize that he is also what they are. . . . At that time [when Dr. Jung was in his teens] it would have been beyond my powers to formulate my feelings and intuitions in any graphic way, for they all occurred in No. 2 personality, while my active comprehending ego remained passive and was absorbed into the sphere of the "old man," who belonged to the centuries. I experienced him and his influence in a curiously unreflective manner; when he was present, No. 1 personality paled to the point of nonexistence, and when the ego that became increasingly identical with No. 1 personality dominated the scene, the old man, if remembered at all, seemed a remote and unreal dream. (p. 68)

These are the utterances of another hero. This one grew up in the Swiss mountains, but he is saying the same thing. Dr. Jung is talking about the One/Twoness of his personality and the split from which he suffered. Most people stop their heroic development immediately when they discern that carrying a number one and a number two, being a One/Two Man, is very painful. Instead, they try to obliterate one aspect of their personality and concentrate on the other aspect. All heroic journeys stop if one does this, and instead a neurotic journey begins.

At this point in our story, One/Two Man has become fully grown, strong and capable. He has all the information he needs to be a mature adult; however, he also has experienced a split. It is after this split that he resolves to rescue his mother, who had been kidnapped and is still held by Old Stone Shirt. This is the heroic test.

Granny hears of his goal and immediately denounces it. "There is no way that this should be attempted, as it will be absolutely fatal to you," Granny says. "Old Stone Shirt always wins, and there is no way of retrieving your mother from his grip."

To understand this portion of the tale, it is necessary to reflect a bit on Old Stone Shirt. He is a man who has gained shamanic powers, but these powers have been perverted in him; instead of a healer, he has become a destroyer. He hoards the feminine gold, just as dragons hoard damsels in distress. One/Two Man must retrieve the feminine, in this case represented by his mother, from the unconscious. It is the feminine principle that will allow creativity and creation. A woman faces many stone-shirted dangers in her own personality as she takes more and more of her masculine birthright. Her masculine side can fall prey to Old Stone Shirt as badly as any man.

When each of us gets in touch with our personal genius, we can apply this power for the good of humankind, or we can take this power and use it egocentrically and thereby accumulate a stone shirt around us that leads to total and absolute isolation. Our story informs us that it is expressly over the area of one's heart that this stone barrier occurs: it is a shirt.

Old Stone Shirt lives in a cave that is guarded by an Antelope who has an eye on the end of every hair. What an appropriate symbol for touchiness. Stone-shirted people are often the most touchy individuals in the world; they are forever getting their feelings hurt, they misconstrue other peoples actions and intentions, and they find misunderstandings where there are none. These characters typically live in a cave, as befits their insulation and isolation, and they have an Antelope that misinterprets reality and finds ill motives where there are none. No one can get by the Antelope who guards Old Stone Shirt's cave.

Fortunately, One/Two Man also has access to certain animal helpers. He has an array of instincts to assist in the task of rescuing his mother. Instincts, that is, the animal nature in one, can serve us well. Simple, traditional people rely upon their instincts and are protected in that sense. Highly conscious people, those who have consented to sleep for four days and four nights on the father's or mother's grave, have generally grown out of a natural relation to their instincts, but still they can gain access to these feelings if they are willing to sit down and listen attentively. Like One/Two Man, we can be well served by our animal friends within.

Old Stone Shirt also has two daughters from a marriage that took place far, far back in time. These two daughters stay at the back of the cave and serve him, bearing bows and arrows that never miss their mark. From this detail of the story, we can see the misuse of femininity in the personality, a feminine power of skill and creativity that occurs in men as well as women. Old Stone Shirt has femininity nearby, but the skill of the women is not used to empower either themselves or the next generation. Instead of serving creativity, the daughters serve their father's destructiveness.

Sad to say, every modern person is, to some degree, invested in stone-shirtedness. Therefore these details of the story are very important to each of us. We may discover our stone-shirtedness by a hardness of heart, but also by the fact that we have become jumpy or that our arrows never miss.

One/Two Man is made aware of the formidable task before him. He consults with Granny, whom he loves so dearly, but she is of no help. She only bursts into tears and advises him not to try this foolhardy mission. So One/Two man gathers around him all the animal helpers of the forest. These are creatures he knew during his carefree boyhood days, his animal friends. Bighorn Sheep comes to the meeting, as do Coyote, Wolf, Mouse, and Rattlesnake. One/Two Man announces his plan to rescue his mother from Old Stone Shirt, and all the animals immediately respond, "No, it cannot be done!" Like Granny, they advise that this scheme will only result in death for One/Two Man.

But One/Two Man is undeterred, and he insists that he will undertake this task even if he must go alone. Witnessing this display of courage and determination, the animals agree to help in any way they can.

This is an appropriate role for the ego—to provide courage and determination. Properly applied, the ego is used not for decision making but as the eyes and ears of God—collecting information, marshaling energies for the task at hand, providing discipline and courage. The heroic ego has an important task, but clearly it must rely upon help from others.

Now each of the animals brings to One/Two Man a special talent. Bighorn Sheep brings a bowl of water that never goes dry, a wonderful asset in very dry country. No venture in the desert will succeed without this essential gift. Wolf has a gift of gab; in fact, he talks and talks until everyone's ears are weary. He is filled with big ideas and plans, and he is absolutely sure of the rightness of every one of them. Coyote has a similar talent, and he interrupts Wolf to announce that he has a still better plan. When Coyote starts to talk, he begins to howl and howl until none of the animals can stand it anymore. When he stops for breath, Wolf begins talking again, and these two go on and on with their big ideas.

During all this talking, Mouse sits there quietly not saying a word and Rattlesnake is coiled in a corner, also in silence. The talk between Wolf and Coyote goes on and on until finally Rattlesnake just can't stand it anymore. He crawls out from under a bush where his color has provided perfect camouflage and leaves the assembly of animals. He slides along the earth and out to the very cave of Old Stone Shirt. He is so well hidden that no one can see him. He gets to the mouth of the cave, and, with a single, lightning-quick strike, he kills the Antelope with an eye on the end of every hair. He then goes back to the gathering of animals and quietly announces what he has accomplished.

"You see," Wolf says, "it was my idea, and it has worked!"

Coyote quickly interrupts, saying, "Nonsense, it was my idea all along, and you all can see that it has succeeded!"

Wolf and Coyote then proceed to argue about who had the idea to kill the Antelope with an eye on the end of every hair. This goes on and on until it exasperates everyone.

I am a bit embarrassed at this stage in our story, because it is such a masculine trait to sit around and put out one big idea after another. I am guilty of this, and I have heard many men sit and talk for weeks about big plans concerning how something should be accomplished. We can view these characters as part of the story only to provide comic relief, but another interpretation is that they are needed to generate a certain amount of energy that is required on the journey.

Whatever the value of Wolf and Coyote, the good news is that the touchy Antelope is now gone, but Wolf and Coyote go on talking for several more weeks, arguing about who should get the credit. Eventually, Mouse can no longer stand it, and he creeps off to the cave of Old Stone Shirt. Mouse knows all about the tiny crevices and small holes in the back of the cave, since that is his focal length and his domain. He gets into the cave, finds the two bows of the two daughters, and silently gnaws at them until the strings are worn down most of the way—but not all the way. They look strong and functional even though they are nearly severed, so that the moment a bow is drawn the string will snap.

This is a nice bit of trickery on the part of Mouse, disarming the daughters with the arrows that never miss. Like an expert in the martial arts, Mouse knows that it is better to depotentiate a destructive power than it is to try to confront it head-on.

Each of us has two daughters in the back of the cave bearing an energy that is sharp and arrowlike in its destructive power. If you try to confront this energy directly, you will probably just end up with an arrow in your chest. However, if you can follow the example of Mouse and depotentiate this impulse, then it does not have to be destructive. We also could speculate that Mouse represents doubt. I am always afraid of someone who claims to know exactly what he or she is doing; I am tempted to look around for a Mouse, someone with a little bit of doubt or humility. If you can carry a small bit of doubt with you on your inner journey and not go off overly confident like Wolf and Coyote, then you will be well served.

So, with the help of his animal friends, One/Two Man is now nearly prepared to deal with Old Stone Shirt. One/Two Man creeps up to within sight of the cave, keeping close to the ground while he tries to figure out what to do next. And while he is hiding in the scrub brush, he spies his mother, who has been allowed to go out for a walk. His heart races as she comes to within only a few yards of him, but Old Stone Shirt is watching her every move. Our hero whispers that it is One/Two Man, her son, come to rescue her. She does her best to hide the shock of hearing this and then insists under her breath that he must go away, since no one can defeat Old Stone Shirt. But before he withdraws, One/Two Man says a very wise thing: "When I am fighting Old Stone Shirt, Mother, you stay away. Go sit by the lake and don't get in my way." Then he silently crawls back to the gathering of the animal helpers.

The work of Rattlesnake and Mouse has taken care of the Antelope and the dangerous daughters, but still Old Stone Shirt remains, and no ax or arrow or weapon of any kind can pierce his armor. If you are dealing with an Old Stone Shirt—whether at work, in a social group, or in yourself—it is important to remember that a frontal attack is not going to work.

The animal helpers debate the best way to deal with Old Stone Shirt. Wolf has a plan, and he proceeds to talk for weeks about it. Coyote can't help but break in and argue just the opposite, and he goes on for several more weeks. The two get to arguing back and forth, until Rattlesnake can't stand it anymore. He is about to go out of his head, so he wriggles off once again. Using his special gift of camouflage, he hides undetected among the rocks just outside the cave, and while lying there he observes that each morning just before sunrise Old Stone Shirt emerges from his cave and walks out to answer the call of nature. On the next morning, Rattlesnake is ready. He positions himself very carefully at just the right spot, and when Old Stone Shirt squats down to answer the call of nature, Rattlesnake bites him in a strategic spot and instantly kills him.

Although Old Stone Shirt is invulnerable in most of his body, he still is unprotected and vulnerable in some very human parts of his being. These vulnerable places are the only areas of personality where one can approach the humanness of a stone-shirted character. No one is ever so completely covered over by his neurosis that he cannot be approached in some human dimension.

There is a story from World War II that Hermann Göring (an Old Stone Shirt if ever there was one) had news one morning that his pet dog had been killed by a car. He was stricken with grief, finished up his morning's work, and went home to grieve the loss of his dog for the rest of the day. The work to be finished was signing documents for the death of another thousand concentration camp victims. Here is a blatant example of an Old Stone Shirt with a tiny remnant of compassion.

Whenever a snake turns up, mythologically or symbolically in a dream, change is under way. The snake, who sheds its skin, represents the capacity for evolution. We know that in the Garden of Eden story when the snake appears, the situation changes forever. The snake here indicates evolution of consciousness. Now One/Two Man can create the heroic quest: he walks out to the lake where his mother is waiting, and the two go back to the village together. Please note the advice that our hero gave to the mother—to sit by the lake. The mother energy in all of us may have a difficult time learning when to get out of the way. I remember a woman who came to me after a lecture on One/Two Man and exclaimed, "Now I know what my son is trying to tell me! He is saying that I should stop mothering him, go out to look at the lake, and let him bring his own power to bear on the tasks he has to do." Wise son. Wise mother. The feminine parallel to this is almost identical. At a certain point in her development, a woman must tell her father to stand aside while she exercises her own inherited masculinity.

～

ONE OF THE CURIOSITIES of this story is that the hero, One/Two Man, relies so much on the assistance of others. As a central character, One/Two Man is the equivalent of one's ego and shadow. In the transformation process, it is not the isolated, heroic ego that saves the day. This is humbling. Our American Indian story points out that there is more to "I" than the ego. There are heroic parts, wise parts, destructive parts, crafty parts—these are all aspects of "I." It is very interesting that there is a minimum of heroism in this story, at least heroism as we have been accustomed to seeing it in movies and on television—the violent, muscular male action hero. Quiet, little-noticed parts of the personality save the day, as represented by Snake and Mouse. The heroic journey has strange twists and unexpected turns to it, and while consciousness is essential to the story, as represented by One/Two Man, it is not sufficient alone for the successful outcome. This underscores that consciousness must learn when to humble itself and to rely upon assistance from other parts of the personality.

My own journey was very similar to that of One/Two Man. After being given the tools for inner work from Dr. Kunkel and Dr. Jung, I set about piling up roots, sleeping on the dry bones of my father, claiming the ax, and then learning to work with the animal helpers to defeat my own Old Stone Shirt within. This was a process that took years, not hours or days.

I have tried to elucidate some of the interior meaning of this story. Myth expresses timeless truths in a universal language, but still it is our duty to mine this gold by searching out the parallels within our own psyches. One/Two Man, the animal helpers, Old Stone Shirt, Granny, the pile of roots, the bones of the father, the ax—these are all figures within each of us.

10

Training with Toni Sussman:

Finding a Religious Life in the Modern World

Over time, the analytical practices that Helen and I established began to grow and prosper, and I became increasingly aware that I needed additional training, though I wasn't sure where to get what I needed. The C. G. Jung Institute in Zurich continued to evolve over the years and add to its requirements, but Dr. Jung himself had insisted that I not join any groups and that I would be better served by apprenticing myself to a master. So I began thinking about who I might seek out. Helen immediately suggested her former analyst in London, a woman named Toni Sussman. I trusted Helen's opinion, but once again my fate was decided not by a rational, linear decision-making process, but by a slender thread. The final decision came from a dream, which presented itself to me as follows:

> I am diving into a pool of water. I love being in the water, and I am swimming around with great ease and pleasure, coming to the surface every now and then to refresh my lungs with air. In my enjoyment, I decide to dive deep down below the surface, and I propel myself so far that I can feel the bottom of the ocean. This amazes me, but in the same instant I realize that I have gone down too far. I realized that there is not enough oxygen in my lungs to allow me to get safely back to the surface. I am in a terrible panic, fearful of drowning, and then I wake up.

This dream convinced me that I should not wait any longer to pursue my training or I would soon be getting myself into real trouble.

That very day I began to make arrangements to travel to London. It is no easy matter to leave a practice for four months, but even that worked out easily. Of course, I had a warm recommendation from Helen, so after an exchange of letters with Toni Sussman, the plans were set. Once again, when you are on the right path, doors begin to open that you could never anticipate. I had planned to stay in a boardinghouse after arriving in London, and then suddenly a friend of Helen's wrote to say that I could stay in her guest room, use her car, and even avail myself of her housekeeper during my stay. All the pieces fell into place so quickly and painlessly that it seemed clear to me that fate was once again at work.

So, in the spring of 1954, at the age of thirty-three, I found another ship passage across the Atlantic, a much more stable crossing than the preceding one, and presented myself at the home of Dame Evelyn Sharp on Sloan Square in London. Dame Evelyn occupied the highest position a woman had ever held at that time in the British government, and I was a bit intimidated by her. She had the feminine equivalent of the title *Sir* and later loved to tell me of the time she had stood before the king as the only woman to be knighted in that official ceremony. Each of the men who were to become knights had been equipped with a small hook on their lapels on which the king could hang the insignia of the order of knighthood. But no one had known what to do with Dame Evelyn in her formal gown. The King came up to her during the grand ceremony and whispered, "What the hell am I to do with this thing?"

"I don't know, Your Majesty, but you could just put it in my hand," replied Dame Evelyn. This the king did, and the greatest honor that England can bestow was conveyed.

Each morning, Dame Evelyn and I would breakfast together. She was so different in character from me that we were both often at a loss for words, so we would talk about the weather or current events.

In London I had four months of free time to devote to my studies, which centered around an analytical hour each day, including Sundays, with Toni. She had sent me directions to her flat that were impossible to forget—I told the taxi driver to go to 34 Baker Street, the famous address of Sherlock Holmes. Sure enough, when I arrived, I found a placard on the wall honoring the famous detective of Scotland Yard, and right across the street was the study of Toni Sussman.

It was Toni's custom that the first meeting with a trainee or a patient should be brief and formal. It was designed simply for the two personalities to sense each other. She felt strongly that you shouldn't talk much but simply be in each other's presence at the first meeting.

It was a positive shock to meet her. It was instantly a meeting of opposites, masculine and feminine, tall and short, young and old, America and Europe, the new world and the old. She was imperial looking, with a regal bearing and formal, though not unfriendly, face. She welcomed me with a proper British greeting, we exchanged a few pleasantries, and our conversation seemed to end before it had even begun. Soon she was showing me to the door and telling me to return at 10 A.M. the following morning.

Toni's father was a Hasidic Jew from Spain and her mother a Swedish gentile. Somehow out of this mix Toni had emerged as an ardent Roman Catholic. She and her husband, an eye surgeon, had escaped from Berlin just as the Nazis were coming to power. Like so many people, they had given up everything and had left Germany with scarcely more than the clothes on their backs. The couple had settled in London, but her husband became ill within a few months of their arrival, dying shortly thereafter. Toni had to find a way to make a living, but despite her training with Dr. Jung she soon learned that the analytical community in London would have nothing to do with her. It was operated as a private club, and Toni was perceived as an intruder. At least that is how she told the story. I suspect that she didn't help matters along with her aristocratic personality. Toni did not suffer fools gladly and was quick to say whatever came to her mind.

On the morning following our first meeting, I returned to Baker Street and took a seat in Toni's office. She looked across her desk at me and informed me that we would meet for one hour each day, seven days a week. I wondered to myself what we would find to talk about with a full hour every day. I was certain that my simple life would be analyzed within a few days. It turned out, however, that seven days a week was scarcely enough to process all that came out of me.

Once the nature of our therapeutic contract was defined, Toni looked directly into my eyes and said, "Well, Robert, I presume you are here because you mean business. You have come a third of the way around the world to work with me. So, let's begin. Whom do you love?"

Her manner was so direct and her presence so intense that I was immediately scared out of my wits by this tiny woman. I sat there like an idiot for nearly a full minute. The silence became heavier and heavier, but I had no idea what to say and she would not toss me a life preserver.

"I am waiting. It's really a simple question. Whom do you love?"

I couldn't think of a phony answer, and so I began to pour out my heart's sorrow, recounting all the loneliness of my life, all the failed attempts at friendship and relationship and community. I said that certainly Helen and I had a special relationship. I was literally sobbing through an unending stream of torment and sorrow.

Toni listened intently, waiting for a pause in my lamentations, and when at last I stopped for breath she replied, "Well, good. Now we have something to work with." And off we went.

Effective analysis is a curious blend of passivity on the part of the analyst coupled with guidance and challenge. Toni was an expert. She never overwhelmed me but was a master at probing into vague places in my consciousness and demanding clarity. She gave me homework assignments. One day she told me to go home and draw my mandala. A mandala is a diagram of the human soul as taught by the Hindu religion; essentially it is a nonverbal way of defining one's character. Toni stressed that it was extremely valuable for a person to draw a mandala and to learn from this about the interior dimensions of his or her personality. That seemed simple enough, and I assumed that I would bring it back the next day, but this assignment began a process that lasted more than a month. I worked and worked on it. I would bring it to her each day, and we would discuss the mandala's evolution. The outward form stayed essentially the same, but I couldn't decide what to put into the circular shape, especially at the very center.

I still have that mandala. It is a very slender, starlike figure with long rays emanating out from the center. Toni told me it was the most extroverted mandala she had ever seen, which totally confused me because I have always been an inward, introverted person. Her comment simply didn't fit. But she insisted that the mandala revealed that I was meant to reach out in the world to a great extent. Within two decades, her prediction would come true, though there was much work to do before I could maintain my essential introversion while lending myself to the world of lectures and books. It is no small task to be a highly introverted person in an American setting and in a public position. I felt as if I were required to square the circle, a medieval preoccupation, in bringing these two elements into some kind of harmony.

It's difficult to describe what goes on in an analysis without making an intense process sound trivial. In a way it is a love affair, without anything personal going on between the two parties. When the analytic vessel is properly constructed, it provides a safety, openness, honesty, and directness that one rarely experiences in life. In my analysis with Toni I could bring up any daily experience, every fear and hope, and there was no need to be tactful or on guard. I trusted her completely, an experience not often available in our power-dominated world. This gift of safety is one of the rarest treasures anyone can give to another. There was nothing I had to do to impress her or to earn her unconditional support and positive regard.

As the therapeutic experience proceeded, I was drawn into its inner intensity in inexplicable ways. I would leave the sessions and make the rounds of London's churches. On some days I would light vigil candles. Other days I would meditate in silence. Mostly I would just walk and observe. Toni understood that analysis can be its own kind of mass, a religious event of the highest order. She also taught me that it is important to store up energy during major life transitions. People rarely store up energy; almost everyone today has their energy mortgaged way into the future. I nurtured myself, trying not to make any major decisions and allowing my unconscious to wander wherever and however it would.

One day I was talking with Toni Sussman and feeling terribly discouraged. I told her that I didn't know how to become a success. Although my analytical practice in Los Angeles had been growing before I left, felt incompetent about turning it into a self-supporting profession upon my return, and I had no sense of how to ingratiate the right people so as to climb up in the ranks of my profession. In my self-pity I was on the verge of tears. Toni, who was often quite sharp and authoritative, responded with great gentleness on this occasion. "Robert," she said, "when you go home all you need to do is leave the door open a crack, and the people who belong to you will come." I believed in her and trusted her advice. That is exactly what I did, and it worked out just as she predicted.

In addition to conducting individual training analysis, Toni also led a group one evening each week. I joined the group, and at first no one knew what to make of the quiet young American. I felt a sense of inferiority, but very early on Toni made a show of presenting to me a certificate. Dr. Jung had authorized her to train analysts in his name and had given her special certificates to recognize the completion of training. These were her most prized possessions, as they were among only a few items that she had managed to smuggle out of Germany. She wrote out a certificate with my name on it and declared to the group that I was from that day forward a Jungian analyst. I was speechless and could not stop a flow of tears. I then felt that I deserved to be among the others in Toni's group. I still have that certificate in a safe deposit box, and it is among my most prized possessions.

Toni was an excitable and passionate person. When inspiration struck her, she would rise to the full height of her four feet, eleven inches and make some pronouncement. I still recall one time when I brought her a dream. I told the dream, and she leaped to her feet.

"Now I see. It is absolutely clear," Toni declared. "It is your job during this lifetime to reorganize the Catholic Church. You simply must follow through and carry out the will of God."

I sat there wondering what to do with such a grand statement. Toni was in a rush of intensity. Before I could object, she reached for her telephone and called up a friend of hers who was a powerful member of the Catholic Church. It was the abbot of Prinknash, the second largest Benedictine house in the world.

"I am sitting here with a very gifted young man who has had a vision from God," she said with absolute conviction. "Well, I believe it is a revelation for the church and that you may be fortunate enough to participate in it."

I squirmed in my chair. I would have laughed, except I knew that she was deadly serious.

"Yes, we can be there tomorrow so that you can meet him. Yes, we will discuss this completely." The matter was settled. Toni dismissed me with a wave of the hand and a pronouncement that the next day we were bound for Gloucester, the town nearest the abbey.

My sleep that night was full of promise.

During our drive from London to Gloucester the following morning, Toni explained that she had been the prime mover in setting up a lay community in affiliation with the Prinknash Abbey. It was organized much like a commune. It began with Toni placing a small, two-shilling advertisement in the Gloucester newspaper. The ad read: "Worthy Catholic cause needs 10,000 pound donation." An elderly woman had answered the ad and subsequently donated 10,000 pounds, allowing Toni to buy a farm next to the abbey and to establish her community in a delightful pastoral setting. Several of the spiritual seekers were former communists who Toni had single-handedly converted to the Catholic Church. I had personally witnessed her powers of persuasion, and though the tale seemed preposterous I thought that if anyone was capable of turning communists into Catholics, it was Toni.

When we pulled up to the farm, the head man from the commune was waiting in the yard to greet us. In the midst of our mutual introductions, Toni startled everyone.

"This is Robert, and he is your new leader. He will be taking over now." She said it matter-of-factly, like one might comment on the road conditions or the weather.

Toni then went on to say that I would be conducting an experimental program that was certainly destined to revolutionize the church and bring it into a new era.

"Soon he will be setting up psychotherapeutic communities next to abbeys all across the world. It will quickly become the Catholic solution to dealing with the ills of the modern world," Toni said.

I gulped hard and smiled sheepishly at the head man. As he stood there silently, I could see that he was as astonished at this outburst from Toni as I was.

In a swirl, Toni led us into the community house. My thoughts were racing. I was thrilled at the prospect of joining a community. It was what I had been searching for all my life, and here I would have therapeutic and monastic aspects of life all rolled up into one neat package. Over a pot of tea I learned that the community lived in substantial poverty, by choice as much as necessity. As I looked about, I could see one middle-aged woman who never seemed to smile and was dressed much like a scarecrow. Everyone at the abbey was very proud of their poverty and showed it off. Already, cracks were beginning to show in my ideal vision.

~

THAT NIGHT, THE ABBOT CAME for a special dinner and sat between Toni and me. Toni had told me to kneel and kiss his ring upon his arrival.

"Whatever you do, do not tell him that you're not a Catholic," Toni insisted.

It seemed to be implied that eventually I would see the light and join the Catholic Church, but in the meantime I was to at least keep up appearances. After dinner we walked down the road to visit the adjoining abbey.

The abbey had approximately one hundred and fifty monks. It was a large institution that had survived the Reformation in England

and had changed little over five centuries. We were given a brief tour. In the chapel the seats were made of beautifully carved oak constructed in such a manner that they folded down but could not be made level. Their natural resting place was at a forty-five degree angle. Monks were not allowed to sleep much in the early days, and the fear was that a flat seat would put them immediately to sleep. After our tour, we were invited to join the monks for a humble dinner.

Toni's enthusiasm had already convinced the old abbot that this idea of an experimental therapeutic community was foretold in scripture. While Toni and the abbot sat and talked, I excused myself on the pretext of exploring the abbey a bit more.

As I walked through the old stone building, I was thinking that my fondest dreams had come true. How many hundreds of times had I fantasized that I might do analytical work in a monastic setting with the power of the church to back up the process? I always believed that analysis, at its best, was really a new statement of the old teachings of the church, and I longed to see the arcane art returned to its source. After all, isn't psychology the study of the soul? And is this not the province of the church? But still something else in me was squirming. Red lights were flashing in my head.

As I continued my walk, I wandered back to the community house. The old scarecrow whom I had seen earlier in a cast-off sweater and shoes that didn't fit was in the kitchen preparing porridge. She stood over a ten-gallon iron kettle, stirring with a large wooden spoon. This lugubrious sight sent a chill down my spine. It was too much like the witches' sabbath in Faust. That moment burst the bubble of my inflation, and I knew immediately that this was a totally impossible situation. Part of me wanted Toni's proposal to be right; I wanted to forget the modern world and to pretend that a medieval existence was still possible. But deep down I knew better. It was a charade. Even the pride that the community took in its poverty was a hoax. Whether I liked it or not, I knew from that moment that I am an irreducibly modern person and that there is no going back to a medieval lifestyle.

We had brought another student of Toni's along on the trip, Kevin, an Irish lad I had made friends with. I hunted up Kevin and said, "Kevin! I need to talk with you!"

"It is about time!" he said. Kevin with his earthy insight had seen me floating off into my inflation and had been helpless to do anything about it. But our urgent talk brought me back to my senses, and I remembered the warning of Dr. Jung, "Don't ever join anything."

How to let this be known to Toni without insulting her enthusiasm? I took the quiet way and said nothing until I was back in America and then informed her that I did not think I could be the head of such an organization even though I wanted exactly that more than anything else in my personal world. An impersonal world had claimed me.

I spent four months training with Toni Sussman, and I gained immeasurably from the experience. If there is a single model for my analytic work it is she. I might have learned as much from Dr. Jung if I had been allowed an equal amount of time with him, but Toni was a master therapist. She had perfected the arcane art of drawing the best out of people, demanding that they explore their own depths but never intruding into the process in any personal way. Each school of psychotherapy and each individual analyst has his own definition where this line should be drawn. I remember a comment about Dr. Jung: this action would be malpractice in ordinary circumstances but it was genius coming from him. It is extremely difficult to define the right stance for a therapist, and each person must find his or her own way in this matter. I remember one day Toni greeted me for my hour with a sigh. "Oh, Robert, I will never learn. I think all my geese are swans." Yes, she had many disappointments, but if there was a swan to be found, she would search him out and demand that he follow his true heritage. It was hard on her, however, to release the geese back to mediocre lives.

I had once thought that it was desirable in the analytic hour for the analyst to keep his or her own thoughts and feelings separate from those of the patient. To bring them into the process was called countertransference and was looked down upon in the psychoanalytic community. However, Dr. Jung believed in selectively sharing such thoughts and feelings, and Toni taught me how to be present in a session as a full and complete human being without contaminating the patient's process.

I also learned from Toni that the analyst must aim for clarity but avoid taking sides with any part of a patient's psyche. Leaning to one side or the other just constellates the opposite force, and the analysis becomes stuck. That doesn't mean that I will not take a stand. Back in my student days in Zurich there was an argument in the Jungian community about whether an analyst has the right to save a patient from some impending disaster that seems to be anticipated in a dream. Some argued that the analyst must fight for that part of the personality that wants to heal and grow, while others insisted that no person has the right to play God and interfere in the fate of another human being. In my analysis with Toni I met a healer who was prepared to battle for my growth, for which I am eternally grateful, and, following her model, I have always tried to do the same for my patients.

Near the end of my work with Toni Sussman, I again had a pivotal dream. It presented itself to me as follows:

I am in Italy on a hot day. It is afternoon, and I am sweating, working very hard carrying a bell in my arms, the bell of the Virgin Mary. It is extremely valuable, I don't know why I have it, but I am carrying it, this precious relic.

It has been known in the church for centuries that this bell would turn up one day, and they have built a basilica for it the size of Saint Peter's in Rome. It is specifically intended to house the bell. There is a niche and a hook in the altar of the church that is just the right size for the bell, since its exact dimensions are somehow known in advance.

There has been a priest on duty twenty-four hours a day every day for centuries, waiting for the bell. I come walking up the central aisle of the basilica and wake the priest to say that the holy bell has finally arrived. He is dazed with excitement. The custom has been arranged that the very big bells in the west tower, which have never been used, are ready and waiting to let the world know that the bell of the Virgin Mary has arrived. The priest goes hurrying down the aisle to let the world know that the bell is here!

I sit down on a marble bench. There is a stone in my shoe that hurts, so I take off my shoe to remove it. Thoughts are furiously rushing through me head: What should I do? If I stay they will make a big fuss over me for being the one who brought the bell. Part of me wants to be the big man, but another part says this will engulf and totally destroy me.

The bells in the west tower are beginning to ring, but I still have time to escape. I am torn between two destinies. I finally get up and walk out the side door of the choir; townspeople are already flocking down to the basilica, marveling that the bells are ringing. I am totally lonely in my anonymity, as I am going the opposite way from everyone else.

This dream foretold the next three decades of my life. I believe that it was an anti-inflation dream, showing how my ego was considering getting everything it possibly could gain—money, power, fame. But another part of me decided instead to duck out and keep my anonymity. It took years before the deep meaning of this dream sank in, before I grew strong enough to incorporate the dream into my life. At the time of the dream, however, I still wanted recognition, fame, and achievement. In fact, my ego tried for a while to turn the meaning of the dream around, perceiving it as a prediction that I would become a big shot, a famous person. I tried to live up to that expectation for a number of years, thinking that I would discover the long-awaited bell and become a big man. But some other part of me has shunned fame. Any time I have been about to arrive, to gain some power or fame, I have tried to slip out the side door. This has been a tension in my life—wanting in but simultaneously wanting to stay out.

This dream comes back to my mind whenever I am tempted to do something big or extravagant, and it reminds me that I am to find the bell of the Virgin Mary (I take this to be a very feminine, introverted, feeling function), but I must let others have the show of putting it on its hook in the church. To do otherwise would be to dispel the power of the process and turn it into personal inflation.

Clearly, the images in this dream are religious. Over the years I discovered that virtually everyone who comes to analysis is in some way facing a religious crisis, a term I prefer to *neurosis,* and every analysis is in some way a religious dilemma.

This is the essence of what I learned from Dr. Jung: listen to your interior intelligence, take it seriously, stay true to it, and—most important—approach it with a religious attitude. His psychological term for this is *individuation*—discovering the uniqueness of yourself, finding out what you are not and finding out what you are. Individuation relates to wholeness, but it is not some indiscriminate wholeness but rather *your* particular relationship to everything else. You get to the whole only by working with the particularity of *your* life, not by trying to evade or rise above the specificity of your life. This is the blending of heaven and earth. This is a truly religious life.

Of course, Jung didn't invent this; it is as old as humankind. Other teachers in my life, such as Krishnamurti, were saying the same thing in their own ways, but Jung presented it in a very practical way and in a language for modern times. After I learned from Dr. Jung the process of approaching daily life with a truly religious attitude, then I could begin to see how the great symbol systems of the world's religions were saying similar things. I had grown up with Christian symbols and rituals all my life, but they had become empty; it is ironic that work with my dreams (and, later, living among Hindus in India) would teach me what those symbols and rituals were really about. Only when I could understand, for example, that the virgin birth was about a birth of new consciousness in me did that story begin to have profound meaning for me.

Dr. Jung linked religious experience to the *numinosum,* a word for dynamic effects not caused by an act of human will, and he distinguished between religion and creed. A creed is a codified and dogmatized form of an original religious experience of the numinosum. Dr. Jung believed that all of the prophets for all the world's religions experienced the numinosum, what I call the Golden World, and over time creeds were developed to help channel the energy and to explain such experiences to the uninitiated. Replacing the immediate experience of the Golden World with an institutionalized set of symbols and rituals has a valuable purpose in defending people against religious experience that might be overwhelming. Direct experiences of the Golden World are glorious but also painful and dangerous, and some people shouldn't try to contain these energies on their own. The church, synagogue, temple, or mosque mediates between the numinosum and the everyday; it is a good place to reconcile the Golden World and the earthly world.

Dr. Jung always tried to return patients to the religious systems in which they had experience, if that was possible. Later, in my own analytical practice, I had many patients in Los Angeles who were German Jewish refugees, and often they were afraid I would try to convert them to Christianity. I never took a Christian standpoint but instead worked with the symbols that came up out of the psyche of each patient. If religious symbolism came up in a dream of a nonreligious Jew, I might ask, "Well, why are you not in synagogue?" and this would completely surprise the person. I wasn't pushing any form of religion, but I was very sensitive to the importance of the religious function in each person.

I do believe that the Christian tradition is etched deeply into the collective unconscious of the West and that the symbols of the Christian Church speak eloquently of the psychological process that occurs in Western people. But for many modern people, the traditional institutions and symbol systems no longer work, and the Jungian approach makes a religious life possible for such people by providing tools to facilitate a direct experience of the divine. While this approach does not provide the sense of community provided by a church or other institution, it also does not mix up the cultural task with the religious task.

Everyone has a double duty in life, to maintain a cultural life and a religious life, and the laws of these two realms are often diametrically opposed to each other. The duty of the church (whatever the creed) should be to assist people with their religious life, which involves seeing past duality and advancing consciousness. The cultural life consists of choosing between good and evil and keeping the human side of life in order and proportion. So many religious institutions today focus on the cultural life almost exclusively instead of helping people cultivate a different kind of consciousness. I have searched the world over for formal religious training that would assist in this process, and, tragically, I never found an institution that satisfied me. I spent decades trying to make collective religious forms work—the Christian Church, monasticism, and various spiritual communities—and over and over again found them inadequate. The best one can hope from an organization is some tools and encouragement. This is the invaluable gift that Toni Sussman gave to me.

After several months of training with Toni Sussman, I decided to take a month off to travel in Europe before returning home. There were several more cathedrals in France that I still wanted to see. I took a ferry at Dover and crossed the English Channel. It was nightfall by the time I arrived in Lyons, France. I knew I was in trouble as soon as I got off the train; once again, I didn't know anyone in a strange city and my inner demons began acting up. As soon as I could find a hotel room, I sat down to have it out with my unconscious through active imagination. I sat up writing most of the night, and the vision that came to me was a Kafkaesque nightmare in which my soul was on trial. Here is the vision:

A prosecutor presented all of the sins of commission and omission that I was responsible for throughout my life, and the list was very long indeed. That went on for hours, and it fell on me like a landslide. I was feeling worse and worse to the point where the soles of my feet were hot. After hours of accusations from the prosecution, a group of angels appeared to conduct

my defense. All they could say was, "But he loved." They
began chanting this over and over in a chorus: "But he loved.
But he loved. But he loved." This continued until dawn, and in
the end the angels won, and I was safe.

Despite being up all night, I greeted the dawn with renewed energy and purpose. I checked out of my hotel and took a train to
Cologne. I tried to visit the cathedral there, but I could not get my
heart into sight-seeing, so I found an express train and channel
crossing back to London. I turned up at Toni Sussman's door and
told her, "I'm back." She said that somehow she was not surprised
and agreed to continue my analysis for several more weeks. That remarkable vision heralded some change that was taking place within
me, though I wouldn't begin to understand the full extent of it until
I returned to the United States.

Return of the Serpent:

Dreams and Visions of Transformation

After returning from London and resuming my analytical practice in Los Angeles, I had another powerful dream, one that in
many ways was a continuation of the archetypal dream that I had
presented to Dr. Jung earlier. Here is my dream:

> I'm on a California beach with a family of friends. The
> woman of the household is a particularly good friend of mine,
> a very wise woman. She and I are a little distance apart from
> the family picnic. We are discussing this holiday crush of people
> on the beach; it seems like everybody in the world is there. I
> can see at least a million people. I like this. I enjoy beaches and
> good fun and good atmosphere—the happiness, the sun, the
> children, the picnics, the sports.
>
> But there is one discordant note. The city fathers have
> brought up a number of old kitchen ranges—wood, gas, elec-
> tric—and have distributed them along the beach, unconnected,
> so that they don't function at all except as funky art. Our party
> has taken up possession of one of these stoves that never pro-
> duce any heat.
>
> My friend and I discuss the American liking for funky, emo-
> tionally shocking, sentimental things as decorative. We agree
> that we don't like it. Nonetheless, our picnic party is around
> one of these stoves.
>
> Suddenly I look up, and who do I see but my snake! The
> same snake that came to me in my dream in Zurich and that I

discussed with Dr. Jung. The giant serpent is wriggling around through the crowd, and no one but my friend and I see him. He slithers along, making no trouble at all. He comes to a pair of upright posts with a crosspiece at the top and wriggles up and does his exercises. He loops and twines, and he goes over himself and back again. I watch him very carefully, because I don't want the snake to find me.

He comes down and begins to wriggle away, and I see that he's moving away from me. I whisper to my friend, "Good, he's going away." But the snake hears this, changes his path, and comes straight for me. I say, "Wouldn't you know it! A million people and he comes straight to me!"

I don't want him to come. I wish he would go away. But for some reason I'm not terrified, and I don't run away as I did in my dream years earlier. The snake comes directly at me. At this point there's a break in the dream. There is some moment of confrontation, but it's just as if a piece of film had been cut out and the ends spliced back together.

When the dream picks up again, the woman is gone and the snake is gone, but a radiant man from heaven—a young fellow who glows—is standing with me. We're friends and we're having a marvelous time. Again, finally, I have my companion, the Buddha.

We walk along and I say, "I didn't realize we were in India." I look again and see that we're not in India—it's just that these blond Americans look so dark compared with the radiant man from heaven that I thought I was among very dark-skinned people. We are indeed on the beach in southern California. And I'm so happy. I say to him, "I know this is extraordinary, but I'm as happy as a mortal could be."

We walk on, looking at the picnic revelry of an American beach. There are chess games going on, body builders are doing their calisthenics, teenagers are courting. I am thrilled at seeing the American scenes that have so often offended me because of their adolescent and sentimental character. But the presence of the man from heaven transforms all these things into a walk across one corner of heaven. He takes me some distance, and we come to a dam. The dammed-up river is immensely wide but not very deep. The man from heaven turns to me and says, "All right. The dam is built, the water is backed up. Now you design and build a hydroelectric system for it, and it will fill the energy deficit for the whole world."

I awoke from this epic dream feeling happy but bewildered. The dream had instructions, but what did they mean? I sat down with a piece of paper and wrote down my personal associations for each image in the dream. (This method is described in detail in my book *Inner Work*.) For example, a hydroelectric system: When I was growing up in Portland a friend once took me to see the construction of the Bonneville Dam. I remember walking around the giant turbine bases where they were pouring concrete and marveling at the great power harnessed by such a dam. Next, I took the dream into active imagination. Over the next several weeks I spent many hours designing turbines for the great dam in my dream, pondering which way they should turn, the position of the concrete aprons, the lubrication system. I proceeded to build more turbines through more active imagination until I got up to a dozen. Then one day, when I felt that the turbines were ready, I turned them on. The water flowed, and my imaginative construction project seemed to work beautifully.

For the next several months I devoted time each day to imagining this great dam and tending to it; I would see myself lubricating the turbines and checking to make sure that everything was in order. One day I sat down to do my active imagination, and in my mind's vision the whole dam was now occupied with turbines, hundreds of them receding off into the distance. I watched and grew intently interested. Then, all of a sudden, I could sense that the Buddha was with me again. He was apparently there to give me some instructions. But there my vision ended.

On one level, this dream reveals the evolution of the Dionysian quality in me, an evolution that has occupied most of a lifetime and that still is by no means complete. The Dionysian quality is one's capacity for joy, ecstasy, the pleasure of earthly physical things. Christianity prescribed a severe curtailing of these qualities at a time when this faculty was threatening to take more than its correct proportion of human life. This diminishing of the earthly element was correct for the early and medieval times of human history but is not appropriate now. We have departed so far from earthly things now that our need is for an increase of the Dionysian element to find the right balance for our lives. The serpent is often a symbol of the Dionysian element. (See my book *Ecstasy* for elaboration on this subject.)

The snake, of which I was once so frightened, had me on the run for years. It turned out, however, that he was protecting me until I could come to terms with him. When he comes to me again on the beach, although I am still resisting him, I am no longer terrified. Since I can now endure the serpent, the promised return of the man from heaven, the fourth Buddha, is possible. I can now receive and work with the heavenly energy, as represented by the great dam. It is there, waiting for me to put it into form for the benefit of all humankind.

The evolution of the images in this dream compared with the dream in Zurich that I told to Dr. Jung represents three decades of work and psychic growth. The first dream left me with the snake still chasing me; the last detail of the dream involved making a circle with my arm and the snake poking through it with his nose, but we were still running. The circle and the fact that I talked to the snake gave Dr. Jung hope that some kind of resolution might be possible. While the ending was encouraging, I was still running from the instinctive side of life. The second dream picks up just where the first dream left off: the snake is still a snake, but I am no longer afraid of him. We have a direct confrontation of some sort, though it is deleted from the dream, and then the snake becomes a holy man or Buddha.

At the time of this second major dream of the snake and the Buddha, I had struggled for years developing my fourth function, which is thinking. I am indebted to the work of the Jungian scholar

Marie-Louise von Franz for the understanding that the arrival of the fourth function is experienced not as an enlightenment but as a breakdown. The third function for me was sensation, and through hard work and discipline I brought this into fruition in my personality. But as Dr. Jung had hinted in our conversation in Zurich, when it is time to develop the fourth function, it is as if the three developed functions fall into the unconscious and are assimilated by the fourth. Perhaps the assimilation of the fourth function can take place only in the unconscious, and this is experienced as though one's world is falling apart. From the point of view of consciousness, this development feels like utter despair, darkness, and hopelessness. Saint John of the Cross called such an experience the dark night of the soul, and others have described the desolate terror of experiencing such a transformation. I was in the process of undergoing something very similar.

Luckily, I had the support of Helen at this time, but soon that, too, would disappear. In the next few years I would step into my place as an author and lecturer, but only after another dive into the depths of the unconscious. My life was about to become like a roller-coaster of highs and lows.

It was at this time that an important international symposium on Jungian psychology, called the Panarian Conference, was organized in Los Angeles. Tom Laughlin, the actor who gained fame as the star of the movie titled *Billy Jack*, was interested in the work of Carl Jung, and Tom financed and organized what at the time was billed as the most important Jungian program in America, perhaps the world. This conference came at a time in which the Jungian world was vigorously ignoring me. This was a time when Helen and I most needed community and the support of mentors, but the Los Angeles Jung Society wouldn't provide any of this. Given my lifelong desire to belong somewhere, I would have been grateful to have been accepted by the official Jungian organization in the city where I lived; it was painful to me at the time that we could not associate with the great names in the Jungian world. Apparently a few people thought we lacked the proper credentials, which was quite ironic in that Dr. Jung himself had told me that the best training would be to apprentice myself to individual analysts, as I had done with Dr. Fritz Kunkel and then with Toni Sussman. In any event, I heard about the Panarian Conference, but Helen and I decided that it would be best if we didn't try to attend.

Then Barbara Hannah, a member of Carl Jung's inner circle and Dr. Jung's biographer, decided to come to America for a visit. Of course, we knew Barbara from our training in Zurich, and when she arrived in Los Angeles she contacted us. Helen and I invited her for tea, and we had a delightful conversation that afternoon. As she was preparing to leave she said, "Well, I'll see you at the lecture tonight."

Helen and I both grimaced and looked at each other, and then we were obliged to tell Barbara that we had not been invited to her lecture. Barbara was shocked by this, but she said she had observed such disputes occurring in other cities, and it seemed to come with all organizations as they grew and became institutionalized.

Barbara Hannah recalled a dream she had just before embarking for her first American lecture tour. She telephoned Dr. Jung to tell him about it. In the dream she was in America for the first time and was standing before a tall skyscraper of a building with the words C. G. *Jung Institute* chiseled into the stone lintel over the door. The building was black. Across the street there was a small house in which two analysts worked quietly with no name over the door. This building was white. Barbara reported that Dr. Jung had burst forth with the following comment on her dream: "Of course! It is always the small and unobtrusive workers who do the best, and it is always the big pretentious operations that go dark." Barbara told us of her dream out of great kindness and empathy, and, as she left our house, she did not fail to point out that it was white in color. That truly amazed me, and her story gave me solace and encouragement, providing balm for my wounded feelings.

The next year, the second Panarian Conference was being organized. I heard about it through friends but continued to hide my hurt and pretend that I had no interest in the event. One day the phone rang and a cheerful voice said, "Mr. Johnson, I am Tom Laughlin's secretary, and I would like to talk with you about the next Panarian lecture. Dr. Marie-Louise von Franz is coming from Switzerland, and Dr. Edward Edinger will lecture."

This was sandpaper on raw nerves for me. I interrupted her rudely and said, "Look, are you really so hard up for customers that you are soliciting by phone?"

She either didn't hear me or had the tact to ignore my rude comment, so she continued. "We would very much like it if you would also agree to be one of our lecturers."

My mind spun around, and I quickly became frightened instead of angry. I didn't know what to say, so I told her I would have to think about it. I hung up the phone, and my head was spinning that entire day. I was not allowed in the back door of the official Jungian world, but now they wanted me to come in the front door. What had changed? I made some inquiries and found out that Tom Laughlin had heard one of my lectures and had liked it so much he insisted that I be invited. Apparently there were protests, but since Mr. Laughlin was providing most of the funding for the conference, his opinion won out.

After licking my wounds, I eventually phoned back and accepted the invitation; then I shook in my boots for the next six months prior to my lecture. I decided to prepare a talk on Tristan and Isolde, the story of two great lovers, and the differentiation of romantic love from human love. I worked and worked on my presentation, making outlines, even typing it out word for word. I rehearsed at home, and finally I got a group of friends together to listen to a trial run of the lecture. Everyone hated it. People were gentle but firm in telling me that surely it was not my intention to make a spectacle of myself at the biggest Jungian conference of the year. I then realized what I had done. I had tried to create a scholarly paper to compete with my famous colleagues, which was never my style. I have always led with my feeling function, talking with an audience as if we were in a very personal relationship. I never lectured from prepared notes. At the very time that I wished to do my best, I had produced my worst because I was trying to please someone else instead of myself. So, the week before the big conference, I scrapped my notes and started over. I made a few notes on what was most meaningful to me about this mythic story and determined that the presentation would be improvised out of what came to me at the moment.

I was the first lecturer on the first day. When my introduction was made, I walked to the podium and depended entirely upon my feeling function to get me through. I knew the risk was that I would ramble into an incoherent jumble of words, but I preferred doing that to producing a dry, inferior talk that bored everyone. I felt I was doing well and was far into the story of Tristan and Isolde, when I spotted Dr. von Franz sitting in the front row. She was one of the great stars in the Jungian galaxy. Just as my eyes surveyed her face, she gave forth a gigantic hippopotamus yawn that stopped me cold. The lecture was recorded for posterity, and I can still hear the total silence on the tape at this moment in the lecture. Standing at the podium, I quickly reminded myself that she had just flown in from Zurich and was probably suffering from jet lag. I regained my composure and managed to get through the rest of the lecture, and I was pleasantly surprised by the applause. The lecture was generally well received, and a few years later I would publish an expanded version of it as my book *We*, which would become a best-seller in many languages.

From this point on, I gained a new confidence about public speaking; I determined to do it in my own quietly introverted fashion, and for some reason it worked. It was incredible in itself that a nobody like me was invited to speak to the top echelon of the Jungian world, and my subsequent success was even more surprising. I seem to be a walking solace for highly introverted, feeling-type people. I've often heard it said, "Well, if shy, retiring Robert can make it, then perhaps there's some hope for me."

Some major transformation had taken place in my unconscious, as predicted by my dream of the snake and the Buddha on the beach. I began to use my thinking function more, and I gained a new self-confidence and inner authority. I had spent so many years developing my feeling function, my most natural form of expression, that now I could risk utilizing my least developed function, thinking. The inferior function is never as stable as one's primary function, but it serves well if used cautiously. It was hardly the power of a hydroelectric plant, as shown in that dream, but it did generate enough power to thrust me out before the world as an author and lecturer. These interior events are probably more powerful than we ever know. About this time I had another important dream:

I am out on a hill, dry like southern California. I am walking without shoes, and there are small cobras around me. I am very cautious, watching carefully where I step. They get more and more numerous, and I am having trouble finding space to put my feet down. I come to Dr. Jung's house; it's the only house in sight. It has a fence and a green yard with flowers. I pass through the front gate. There are no cobras there in the yard. I ring the bell and Mrs. Jung is there. I explain my plight and ask if she has any shoes. "It is too dangerous to go on this journey without shoes," I say. She says she will see what might be done and invites me in.

Mrs. Jung then goes to get Dr. Jung. I explain my predicament to him, and he tries to be helpful and looks all over the house but cannot find any shoes for me. He would do anything for me that he could, but he has no shoes that will fit me. I go out the back door, thanking him for being so kind to me, and I go out the gate to a dry, brown place again.

Now the cobras get thicker and thicker as I get some distance from the house, until there is no place to put my foot down without stepping on a cobra. There is nothing to do but stand still. So I stop, and an extraordinary thing happens. The cobras make a circle in a curious way. Each one takes on an S shape. They lie close to one another, radiating out away from me, hundreds of cobras surrounding me. I am tired and sit down. I don't know what to do, when a thought comes to me:

are they facing me or facing out? When I look the tails are toward me and the heads are all facing out. Good God, I think, they are protecting me and I didn't know it. I talk to the cobras and say, Look fellows, if I make an agreement not to move from here, if I promise not to move, will you ease up on me? Instantly, all the cobras coalesce into one white cobra, three or four feet long.

In mythology, there is a white version of every animal, such as Moby Dick the white whale, the white buffalo in Native American lore, a white tiger, and a white elephant in the stories of India. It is the archetypal form of that species. The white elephant is something infinitely valuable; we use the term to refer to something that is worthless only because we can't afford to keep something so valuable. Next the dream continues, with the white cobra coming to me and winding up my body. I am frightened when he gets to my shoulder and climbs to the top of my head.

I am not repelled by snakes, but this is a bit much. He climbs up and winds across the top of my head with his head rising up from his coiled body looking in the same direction that I am facing. The dream ends with the two of us sitting there very still.

This was an extremely powerful dream, from which I learned that while it is very human, it also is naive to look to Dr. Jung for protection from the cobras. I'm sure that Dr. Jung would have had a great laugh over the dream. The dream also takes me back to doing nothing. It suggests that I sit down. In any personal sense, it tells me that I am nobody. I have gotten used to the fact that it is best in life when I accept that I am nobody. I am aware that many people have read my books and heard my lectures; I am not naive about the impact I have had on the world, however modest, but psychologically this dream tells me that the safest place is the nothing place. So long as I will consent to accept my nothingness, the slender threads will continue to take care of me.

WHILE MY SUCCESS IN SOCIETY was taking off for the first time, the foundation of my life was starting to unravel. Near the end of our years together in Los Angeles, Helen went into a profound introversion in which she gave up her analytical practice. Eventually even the hustle and bustle of the household was too much for her, and she began spending alternate weeks in a convent near Los Angeles. Mrs. Mitchell and I worked together taking care of Helen's two boys, who by this time were teenagers. The older boy, Nicholas, decided to attend the Royal Academy of Drama in London. Eventually he elected to revert to English citizenship.

Helen's other son, Rob, came into my room one day, dropped himself into a chair, and announced, "Bobsie, I have to be a musician." There had been music in our house for as long as we had known each other, and I had taught him to play the harpsichord at a young age.

I replied, "Don't set your sights on becoming a musician if you can help it, but if you are certain, I will do everything I can to help."

I inquired what instrument he thought belonged to him, and he replied that it would be a stringed instrument of low pitch. Within a week I had found a viola da gamba, the cellolike instrument that was the predecessor of the modern cello. Next, I found a teacher for him, and we began one of the most remarkable experiences of my life. We played together—harpsichord and viola da gamba—for thousands of hours over the coming months. Once Rob was capable of playing publicly, we devised a trio with a flutist and began hiring ourselves out as a baroque ensemble, playing at colleges in the Los Angeles area. We cut a spectacular figure with a two-manual harpsichord by Johannes Ruckers dating from 1617 (one of my most prized possessions) and a viola da gamba, an eighteenth-century instrument that was seldom heard in modern times. Rob went on to attend the Royal Academy of Music in London, followed by a prestigious appointment as a professor of early music at Wesleyan University in Illinois.

Despite these happy times with Rob, it was a most difficult period in which our household was losing its balance. Helen seemed to be undergoing her own dark night of the soul. Anyone who takes a religious life seriously probably goes through dark times like this, and it is easy to misunderstand such an experience. It is an extremely dark time of great suffering, as it involves the giving over of one's life to a higher center of intelligence than the ego can provide. This precedes the flowering of creativity in anyone who has the capacity for genius—so it was with Helen.

When Dr. Jung was once asked what the meaning of a human life was, he replied that it was to relocate the center of gravity of the personality from the ego to the Self, another way of saying what the apostle Paul once observed: "I must decrease that He may increase."

Soon after Helen recovered from this painful restructuring of her life, she decided to go to an Anglican convent in Wisconsin to live. Later she would establish a retreat and study center in Michigan. The boys were, by this time, launched in their careers. I suddenly felt as if my life had come to a standstill. Helen and her two boys had been my adopted family, providing the balm for my loneliness that I had sought for so many years. They were, in fact, my only tie to Los Angeles, and I couldn't envision life there without them. Once again, I was thrown back on my own resources, searching for a way to balance the Golden World and life in the earthly world. So in 1961, I dismantled my Los Angeles life and moved to a Benedictine monastery in Michigan.

12

Monasteries, Medieval and Modern:

The Search for the Holy Grail

Joining a monastery was one of the least intelligent things I ever did, primarily because I made that decision for the wrong reasons. I was not running to meet God, I was running away from life. I wanted to warm the misery of my isolation and loneliness, but instead I jumped into a more severe form of just that. Of course, I was not alone in doing this. I have to confess that most of the monastics I have known are more motivated by escape than by devotion. I think the monastic form was often valid in the medieval world, but I have rarely seen a modern person making a valid life out of that form. The solitary life (the word *monk* derives from *mono*, meaning alone) is correct for a small percentage of people in every age, but the form varies from one age to another. Solitude in the modern world was—for me—to be lived in the midst of ordinary life, not sequestered away from life, but I had to learn and relearn this lesson.

In joining an organization, I did precisely what Dr. Jung warned me never to do, but I was intensely lonely again and wanted badly to belong somewhere. I knew in my head that it was my destiny to lead a solitary life, but I did not yet have the strength for it.

I selected a monastery in Michigan and arrived there for an initial three-week stay; this provided a time for the monastics and me to size one another up. At the end of those three weeks I understood at some level that this was entirely the wrong thing for me to be doing, but I couldn't think of what else to do with myself, so I stayed. The demand to gather some kind of community around me to replace what I had lost was more powerful than my insight. As I look back on it now, this time was in some ways my midlife crisis; I was forty years of age.

An agreement was worked out by which I would be allowed to live in the monastery while also serving as a counselor to the monks and novices there and the many guests. This arrangement took a lot of weight off the abbot, who had an endless stream of people coming to him with problems and difficulties of various kinds. There were about a dozen novices coming and going, beginners who were trying out what it was like to live a secluded life away from the world.

The monastery was built next to a small lake on what had once been a farm. To complement the old farmhouse, the monks had built a chapel and a guest house. They no longer worked the land other than to keep a garden; guests were their chief crop. The schedule was a noble one, and it pleased me to arise before dawn to thank God, but I quickly learned that these customs did not take me closer to the Golden World. When I was leaving Los Angeles to go to the monastery, a Jewish friend had challenged me, "Robert, how do you think you can talk to God in a monastery? You don't know Hebrew." Neither did I possess a medieval mentality, and this proved to be the gulf between the monastic way—essentially a medieval way—and me.

In many ways, living a monastic life should have been a step toward the Golden World. When a novice takes his final vows, there is a ritual in the monastery that celebrates his funeral. He lies down near the altar, they put a ten-foot-by-ten-foot black cloth over him, and his fellow monks recite a funeral mass. Then they take the cloth off, and he changes from novice clothing to a monk's robes. It is a death of sorts, as when it is done properly the monk must die to the ordinary world. This is noble language, and it might have touched me very deeply and contributed to my interior solitude. But there was so much hypocrisy in the system at the monastery that no ceremony could cut through it. One can be a legitimate monk only by being a true medieval or by being a deeply conscious modern person. I am sorry to say that there are few of either in our society.

My therapeutic work at the monastery was exciting, fulfilling the potential that Toni Sussman had envisioned for me years earlier in London with her dream of marrying the insights of modern psychology with the traditions of the church. My patients were protected in a safe environment with few of the material pressures of the outside world, however they still suffered the ills of modern life, that is, they faced inner conflicts. Each summer twenty young novices came as part of a vocational program, and by May I was placed in charge of them. I did my best to teach them what I knew about religious experience, and we also worked together to create a sense of community. Everyone accepted different kinds of manual labor—I was a baker and dishwasher—and we did our best to make every part of the day a prayerful, here-and-now experience.

I soon learned, however, that there was a distinct social hierarchy, even in a monastery. The abbot was a tired man who seemed to have given up on creating anything of worth or dignity. He went through the motions of his station but delegated much of his authority. The second-in-command, an elderly Englishman, was bitter, and he made life miserable for everyone whenever the abbot was gone. He ruled with a cold brutality and, I was soon to learn, sad hypocrisy. I had not been in the monastery for long before I learned that almost no one was safe from the hypocrisy of a system that had lost its validity and no longer spoke to the present time. After I voiced dissent, I was placed on an invisible blacklist. For example, one of my great joys was baking hot bread and serving it to the novices in the afternoon. It was not long before this assignment was taken away from me. A few more months went by, and it was decided to deny me the vocational teaching program for the young novices. It was explained to the novices that they were not to speak to me since they now had to learn to be true monks; they were told that hot bread and honey on baking days was not part of a monk's regimen. None of the novices stayed on that year or for many years to come. I believe if the monastery could have addressed the universal loneliness (not solitude, for that is the basis of monasticism) of its novices and offered them a valid form of relationship, they might have stayed.

By this time I realized fully that my dreamed-for community was not to be; in fact, I had never felt so lonely in my entire life.

In some ways I enjoyed the monastic life; the monastery was a perfect place to provide counseling with a religious orientation, which was my ideal. In theory, a monastic life should provide the ideal balance between the Golden World and the earthly world. I felt that many of the men who came for retreats as part of the summer programs were sincere seekers who were honestly looking for ways to serve God. The order and the tranquillity of the environment worked wonders for many of our guests. But those who stayed for very long soon were caught up in the system. The political intrigues and vendettas were degrading. One night I had a dream that told me it was time to leave. It went as follows:

> I am in the crypt, the basement of the monastery, and the four great arches that support the A-frame church above are standing on four great pillars. A gorilla is chained to each of the pillars. Three of the gorillas are dead, and the fourth one is dying. End of dream.

It didn't take any great insight for me to see that the instinctive animal life within me was in great peril. When I awoke from this dream the issue was settled, and I left the monastery very soon afterward.

In some ways, my life has been a search for a monastic life that is appropriate for the modern world. In running away to a monastery set up in the medieval form, I learned firsthand what I should have already known—that consciousness cannot go backward, it can only go forward. My consciousness was far too differentiated to reunite with the Golden World without profound inner transformation. If someone has been driven from the Garden of Eden, he or she may never return to that paradise—no matter how strong the yearning—but may go ahead through the process of redemption to the Heavenly Jerusalem. Many people use the energy of their nostalgia for paradise trying to get back to a previous state of grace, back to childhood. This is not possible, and people are wiser to use their energy to progress to the Heavenly Jerusalem. Regression is deadly; progression wins one's soul.

The modern world engages in a terrible heresy in assuming that everyone is born like a blank page, assuming that the experiences of life form our character. That is half true. The other half is that each person is born with a mythology built in. This personal myth determines much of our experience of life, and it is extremely important for a person to discover and understand his or her fate. Life is easier if we cooperate with that myth rather than continually pull against it. In my own life, when I decided to honor my introversion and strong feeling function, life began to flow with much greater ease. It was only after living in India during my fifties and being among others of a similar temperament that I gained insight and courage enough so that I could come back to America and live an introverted, feeling life without continually bearing a sense of inadequacy.

Much of my own mythology, the myth that was incorporated in me at the beginning of my being, seems to be related to the archetypal image of a monk. If I had lived in the medieval world, I most certainly would have been a monk. Although I no longer live in a monastery, wear curious clothing, or take on the other clichés of monasticism, my life very much corresponds with the pattern. I have worked out a way to live this myth in modern form. Some friends have called me a mystic, a title that I don't object to. Mysticism is a hallowed tradition in the religious life, and there have always been people with the job of tending the border between the two worlds. Here again, words fail me. I speak and write of two worlds, when in fact the two are one. To everyday consciousness, however, there is a veil between the Golden World and the earthly world. In all my experiences of the divine realm, I have always maintained the sense that I existed—I didn't just merge into the Golden World. It takes an observer to experience the existence of heaven.

Apparently, one must separate from God so that there is an objective standpoint from which we can observe. In my own homespun theology, I believe that perhaps God wanted human eyes in order to be able to see the splendor of the Golden World. If so, then it's our business to be the eyes and ears, to see and hear the splendor or God, but it requires that we stand apart from God. To be a discrete observer necessitates that one is separated from what one is observing. That is the alienation of a human life. One is reminded of the Zen comment on the intermediate stage of development when "rivers were no longer rivers and mountains were no longer mountains."

That sense of being separated is the ego. In arriving at adulthood we all have built an ego structure, a separate sense of "I," but it is precisely that distance from all else that makes us feel so lonely and alienated. One then must find a way to restore the unity with God, to worship. This is the Zen stage when "rivers are again rivers and mountains are again mountains."

It is our human duty to witness the splendor of God, which is my sense of worship. What makes all of this so difficult is that our duties are in conflict. These principal duties are to separate from oneness (the childhood paradise), develop an ego, and live a cultural life; and then to reunite with the oneness of God. Generally the early part of one's life is taken up with the necessary distancing from God: learning about the cultural requirements of the society in which one lives, leaving the house of the parents, developing one's independence and sense of personal self. There is a constant pull back to the sense of unity from which we came, and in Jungian psychology that is called the mother complex. There is a regressive pull in each of us to quit this business of winning independence, to escape the painful human process of becoming a distinct, separate personality. Physical suicide is the ultimate expression of the mother complex, but it takes many other forms, such as the use of drugs and alcohol or mindless consumption of food or material goods. When people come to my consulting room with a drug problem, I tell them that they are addressing the right problem but in the wrong way. They are trying to go back to a paradise when they need to go forward to a paradise.

We must separate from God before we can reunite with God. We must create a useful life, learning the customs of the society in which we live. You cannot put back together again that which has never been adequately differentiated. Consciousness must separate before it can reunite. Many of the spiritual communes, monasteries, and spiritual practices in this country are nothing but institutionalized mother complexes, with selfishness and ego regression running rampant in the name of spirituality.

It is a legitimate question to ask just how far one really needs to push this differentiation before one can legitimately seek to reunite. That is an individual matter. A very simple person may not be differentiated to any great degree, and I have seen this among the traditional peasants who live in the small villages of India; they have the right to put things back together again without a great deal of differentiation. But educated Westerners go much further in developing their consciousness, becoming so split that it is difficult to become whole again. The cultural laws of Western society encourage us to get as separate, as specialized, as unique as we can get. To get a good job today you must have a college education, and a professional degree or a Ph.D. is better still. We are trained to become more and more specialized. Then on Sunday at church we are advised to merge ourselves with God. It's no wonder we've become a neurotic society; the wonder is that we are not all schizophrenic!

Once we have built a strong ego, we must then link it back to the matrix from which it has grown. Differentiation of consciousness is only one-half of our life journey. But to say, "I want an experience of God" is a total oxymoron; if there is an "I" seeking an experience, that is precisely the problem, since an "I" that sees itself as separate from God is the cause of suffering in one's life. There's a Christian proverb that says he who searches for God insults God, because a search implies that God is separate. Zen Buddhism also is very articulate about this, stating that the very motivation for satori or enlightenment is suspect. You find the kingdom, not by seeking, but only by grace. Seeking after the splendor of God is a highly egocentric and fragmenting thing to do. I now understand that the most profound religious life is found by being in the world yet in each moment doing our best to align ourselves with heaven, with the will of

God. However, I was still learning this when I tried to find the answers in a monastery.

When I went to the monastery I had sold most of my possessions and had spent much of my savings sending Helen's two boys to school in England. When it became clear that I had to leave, I wasn't sure where to go. I did have a friend who ran a prisoner rehabilitation program at a hundred-acre farm only a few miles down the road from the monastery. The farm had been a failure, and the prisoner rehabilitation project had lost its funding and been closed down. At the time, the property was sitting vacant, and I knew that they needed someone to serve as caretaker and to safeguard the property. I immediately called my friend and volunteered for the job. I was loaned the farm on the spot, so I packed my bags, bid farewell to the monastery, and walked down the road to my next adventure.

When I arrived at the farmhouse, I found quite a mess. Various charities had donated items, and the house had stacks of canned goods and bags of grain piled up in the kitchen. There were twelve bedrooms in the old farmhouse, and for the first week I did nothing but clean up the mess that had been left behind. I arrived the day before Thanksgiving with five dollars in my pocket, a pretty thin padding between oneself and the cold world. I decided that I would try it for a week, and if after that time I had more than five dollars I would stay. Some friends came by and created a fine Thanksgiving dinner; they encouraged me to live at the farm. Slender threads were at work again.

It didn't take long for word to get out about my new address. I had a small therapy practice built up at the monastery, and many of the people who had been going to see me there now drove down the road for therapy sessions at the farmhouse. I hadn't charged for my work when I was living at the monastery, but now I needed an income, so I devised the sugar bowl method of payment. I simply set out a sugar bowl and asked my patients to make whatever contribution they could.

I struggled along for the first month, and soon after I had the place cleaned up, people started asking me if they could come to the house for weekend retreats. Before I realized what was happening, I was running a therapy practice and a weekend retreat center. I was creating my own version of a monastic life in which I lived close to the Golden World, with long stretches of time in solitude, but also with access to a community of like-minded individuals.

The next summer some volunteers helped me repaint the interior, and someone donated aluminum siding for the exterior walls. I was having a great time, and I began to believe that perhaps I had stumbled into a real, viable way of life. But when I tried to buy the farm, the archdiocese that owned it refused to sell. It made no sense to invest my own money continuing to repair the old buildings, so eventually I determined that I should move on. But I had created the blueprint in my mind for a new kind of program—a retreat center that combined psychotherapy with monastic life. The next step was to make that dream a reality.

While I was living in the Midwest, an Episcopal priest from Minneapolis started an analysis with me during a retreat. The experience was so powerful for him that he suggested that I travel to Minneapolis for one week of every month to provide counseling hours for parishioners and to lecture for his church. This worked very well for some time. One day in Minneapolis I was walking down a street, ten blocks or so from the church where I worked, when suddenly I heard a demand from heaven. I didn't exactly hear words, as from a voice in the clouds, but the following command came into my head: "Now make up your mind: either everything in the world is the body and blood of Christ, or nothing is. Make up your mind."

That was such a shock that I still recall the angle of the sunshine, the color of the trees, the type of cars driving by on the street—it was a terrible/wonderful moment. I knew the answer immediately, but I didn't know what to do about it. If I said that nothing is the body and blood of Christ, I would die immediately from a lack of meaning in my life. Life is not possible without meaning. You can live for thirty days without food, for three days without water, for three minutes without air, but you can only live three seconds without meaning. Therefore, it was clear that Christ must be everything. But how could I live that truth? It seemed too big to take in. I have been struggling since with the implication of that sudden vision.

A few months after I began lecturing in Minneapolis, I had a similar offer to affiliate with a church in California. I decided to move there and commute back and forth to Minneapolis once a month. This seemed like the perfect arrangement. Everything went well in Minneapolis, but the program in my new California setting was not well founded. I found I had made another blunder and had gotten myself into a situation where I did not belong. It has taken the most stringent efforts of fate to keep me away from my hunger for a personal sense of belonging to a community.

It was at this time that another great dream again pointed the direction for my life.

A very great lighthouse is being built on the coast of England. It is almost finished but is not functioning yet. It has been placed some distance inland so that there will be enough height so that the light from the house will go far out to sea, almost infinitely far out.

It is a traditional, tall, and circular lighthouse, with glass on the top and a spiral staircase on the inside to ascend to the top. Though it is not yet finished, it is already a pilgrimage place, and great numbers of people come to see this monument. I am there alone, dreadfully lonely. I spend three or four hours in a long but orderly queue waiting for access to the structure, with the line of people slowly winding in a serpentine path up to the base of the lighthouse. Eventually I begin to ascend the spiral stairway inside, one revolution after another. Every time I make a new revolution I understand something more. I gradually learn that the lighthouse is nearly finished, and I discover that the source of the light is going to be a dead body lying in a sarcophagus.

The body of the holy man, like a relic, is to be the source of the light. The last revolution to get to the top is outside the body of the lighthouse; it is perfectly safe, as there is an iron railing and iron steps, but it is at a terrifying height, and I can see through the weblike metal steps all the way to the ground below. Now the most astonishing bit of information is revealed to me. I find that it is to be my body that will be in the lighthouse when it is functioning!

When I make the last revolution, I walk into a chamber at the top with a stone sarcophagus. It is empty. I realize that this entire project is under the control of a cold, stainless steel man with no humanness or kindness in his personality. He is all business. He recognizes me and says, "Aha, you're here. You are no good to us until you are dead, but since you are here, let's see if we got the sarcophagus in the right shape."

I then lie down in the sarcophagus. It fits perfectly, so he orders me out, saying, "Get down out of here now. You're no good to us yet."

So I go back down the winding stairs. I don't remember the descent, but when I arrive at the bottom, it is nearly dark and raining. I walk away crying, thinking that they will make so much fuss over me when I am dead but they don't give a damn about me while I am alive. Then I walk off in the rain feeling miserable. End of dream.

Dreams are strange things, and big ones like this difficult to relate to. I shudder at the word *interpretation,* because it is audacious to try to interpret a dream like this, but I must relate to it somehow; I can't pretend it didn't happen. One way of putting it into perspective is to observe that many dreams are compensatory. If one's personal life is too far in a particular direction, one will have a series of dreams in the opposite direction to bring balance to the personality. This dream occurred during a lonely, isolated, and desolate time in my life. I thought that my vision of the lighthouse tower was going to lead to great success, but then it also failed. The dream accentuates to almost a ridiculous degree the opposite that I needed to bring my life back into balance: I needed to be reminded that the great worth of a person is most evident from a less personal viewpoint. Everything is exaggerated in this dream: my life was not so lonely as the dream depicted, nor was my vision of "shedding light" by creating a new kind of religious retreat so glorious as the dream portrayed. The dream and my life were seeking a balance, my conscious and unconscious trying to work out a middle path.

In addition to being compensatory, the dream also seems to be a treatise on the fact that someone of my temperament and closeness to the collective unconscious is most useful when dead; when I am alive, the dream points out, I am scarcely worth feeding or keeping alive. There was a certain bitterness in me at the time of this dream, a feeling that the world did not appreciate me. That resentment would diminish over the coming years, and, in fact, I was just on the verge of gaining more worldly success than I ever thought possible.

Aside from personal issues, the dream can also be looked at from another perspective. If one takes the word *dead* in a metaphorical sense, and not as the physical death of one's body, then it can be seen that one is useful on the face of the earth and has a far-reaching effect if one will consent to an impersonal manner of life. This is the depth of the Grail Castle question, Whom does the Grail serve? If one answers this question by saying the Grail serves oneself, one is caught in a personal view of one's own meaning; if one answers, the Grail serves the Grail King (God) then one is capable of seeing more than one's own limited ego. The dream seems to be saying, "Do your work, follow your duty, then you will have an effect upon the world. Your life, work, and suffering are not without meaning." But the personal dimensions of one's life are as small and unremarkable as the dream seems to suggest. I am there at the lighthouse alone. I see all this magnificence and gain information, but it is no solace to my personal life. I am as alone as ever, but one can't be lonely unless there is a vision of sublime relatedness to accentuate the aloneness. In a personal sense I may not be worth much, but in an impersonal sense I may be contributing something of great value to the collective unconscious. This is my general view of such a dream.

Within a few days after having this dream, and only six months after moving back to California, I met John Sanford, the rector of Saint Paul's Church in San Diego. John, who is an Episcopal priest and also a certified Jungian analyst, was very excited by my efforts to create a new form of monastic life that combined psychology and religion. He offered me my own office at his church, a steady stream of patients, and an appreciative and understanding ear. So in 1967, in my midforties, I moved south to the San Diego area, where I have lived ever since.

My first joint venture with Saint Paul's in San Diego was to take part in a Wednesday night adult education program; this was so well received that it eventually became its own organization, the San Diego Friends of Jung. Soon I was doing well enough to purchase a small house perched on a cliff overlooking the Pacific Ocean. It only had three guest rooms, but it was my humble version of a retreat center. I presented my lectures as well as exploring other myths and stories and drew out their psychological lessons for modern people.

Here again, I seemed to be finding a version of monasticism that would work for me. Joining an existing monastery had ended in failure, which I should have known from the advice Dr. Jung had once given me. Monasteries that still try to adhere to the medieval model provide community but not a set of personal relationships. As I developed my work at Saint Paul's in San Diego, I developed good friends, people who valued me highly, while I continued to live my own version of monasticism. I was searching for a balance.

⁓

IT WAS AT SAINT PAUL'S in San Diego that I developed my lectures on Parsifal and the Grail legend. My first book, *He,* grew out of a series of four lectures that I presented at Saint Paul's. John Sanford had it recorded and asked the church secretary to type up a transcript. John then tidied it up a bit and sent the manuscript off to a small publisher of religious-oriented books in King of Prussia, Pennsylvania, before I even knew what he had done. Surprising to all, they accepted the book and agreed to publish a few thousand copies. Before I knew what was happening, Harper & Row, one of the world's largest publishers, became interested and purchased the rights to my book. Apparently they saw potential, and when the reprinted version was distributed it began selling in great numbers. *He* is now translated into thirteen languages and can be found in bookstores around the world.

At the time I wrote the book, I had wandered into the Grail Castle once, having seen the Golden World at the age of sixteen; (one might say that my hospital experience at age eleven was the first experience of the Golden World. But at sixteen I had the first chance of experiencing it consciously), at that time I was dazzled out of my wits and could not contain the experience. I was taking a writer's liberty when I wrote in *He* that we all get a second chance in the Grail Castle. This was based on hope and theory but was not yet my own experience.

The story of Parsifal is, in many ways, the story of my life. The Arthurian legends were part of my childhood, and I knew the Parsifal story from a young age. I was drawn to it long before I heard Emma Jung lecture on the Grail myth during my training in Zurich, although her interpretation of the book immediately intrigued me. The story kept popping up in my life in unexpected ways. While I was studying in Zurich I rented a room in the top floor of a house from a kindly couple. They would invite me down once a week for tea and a visit. One day they announced that they simply couldn't call me Robert anymore because it just didn't fit my personality. Instead, they wanted to call me Parsifal. I thought that was a bit odd, but I accepted their wish as some Swiss idiosyncrasy. A few weeks later, when Mrs. Jung began her lecture on the Parsifal story, I learned that the name Parsifal means "innocent fool." When I learned that, I went back to the next tea party, thinking I would impress my hosts.

"I bet you don't know what *Parsifal* means," I said proudly. "It originally meant an innocent fool."

"Oh, yes, we knew that," I was told.

That took some of the wind out of my sails, and once again the Parsifal story seemed to be my story.

At the start of this myth, Parsifal is a simple, naive young man who lives with his widowed mother. Her name is Heart Sorrow. One day the adolescent Parsifal sees five knights riding by on horseback. Dazzled by them, he dashes off to tell his mother that he has seen five gods and wants to leave home to join them. His mother weeps at the loss of her son but gives him her blessing and sends him off wearing homespun garments. Parsifal never finds the five knights, but he does have many adventures. One day he finds his way to the great castle of Gournamond, who trains him to be a knight and gives him a special instruction: if he ever reaches the Grail Castle he must ask, "Whom does the Grail serve?"

After much travel and adventure, Parsifal meets a solitary man fishing from his boat. The fisherman invites Parsifal to stay the night in his humble abode, which is to be found by the following directions: "Go down the road a little way, turn left, cross the drawbridge, and you will find my house." When Parsifal reaches this house, he finds himself in the Grail Castle, in which is kept the Holy Grail, the chalice of the Last Supper. The Fisher King has been severely wounded and is too ill to live yet is not able to die. He is called the Fisher King because he was wounded early in his life in an incident that involved a fish. While wandering in the forest, the young king had reached a camp that was empty except for a spit on which a salmon was roasting. Being hungry, he took a piece of salmon but burned his fingers badly. To assuage the pain, he put his fingers into his mouth and tasted a bit of the salmon. At that moment he had a taste of something that he could never forget, a taste of the Christ nature (the fish is one of the many symbols of Christ). But its effect on him was a wounding, not yet a revelation. The wound was in his thigh, meaning that his suffering was in his creative or generating capacity. His virility and strength were severely wounded. As a result, from that time onward the king had to be carried on a litter, though he gains a little respite from his suffering when he is fishing.

It is this Fisher King who presides over the castle that Parsifal has wandered into. It is also the castle where the Grail is kept, but the power of the Grail does the Fisher King no good. He cannot touch the Holy Grail despite its being so near. As the king suffers, so does his kingdom. The entire country is in desolation. The king and the kingdom cannot be healed until an innocent fool enters the castle and asks the right question: "Whom does the Grail serve?"

As Parsifal enters the castle, the drawbridge strikes the back hooves of his horse as it closes shut. He is met by four pages who bathe him and lead him into a banquet room filled with four hundred knights and ladies. A grand procession is taking place, and Parsifal sees the Holy Grail and a sword that drips blood. He is so astounded by this experience that he forgets to ask the crucial question, and the next morning he finds that the Holy Grail, the Fisher King, the people, and the castle have all disappeared.

It takes many years for Parsifal to find his way back to the Grail Castle though he searches and searches for it. When he does find it again, he immediately sees that the Fisher King is still suffering. This time Parsifal asks the question "Whom does the Grail serve?" and the answer is given: "The Grail serves the Grail King." We learn that the Fisher King is only the lord of the castle while the Grail King lives in unseen eternity in the center of the castle. When Parsifal learns the difference between these two interior parts of the human psyche, the Fisher King is healed and the kingdom can once again be productive and peaceful.

This story is not only about a personal quest, it is also about the evolution of consciousness for all humankind. The Grail Castle, which brings the greatest joy that a human being is capable of, is that visionary, mystical, interior world that is always just down the road. It is never very far away. But it must be earned. It isn't just what you do in life, but the attitude by which you live. This is epitomized in the question "Whom does the Grail serve?" Each modern person must ask himself or herself this question. Is your life just about serving the ego? Is it about how much money you can get in the bank? Or does it serve something deeper and more enduring?

"What's in it for me?" is the approach that many modern people take to any activity. That serves the ego. But the understanding that is crucial in the Grail Castle is that the Grail must serve God, that which is greater than "I."

It is painful to live at the end of an era, as we do now; everything seems so tenuous and uncertain. It must have been much the same in the twelfth century, when the Grail story was being told and recorded. There were stirrings and undercurrents of a new age, but all people saw around them was disintegration, old experiments gone awry. I feel that a major psychological burden for modern people is an overwhelming sense of loss, yet we are not quite sure of what we have lost. I see many people puzzling over this. In our culture, we see people tearing things down, but we don't see anything really new. This is true in politics, in the arts, and across our culture. It is a time of transition, and the great legend of Parsifal is an important story for such a time.

~

WHEN MY BOOK *He* unexpectedly became popular, I soon found that I was working harder than I had worked in years, preparing new lectures, seeing many—eventually too many—patients in my growing practice. Soon my publisher was asking for a second book, then a third, and my career as an author and lecturer took off. I hardly knew what to do with this unexpected success.

As a result of my increasingly full schedule, I was no longer sitting down at my computer to do my own active imagination and to dialogue with my inner self. A busy winter passed filled with appointments, and it wasn't until the following June that I could find time to go to the desert and catch up on my inner life. My plan was to meditate as intensely as I had been working for the previous six months. After two days of adhering to a strict and austere schedule, I had still another informative dream.

I have gone to a high place, a campground in the mountains. I am with friends who tell me there is a wonderful view on up ahead. "You should see it," they marvel "What an inspiration!" I listen, but I also know that I could never walk that far.

But as is often the case with dreams, the scene shifts suddenly and illogically, and I find myself in this high place all alone; it is indeed a magnificent spot, like the edge of the Grand Canyon with a one-hundred-mile vista. I look around and notice that there is a man-made building with a flat roof built right on the edge of the canyon. Projecting out from this odd little building—right over the abyss—is a diving board. I am so inspired by the beauty of the vista that I walk over to the board, lay down on my belly, and wriggle my way out to the edge of the diving board. Then I crawl out a bit more so that my head is actually looking over the very edge of the board. I am thrilled, but soon I get dizzy from the height.

After a few minutes of this ecstatic view, I decide it is time to go back, but when I try to wriggle my way back to the building I find that I am paralyzed and cannot move a muscle. First I freeze, then I try going forward one inch more in hopes that doing so might break my paralysis. I can move forward, but not back. Now I really begin to panic. I lie there breathing heavily, gripping the sides of the diving board with sweating palms. With all the willpower I can muster, I order my muscles to wriggle me back. They moved ever so slightly, a fraction of an inch at a time, until I am back off the board and standing safely in the building. I scurry back down the mountain to the camp where everyone else is waiting. Someone sees me coming and says, "Oh, so you've been up there to the lookout; isn't it great."

"Yeah, real great," I reply.

The next morning I thought about this dream, and I could see the folly in what I was trying to accomplish at the desert house. I had become inflated with the success of my work and was in danger of a fall. I had been doing far too much and ignoring my inner life. I went to the desert thinking I was going to make up for six months' worth of too-muchness by a week of intense meditation. The dream told me straightforwardly that I could not find my balance by going from one extreme to another, it was just going to make me dizzy and in grave danger of a mortal fall. It's like eating too much and then fasting; it just makes you sick. Once again the wisdom of a dream came to my rescue, reminding me that I had to find a balance each day.

13

The Reemergence of the Golden World:

Journey to the East

I always knew that I would go to India someday, but my ego never quite had the courage or my body the stamina to make it happen. During my studies in Zurich in 1949 I had read a passage in the works of Carl Jung that said an Indian who follows his religious tradition with sincerity is incapable of suffering neurosis. Dr. Jung had visited India, and his comment seemed to jump off the page at me; it set me on fire. To imagine someone who is not fragmented, torn, and worried half to death—this was almost inconceivable to my Western mind, and I knew then that someday I would have to see for myself if this was truly possible.

I don't know what changed in me, but at the age of fifty-one I finally decided to make a pilgrimage to the East. A couple of trips with a youth group from Saint Paul's down into the desolate Baja peninsula had helped toughen me up and had provided some confidence that a demanding journey was within my capacity. So in December of 1972, I announced to my friends that I was going to India. Most people immediately advised against it; friends worried over my health, and professional colleagues said it was foolhardy. Only the adventurous young men whom I traveled with to Baja were in favor of the idea—they thought it was a grand adventure! So I began inquiring about where to go and what to see in India. One Jungian analyst I knew in Los Angeles had spent six months at the Sri Aurobindo Ashram in Pondicherry working on his Ph.D. dissertation, and he advised that this would be an excellent place to stay since English was spoken there and precautions were taken to ensure the health of Westerners. I wasn't sure if that was the part of India I most wanted to see, but I tucked the information away in the back of my head. Pondicherry is a hundred miles south of Madras on the east coast of the great Indian subcontinent.

In scouring a large map of India, I found that New Delhi was the nearest place to Pondicherry that received international flights, so I talked with a friend who worked for British Airways about how I could get from San Diego to New Delhi. He took care of everything, booking my trip with departure on January 6, 1973. When the tickets arrived in the mail, I could scarcely believe that I was actually going to make such an adventure!

Jet travel is truly a modern miracle, and I often wonder about the effect this technology has on our psyches. Approximately twenty-four hours after boarding an airplane in Los Angeles, I was stepping out into the airport at New Delhi. I had traversed halfway around the world and across a span of centuries. These early adventures in India made me think I had at last recovered the medieval world that I had always had an affinity for. But later pondering convinced me that I had gone back to the ancient world. At least it was the ancient part of India that fascinated me; I have little interest in Westernized India. It seems mostly to be absorbing our worst qualities while losing its own beauty.

Once again, the stage was set for a breakthrough in consciousness. It was 4 A.M. local time when our plane pulled up to the gate, and I was exhausted, deprived of sleep, excited, and scared all at the same time. I had passed thirteen-and-a-half time zones. It was January and, though the cool season for India, it was still an extremely humid eighty-five degrees even in the early morning darkness. I didn't know a soul in India, and when I went to the baggage claim I was told that my suitcase had apparently been lost (it turned up five days later in Hong Kong). Despite all of this confusion and disorientation, I was exulting in happiness. I felt a sense of homecoming as I stumbled out to the curb and a mob of taxi drivers descended on me. This was the beginning of my education in Indian ways, and even though I was tired and dazed by the long trip, I knew instinctively what to do. I chose the most alert of the twenty or so taxi drivers who were battling for the last fare to come out of the building and asked him to take me to a good Western-style hotel.

The taxi driver must have thought I looked a bit down at the heels, as he took me to a stately but worn-down building left over from the days of the British Raj. It was located on a noisy street, the lighting was dim, and the crushed velvet sofa in the lobby was well worn and smelled of must, but the rate for a single room was only ten dollars a night. I was not in a mood to shop around, so I checked in without even looking at the rooms. By this time it was nearly 6 A.M., and I was becoming terribly exhausted. I needed to rest, and I followed the bellboy to the elevator, dragging along my only remaining possession, a carry-on shoulder bag. My room was on the tenth floor. The decor was run-down Victorian, but I didn't much care, and as he pulled open the drapes on an east-facing window I could see the ancient city of Delhi outside. The first light of dawn was about to come up. I absentmindedly handed him a handful of coins, he departed, and I stood there staring at the minarets of a great mosque—and then it happened. I was no longer just watching the sun come up, I was overtaken by a vision of the Golden World. All my senses were set spinning, I heard the music of the stars singing; it was the same intensity, the absolute glory and joy that I had experienced thirty-five years earlier on a mountainside in Portland, Oregon. Once again, I was caught in the grip of a divine ecstasy.

The return of the Golden World! I had prayed for this moment, reaching for it in my passion for music, searching for it in my stay with Krishnamurti, getting a glimpse of it in my dreams and my talk with Carl Jung. I had even written about it in my first book, *He*. In that book I made a bold claim, based upon the Grail myth—I stated that it was possible, indeed essential, to visit the Grail Castle a second time in one's maturity. According to the Grail myth, any fool can wander into the heavenly realm as a youth, but those who are privileged to visit it again in maturity are given a gift beyond price. I had stood before audiences and declared that we all are given a second chance to taste heaven, an opportunity to redeem ourselves. These brave words were based upon faith, however, not personal experience. Now my faith was vindicated! It was possible to find one's way back to the divine realm.

Again, my vision lasted only minutes in clock time, though it seemed like an eternity to me. Eventually the sun was fully up and the radiance of the experience gradually receded. No one can live in such intensity for long without burning up, but on that glorious day in India I gained a presence that never again entirely left me.

After the intensity of the vision began to fade, I found myself so tired I could scarcely stand but so excited that I could not sit still. I didn't know what to do. There was no one to tell about the glory that I had just experienced. I felt like running through the streets shouting, but such behavior by a foreigner would surely lead to my arrest as a madman. I tried reclining on my bed for an hour or so, but there was no way I could sleep. Finally, I gave up on resting and took the elevator back down to the lobby of the hotel. I smiled broadly at the front desk clerk and saluted the doorman with affection. They nodded with serious expressions and great dignity. As I descended out into the street, I was surprised to find that my taxi driver from the airport was camped out at the front door as if waiting for me, and he quickly offered to take me to all the tourist spots. I told him I was not interested in tourist spots, but I did want to experience traditional India. Eventually he got it through his head that I wanted to drive through the old city without an itinerary or an agenda, and off we went.

My memory of that morning is as clear as if it happened yesterday. We drove around the old mosque that I had spotted from my hotel room. My mind was recording every detail photographically—the faces on the street, the fruit stalls, the sacred cows lumbering about at will. I could smell a hundred scents on the air—spices, laundry, human waste, rotting vegetables and fruits, incense, gasoline fumes—all competing for my attention. The light, however, made the riot of activity before me soft and impressionistic. Everything before me seemed holy and touched by God—even the beggars!

I was half out of my head with all the sights and sounds of India as we drove through the narrow streets. Some shift was taking place in my inner life, some healing, an inner reconciliation that I could not name or understand at the time. I was happy in an intense way that I had seldom felt in my life. We toured about for several hours, and then I told the taxi driver to take me back to my hotel. I quickly learned the Indian art of embracing you with one hand while dipping into your pocketbook with the other hand. My driver had no meter, and I violated all guidebook wisdom by not settling on a price beforehand. But when our brief tour ended, I didn't even haggle or raise an eyebrow at his fee, which made both of us enormously happy. I doled out the Indian rupees like Monopoly money and walked back through the hotel lobby and up to my room as though in a trance. Then I fell upon my bed fully clothed and slept for the next twenty-four hours, peaceful, content, fulfilled.

My plan had been to rest for a day or two in New Delhi and then follow the advice of my Jungian friend from Los Angeles and travel by a domestic airline to Madras in southeast India. My home base was to be the Sri Aurobindo Ashram in Pondicherry. As soon as I was rested, I inquired at my hotel about the next departure for Madras. My airline friend had purchased the ticket for me but had underscored on at least four different occasions that I would have to confirm the flight after I arrived in New Delhi. The hotel clerk provided me with a phone number to call the airline but also politely informed me that there was no point in calling, since the airline that flew from New Delhi to Madras was in the midst of an employee strike. I asked the hotel official if there was any other way that I might get to Madras, and he replied that it was "very impossible at this time!"

Ordinarily, such a disruption in my plans would have been upsetting, and I would have set about calling travel agents and scrambling to find alternatives. However, that phrase caught something in me and set off an explosion of humor and energy. How could one do anything but love a people who can find something "very impossible"? The very fact that something is very impossible lets it be known that there are degrees of impossibility, and if there are degrees then perhaps there is a way after all. I have a profound respect for a people who allow impossibility to have degrees and at least a hint of flexibility. Who knows what stone walls of impossibility are only "very impossible"?

I learned that it was, in fact, somewhat possible to get to Madras, but I would have to travel by train, and the trip would take two days and two nights "if all went well." I didn't think I could possibly cope with train travel during my first week in India, so I resigned myself to staying in Delhi until the labor strike ended (though no one could predict when that might be).

My contentment was surprising, but for one of the many times in my life I felt as if everything was exactly as it was meant to be. If there was an airline strike, then I was supposed to be in Delhi, some slender threads were guiding me, and I would give myself over to their wisdom. What a release of anxiety! It was not up to me to control the world around me; all I had to do was be attentive to its design and follow the slender threads. There was absolutely no use in trying to control India, so I would just let India carry me along.

Just to go for a walk on any street in Old Delhi was a revelation to me. There was no ordinariness about any aspect of this ancient land. I looked at the people and how they walked; I peered into mysterious shops; I walked and walked until I was exhausted.

Before I ever got to India someone explained to me that Americans are homogenized people but that in India I would see true saints and devils in human form walking the streets. It was so. One such face is still indelibly etched in my mind. He was a coconut vendor who sold green coconuts for two rupees (a rupee was only about three cents in American money at that time). This coconut vender would slash off one end of his produce with a huge machete and hand me the coconut to drink the cool sweet milk. His face was so primitive and his skin so glossy black that I nicknamed him the Missing Link, but soon he made friends with me, and after that there was no paying him for a coconut. The coconut milk from that kind man was the sweeter for its being a gift.

I also had been instructed by friends to ignore the beggars. This I did for a time since I knew nothing and was content to obey custom. But soon my Western sense of compassion would no longer allow me to ignore the terrible suffering around me. One morning I was out walking and I encountered a leper who suffered from horrible disfigurement; I felt such compassion that I offered him a small coin, and I was immediately surrounded by a ring of lepers pawing at me with their mutilated claws of hands. I am ashamed to say that I fled in terror, showered with soap (leprosy is highly contagious), and would not go out of my room for hours until I had come to some resolution inside myself. I finally came to the expediency that I would adopt one of the lepers and care for him and ignore the rest. I chose one of those terrifying derelicts of humankind on the street—no one is more terrifying to look at than a leper with his hands, feet, ears, nose, and so forth eaten away by that relentless disease—and gave him a coin every day. The others quickly learned that he belonged to me and that I would not give coins to anyone else. This was the best I was able to come up with as a makeshift solution.

My taxi driver continued to camp out at the hotel door and was available at my beck and call any time of the day or night. One day he talked me into a trip to the Taj Mahal, about a four-hour drive from New Delhi. We started early and arrived to see its spectacular grandeur; even the throngs of tourists could not tarnish its regal beauty. But it was not the famous sites that spoke most powerfully to me, it was one small thing after another. The grand and glorious "must sees" touted in the tourist books were magnificent, but the little out-of-the-way places in the nooks and crannies of Old Delhi never ceased to hold miracles for me. What pleased me most were the human dramas of the Indian character, which is so transparent in its feeling quality. Indians have a wonderful custom of making themselves known to others: if you want to make friends with someone you need only stand near him or her for a time, not looking directly at them, or talking, but just making your presence known. If the other person wishes to acknowledge you, they will let you know by some small gesture and a conversation will follow.

This delighted my highly introverted nature for I am clumsy at beginning a meeting with casual talk. I loved being charmed by one unexpected experience after another without feeling any fear or dread that harm would come to me. I learned quickly, more by feeling than by rational thought, that I could walk on the darkest narrow streets of India at any time of day or night with a safety I did not have in the main park of San Diego at night. There is a respect for human value in India that far exceeds our Western attitudes. This is beginning to crumble in the big cities with the Westernization of India, but it still remains true in the less urbanized sections of the country.

Finally, after ten days, the air strike ended, and I gained passage to Madras. By this time my suitcase had arrived from Hong Kong, and, amazingly, everything was intact. When the time came to depart to the airport once again, "my" taxi driver took me there but then refused to leave. I didn't know what to do, and since there was still time before my flight, I invited him to lunch. When our parting could be delayed no longer, he was in tears, and consequently so was I. He asked for my address in America, and for years after that he wrote to me in rudimentary English, letters filled with tales of all that was going wrong in his life and how desperately he needed money.

My flight to Madras went well—only two hours late, which is considered on time by Indian standards. I had the name of an Indian hotel at which to stay until I could catch a bus for the last leg of my journey to Pondicherry. The guidebook advised that I bring my own padlock to secure the room, so I had purchased a combination lock in New Delhi. India prides itself inordinately on the huge padlocks that adorn, strengthen, and bolster every place that marks private property, privilege, or sanctity (respect for property does not lie in the same category as personal safety; anything that can be carried off is fair game for the thief castes who make their living in this manner). In a land of thievery, locks do their important work as much by appearance as by physical strength. A lock weighing less than ten pounds is public announcement of weakness and ineffective function. A truly majestic statement of privacy will weigh in at around twenty pounds. The accompanying keys, which I had little to do with, fortunately, are correspondingly great. To carry such a key or to be custodian of it is to announce one's dignity and worth. My lock was puny and mostly symbolic, but I applied it anyway.

After settling into my room, I immediately went out to walk the streets of Madras and absorb the atmosphere. Again, I was happy as could be. Despite the grinding poverty that I could see everywhere around me, I felt entirely safe and comfortable, and I was so at home that tears would come to my eyes for no apparent reason.

When I went to dinner that night, the waiter seemingly played a trick on me. He asked what I wanted, and I replied I didn't have any idea because I could not read the menu, which was written in Tamil.

"How about a meal of food native to Madras?" he asked.

I nodded, and he disappeared into the kitchen. He brought back a curry dinner consisting of an empty plate with a dozen little bowls around the edges, each one more spicy than the next. I sampled them all, and the only one I could really enjoy was the yogurt. The waiter stood behind me and waited like a vulture; just to satisfy him, I ate the entire contents of every little bowl, one of which was filled with a vile concoction of powdered peanuts and red pepper. Only when I was all finished did he nod and depart again for the kitchen. He arrived moments later with a large platter of rice, which I now know should have been served with the assortment of spicy condiments. I'm sure he had a good laugh with his friends back in the kitchen, but even this could not dampen my joy and enthusiasm; I found myself laughing along at the foolish American who scorched his tonsils because he did not know enough to ask for rice.

After dinner I walked back to my hotel and headed up the stairs, only to find that the corridor to my room was so dark that I could not see my hand in front of my face. There was one small light bulb in the middle of the hallway, but I could literally see the spurts of electricity struggling to crawl around the dim filament of the bulb. I stumbled down the hallway, grabbing out to touch the wall like a blind man. Only when I got to my door did I remember that it was secured with my sturdy combination lock. It was now impossible to see the dial of the lock, so I fumbled through my pockets to find a book of matches. I had quite a time holding the match, juggling the lock, and dialing the combination. It was a three-hand job, but eventually I got back into my room and fell across the bed, totally exhausted by my venture out for a simple meal but still happy and chuckling at my own human foibles.

The following day I inquired about my trip to Pondicherry and was informed that indeed there was a bus, and it left at 6 A.M. I got up very early the next day and took a taxi to the bus station, which it turned out was a one-block-square parking lot filled with mud. There was nothing so formal as a gate, let alone a number, so the buses would just pull in and park at the shallowest mud puddle their drivers could find. I was completely lost and befuddled at this point, so I looked about and found a middle-aged Indian man dressed in Western clothing who looked approachable. I edged up to him cautiously.

"Do you speak English?"

"Yes."

"Could you help me find the bus for Pondicherry?"

"Yes, I am going to Pondicherry; will you please come with me."

So I tagged along as he took the suitcase out of my hand, an act that my guidebook insisted one should never allow. I nervously followed him, half suspecting that he was going to take off at any moment with all my belongings. We walked to an old derelict bus that had no glass in the windows and scarcely more paint than rust. My suitcase was handed to another man and then hoisted up to a rack atop the bus. I was certain it was the last time I would ever see it. My newly found Indian friend, however, did not deserve such suspicion; he was being very good to me, and I joined him on one of the hard wooden bus seats.

He spoke excellent English, and in a polite, formal manner he inquired about my family and what brought me to India. As the bus gradually filled up, we exchanged pleasantries. Eventually, we pulled out of the sea of mud and into a mess of traffic.

Indians drive with their horns; I have heard that if there is a traffic accident in India and you can prove that you were blowing your horn at the moment of impact, you are entirely exonerated from any blame; it must be true because there was a cacophony of sound and total chaos on the highway. Children, dogs, chickens, even cows were running in and out of traffic, barely escaping being pulled under a wheel of the bus. The distance from Madras to Pondicherry, a city of half a million, is only about one hundred miles, but it takes more than four hours to traverse it. The narrow, two-lane road would make an excellent training ground for stunt drivers. In many places farmers had piled grain on the pavement so that the passing cars and trucks would thresh it for them. The driver dodged these hazards along with potholes the size of a telephone booth. I took all this in along with the red dust filtering through the open windows. I didn't give a whit about the chaos that surrounded me, however; I noticed once again that I was in an unexpected reverie of happiness. I was so happy that it nearly made my bones ache with pleasure.

After about two hours, the bus ground to a squealing halt for a rest stop in a small village. By this time I knew my traveling companion well enough to ask him where I might find a toilet. His dignified reply: "If it is not serious, just go here on the street. If it is serious, please go around the corner then on the street." I did as I was told, looking out of the corner of my eye for passersby and expecting every second to be arrested.

I walked around a bit to stretch my tired body, and then our journey resumed. When we arrived in Pondicherry, I was preparing to bid farewell when my newfound friend asked where I was headed.

"The Sri Aurobindo Ashram," I replied.

"That is good, I was hoping as much. I am a monk in the ashram, so please be so kind as to follow me."

This was my improbable introduction to Shankar, my first Indian friend. Over the coming twenty years we would become very close. The fact that I would have picked him—a monk who was going exactly to my destination—at that mud puddle of a bus station is one of those slender threads that still amazes me.

Shankar took me directly to the ashram and found me a place to stay at a guest house. The ashram housed more than two thousand members at that time, plus hundreds of guests and a resident school (children came from long distances to this famous school). The Sri Aurobindo Ashram is named after Aurobindo Ghose, who was born in Bengal in 1872 and who died in 1950. Sri Aurobindo was the son of a medical doctor, a Kshatria (the warrior and ruling caste) who sent his son at an early age to England so that he might be schooled in Western thought and escape the "mystical nonsense" of India. Sri Aurobindo spent his early years, from age five to twenty-two, in England and came home to India with a first-class degree from Cambridge University, fluent in Greek, Latin, French, and English—but with no knowledge of any Indian tongue. His father had died during his English years, and Sri Aurobindo immediately allied himself with the anti-British group in India and lent his excellent knowledge of the English and their language to routing the oppressors. He was caught and jailed, along with Gandhi, and was sentenced to death. During his imprisonment, someone in the jail taught him yoga, which proved to be so native a language for Sri Aurobindo that he very quickly changed his allegiance from politics to mysticism. His father's efforts to protect his son from the highest levels of consciousness known to India were entirely in vain. The British had to release him on some technicality but planned to arrest him the next day to proceed with the death sentence. Sri Aurobindo escaped to Pondicherry, then a French colony, where the British had no power to arrest him, and it was there that he founded the ashram that now bears his name. The ashram has become famous for trying to bring the mysticism of traditional India into modern focus and to provide a community embracing the best of old and new as its ideal.

One of the first joys for me at the ashram was the food, which was sanitary, nutritious, and tasty. It was the first good food I had eaten in India. In fact, nowhere in my life have meals been attended to with as much warmth, companionship, and dignity as they are there. The ashram's dining hall is located in an old French colonial state building converted for ashram use, as are so many of the fine structures in Pondicherry. Classic pillars two stories high, steps, a fine garden—all the dignity of colonialism—lend grace to the setting.

On the day after my arrival at the ashram, Shankar found me in the dining hall and asked if he could come visit me at my room the following day; he suggested 4 P.M. I said that would be fine. He then looked at me quizzically.

"I said I would come at 4 P.M."

"Yes, I heard you."

"And what, Robert, do you think I mean when I say 4 P.M.?"

"Well, you might be here by 5 P.M., more likely 6, but there is a chance you won't be here at all until the next day."

He slapped his thigh and laughed. "Very good, you already know how to tell time in India."

He did come the next day about 6 P.M. I would soon learn that Shankar taught school and had access to a motorcycle that was owned by the ashram. I had never been on a motorcycle in my life, but he invited me to join him, and I was so enthralled with new experiences that I threw caution to the winds and climbed on for a ride. It was great fun, and soon we began a daily tour program in which he would arrive late in the afternoon after school was finished and take me out to see the sites in and around Pondicherry.

Shankar followed the usual Indian custom of testing me out for several days, always talking formally and politely while remaining cautious and guarded. Each day there was stiff, stylized conversation, as he inquired about the health of my parents, my own health, how I was enjoying the weather, and other such trivialities. I tried to be patient, giving him the same polite answers day after day. Then all of a sudden it was as if I had passed some test, and I was worthy of true friendship. After a week of this sparring, our real friendship began. In our afternoon visits Shankar began to shower me with good cheer and warmth, and our relationship entered a closeness and community that I had seldom experienced in my life.

My days in Pondicherry would invariably begin the same way. In the early morning hours there is a tranquil peace that is as ephemeral as the fragrance of jasmine on the cool air. I awaken very early to the sound of stillness and treasure it for an hour. But a half hour before daylight the raucous sound of the crows breaks the tranquillity. Perhaps it is the rooster who awakens the Western sun, but in India it seems to be the crow, Shiva's bird. Shortly following the cawing of crows, the muezzin cry comes from the minaret of the mosque down the street. The man with the loudest voice is chosen for this task since the whole community must hear that there is only one God, his name is Allah, and his prophet is Muhammad. There is no vibrato in the tuneless sound, and the flat reediness of it etches its message deeply on the ear. The muezzin sings in quarter-tones, something the Western world knows little about. These are pitches that would be in between the keys of our modern piano keyboard, and these notes skid about, destroy form, and defy order and location. It is an eerie sound not known to Westerners except in the singing of a Jewish cantor heard in an orthodox synagogue.

After the muezzin cry, every tea house or shop turns up its bid for attention, using whatever loudspeaker system it can afford. The temples then begin blasting their music, and every moving vehicle strives to clear a path before it with whatever noisemaker it can boast. With that, India is awake and a new day has begun.

About two weeks into my stay at the Sri Aurobindo Ashram, I got terribly sick. Shankar came and took me to the ashram hospital, a place called Tressor Hospital; I misunderstood and thought they said they were taking me to a "Treasure House," which soon ceased to be amusing, as I didn't leave that treasure house for ten days.

The staff at the hospital must have seen my apprehension upon checking in, as they tried to assure me that they were a very modern facility. "We have a thermometer," a nurse reassured me. I later found that their one thermometer was passed from one patient to another. In between patients they held it under the water faucet— just to be safe. My temperature reached 105, and I had terrible diarrhea and stomach cramps. Somehow I survived, not only my illness but also the medical treatment, and when I regained my strength I asked my Indian doctor, "What on earth did I have?"

"Oh, I don't know. Probably one of our ten thousand viruses," he replied.

From the nature of my symptoms, I think that I suffered from dysentery. As part of my treatment, they performed an X ray, gave me unknown medications, and fed me for ten days. The bill was twenty-eight dollars.

While I was hospitalized, my new friend, Shankar, came every evening to visit me and slept each night on the floor under my bed. Of all my experiences in India over the next twenty years, that was perhaps the most touching. When I was sick, my friend slept near me so that I wouldn't be frightened or lonely.

Shankar not only slept on the floor in the hospital room. One day he stood at the foot of my bed and said, "Robert, I want to tell you a story about Baba and his friend. This friend got very sick, and Baba came and stood beside him and told him, 'Only say the word, and I will go to die so that you can live.' Robert, for you, I am Baba. You have only to say the word, and I will die so that you can be better."

At first I was shocked by this story, but I had the presence of mind to say, "Thank you, Shankar, for this great gift; however, I think I have enough vitality left in me so that both of us can continue to live."

I never forgot the depth of tie and the profundity of relationship implied by this exchange between Shankar and myself. Shankar presented me with a kind of relatedness that I had never known before.

From the very beginning, India was for me a feast of feeling and relatedness. One day, shortly after recovering from my illness, I was riding a bicycle outside the ashram. An Indian stranger came up from behind me riding another bicycle, and when we were abreast he reached out, touched my hand, and smiled. The two of us traveled that way for a block, then he turned and went on his way.

As I have noted earlier, Sanskrit-based languages have ninety-six words for love. This allows a precision for feeling unknown in a Western language, for there is a word for love of your mother, a different one for your father, your horse, the sunset, your buddy, or the delight of a fine poem. I wish I had an English vocabulary of ninety-six words to discuss love, but I do not. In India the broad vocabulary for different types of relatedness allows people to show affection freely without setting off concerns and fears about what it might mean. There also are words to convey the friendship shown to me by Shankar that night he slept on the floor of my hospital room. Encountering such relatedness, most of us in the West would immediately ask ourselves what this person was after, but I quickly learned in India that warmth and feeling is possible without any implication of power, control, or sexuality. It is a certain indication of an undeveloped faculty when there is a paucity of terms for that faculty. India honors its feeling function with a rich vocabulary; ours is very limited. I am only half joking when I say that India has ninety-six words for love but none for nuts and bolts (they have imported our Western terms for these practical things), while we have ninety-six words for nuts and bolts but only one for love. I set to work to adopt the best of both Eastern and Western worlds.

I once asked Shankar about loneliness, admitting that it was one of the most painful dimensions of my life, and he replied, "I'm sorry, Robert, but I can't contribute anything on this subject because I have never been lonely in my life." His answer stopped me in astonishment; I thought for days about what it would be like to have a life where you were never lonely.

~

WHEN I PRAISE INDIA TO FRIENDS, I often tell people about esoteric things such as the quality of the light, and it's true the sunrise looks different there, which may have to do with something as mundane as the humidity or the pollution in the air. In truth, it is not the light, the heat, or the humidity that bathes me in warmth in India, it is the people. America is, collectively speaking, an extroverted culture that prizes rational thought above all else and values people accordingly. We also place a high value on material things and how much money one can collect, and in that way we are a sensate culture. Our thinking and sensation functions have brought the scientific, technological, and mechanical aspects of existence to an apex in the West, of which we are justly proud. But we have done this at the expense of our feeling. Practically everyone in the West becomes lonely, discontented, and uneasy because our capacity for feeling is in a terrible state of disrepair—worse than India's roads.

Politicians and officials lament the loss of family values in American society and rack their brains trying to figure out how to repair our social order. Perhaps the root of the problem is that our feeling function is nearly bankrupt. As an individual, I have spent much of my professional life working as a therapist to help patients develop and gain access to their feelings. I am, by birth, an introverted, feeling person—just the opposite of what is prized in American culture. One of the things I want to argue with God when I get the chance is this: Why on earth did you drop someone like me into that kind of family, in that kind of society, and in that century? I was a total misfit!

In any case, in India I was in the majority for the first time in my life, for the culture there favors introversion and feeling. Even at a young age some instinct in me must have sensed that India was home for me in a psychological sense; by reading the tales from India, I felt a kinship to the people and the culture there. And after arriving on Indian soil I gradually understood why I was continually bursting with happiness: my feeling sense and my quiet, introverted nature were respected and even valued. I also found the people there to be so much happier than I had ever encountered before. In the days and weeks ahead, I would find peasants in rural villages with greater contentment than most Americans I know.

Once Shankar became my friend, it was as if we were blood brothers for life. This was not an unusual situation by Indian standards. In traditional India it is expected that a young person will have a buddy or mate, a close friend of the same sex. There is even a ceremony for adolescents in which the skin is pierced and the blood of close friends is mixed. If someone gets into trouble in a village, they will seek out that person's blood brother. We have remnants of such camaraderie in America, as can be seen in fraternities, sororities, and—most unfortunately—gangs. But these have lost most of the sense of true relatedness and feeling.

My friendship with Shankar continued to grow. I gradually learned that he had been sent to the ashram at the age of twenty.

His father was a poor man, and since the ashram does not work on the money system, it provided a good home for Shankar. As we became "brothers," it was also expected that we would share worldly possessions. Shankar was delighted to have joint ownership of my pocketbook, and though at first I resisted, eventually I allowed this, and I found that he never took advantage of it. I did not pay him for taking me on tours, yet he would take just enough money to pay for necessities. Our relationship was not based on economics or sexual attraction or selfish needs. It was based on a kind of relatedness rarely known in the Western world and a quality we have no terminology for. I think I had been hungry for that kind of relationship all of my life without the means for finding it in a society that seldom experiences such a subtle bond.

One of the most important gifts given to me by my Indian friend was an invitation to visit his home village. This was an honor of the highest sort. Located in the center of India, Halasangi appears on no maps. It is desperately poor there, and, before me, there had never been another white-skinned visitor to the village.

To get to Halasangi, we departed the ashram in Pondicherry and took a train to Shallipur, which was the nearest station but still about thirty miles from our destination. Then we took a bus to within a couple of miles of the village. I was very tired by the time we got off the bus. If Shankar felt like walking ten miles, he presumed that I could do the same, so I had to tell him over and over that my limit was two miles. This time, however, he had anticipated my weariness, because when we got off the bus, there was his brother, Allamprabhu, waiting for us with an oxcart. Allamprabhu had been to the ashram in Pondicherry for a visit, so we were already acquainted.

It was February, and the evening air was fairly cool as we climbed up on the cart. There was not a light anywhere save for the stars and the pale moonlight, so I surrendered my well-being entirely to their care. We progressed slowly, rumbling over uneven ground, crossing streams, and pitching back and forth in the oxcart. No one felt compelled to say a word, so I could drink in the mysterious sounds and smells of animals, the vegetation, the living breath of India. So many people in America immediately feel compelled to fill up any empty space with sound. It was a peaceful, harmonious silence in our oxcart, and after nearly an hour's travel we arrived at our destination. A few dim oil lamps were all that could be seen as Shankar helped me out of the cart, took my arm, and escorted me through the doorway of his family's house.

"Will you honor my poor house with the dust of your noble feet?" This is a common saying in India, and it certainly expressed the essence of how I was welcomed into the home of Shankar's family.

The wooden door opened into a twenty-by-twenty-foot stone house with a dirt floor. The embers of a fire smoldered in the center of the room, and the smoke escaped through a hole in the ceiling. Shankar motioned for me to sit down on a worn rug, and I don't know who was more astonished, Shankar's family or me. Many pairs of dark eyes stared at me in the half light; twenty-seven people were living in this tiny abode. I was treated as an honored guest (I found out later that they had applied a fresh coat of watered cow dung on the floor just to keep the dust down for the new visitor). Shankar spoke in Kanada, the native tongue, and motioned to a young woman to bring me water to wash my hands, followed by a banana leaf place setting. Next out came a clay pot, and rice was ladled upon the leaf, followed by two kinds of vegetables, both highly spiced. I was a bit frightened to eat their food, but I could not refuse without insulting them deeply, so I hoped that my cast iron stomach would carry me through. There were no utensils, so I used my fingers, as is the Indian custom.

Shankar and his older brother, Allamprabhu, did all the speaking. Shankar had five brothers and a sister. Their father had been dead for some time, but the old mother sat on the periphery and silently watched my every move.

Concentric circles of people sat in the lamplight watching me eat. Some of the children had climbed up a ladder to the roof to get a better view of this man who fell down from the sky into their village. There was little conversation during the meal, but when I was finished and the banana leaf was cleared away, Allamprabhu spoke as the elder male of the household, with respect and great dignity.

"We know our Indian scriptures and the sayings of our wise men. Please tell us some wisdom from your wise men," he said.

This put me on the spot, and I searched my mind for something appropriate to say. Finally I remembered something from Meister Eckhart. "Well, one of our wise men says that the eye by which we see God is the same eye by which God sees us."

Allamprabhu translated this, and a buzz went through the group. They left considerable space before responding to me. Allamprabhu was sitting there cross-legged on the dirt floor across from me. I was sitting as cross-legged as I could, and I felt awkward being twice as big as anyone else.

After several minutes, Allamprabhu said, "I don't understand, what does this mean?"

"Well, it means that God needs us as much as we need God."

The man fell over backward with a clump on the dirt floor. I couldn't see if he was laughing or if he was insulted and angry. When he sufficiently recovered and sat back up, he said, "Robert, we have never had such a thought as this."

It was soon time for bed, and thus began one of the most re-markable experiences of my life! Shankar and Allamprabhu took me out to the oxcart again, put me on a mat on the floor of the cart, and went about a mile out from the village to deposit me in a stone building that was to be my sleeping quarters for the next several weeks. I could see only by the stars and the light of the tiny oil lamp that they had brought along for me. The building was small and made of marble, a single room with a roof held up on four pillars. I was set down on the floor, blessed, and left for the night.

Fear was rarely an element of my relationship with India. Only once in Calcutta was I overcome with a sense of panic at the unknown experiences that India presented, but fear was not present as I curled up on the stone floor to sleep. I don't count myself to be a very courageous person, but this experience did not elicit any apprehension or panic in me. I was safe, I was at home, there was only a stone floor with no blanket to sleep on, but I was strangely peaceful and content. I thought once of cobras, which are native to this part of India, and the mosquitoes played havoc with my light skin; but they seemed a part of the experience of that astonishing night. I slept well.

In the morning Shankar appeared at daylight driving a female water buffalo. He milked the buffalo, boiled the milk in a clay pot over a tiny fire, and presented this to me as my breakfast. The milk was strange only in its thick richness.

I was to sleep in this stone building, alone, every night for many weeks. It was only slowly that I learned—a bit at a time—that the stone building I was in was the tomb of a saint of the village who had died a generation before but who was still remembered by the very old people. Upon my appearance in the village, they had decided that I was the reincarnation of their saint returning to them; accordingly, they had put me out in the mausoleum to be properly housed with my former body. In addition to sleeping there, I spent long daylight hours in the mausoleum and was introduced to the custom of darshan, a procedure I was not aware of before this time. Darshan consists of people coming into the presence of a holy or revered man or woman, just to be in that presence. No words or actions are exchanged; just sitting in the presence of a revered person is sufficient to establish a sense of relatedness with that person. Villagers came often during the day to do darshan and would sit quietly for a few minutes and then leave.

So I was introduced to the strange art of sainthood. I learned the simple but astonishing fact that sainthood is conferred on someone by a group of people without much reference to the character or even the consent of that person! It was enough that I came from far away, had strangely white skin, and was a quiet person for the village to come to the consensus that I would be their old saint returned for their safety and protection. After some weeks of this, Shankar came to me one day and laid out the proposal that I stay in the village and be their local saint. This was a giddy thought in my head, and I got a bit dizzy at the prospect. "But how would I live?" "We will care for you and take care of your every need," replied Shankar. "But what about my visa?" "No one knows anything about visas here, and official India will never know you are here," replied Shankar. "But what—?" and my thought processes came to a halt. Never before had I been offered a job like this!

I contemplated this possible vocation and quickly decided I was not cut out for the work and informed the village that I had to return to my own village and could not stay with them.

I have meditated on the subject of sainthood many times since this experience, and I find a bit of wisdom in understanding that saints are people who suffer the projection of unlived holiness from a group of people and are made to serve in this strange role whether they like it or not. It is only the other side of the coin of scapegoating, in which a group chooses an individual to carry the dark side of their own personalities, which they are unwilling to own for themselves. This idea has been borne out by careful examination: every group I have ever experienced has done this living-out-by-appointment of the human elements that are too good or too bad for an ordinary person to accommodate in his or her own life. The group gives that overwhelming characteristic to some person nearby. God help the poor person who is landed with either of the excesses that humankind finds equally difficult to bear.

Early on during my stay in Halasangi, one of the small boys in Shankar's family mustered up enough courage to come sit in my lap; before I knew it he was rubbing my arm, apparently to see if the white of my skin would come off. I asked what he was doing and was told he was trying to get the dust off me so that I would be the right color. The children also were fascinated by the fillings in my teeth, which they had never seen before. I must have been quite a spectacle for the residents of this rural Indian village, yet they treated me with more grace, dignity, and sensitivity than I have ever felt in my life. I was a minority of one, but I never felt insecure or separate.

It was about this time that I was invited to address the students at the village school, which provided the most basic kind of education up to the fourth grade. The language spoken in this part of India is Kanada and the schoolmaster agreed to translate my words to the children. I would say a few words, then the schoolmaster would talk; I didn't understand a word he was saying, but I did notice that the students were unusually attentive. They sat there quietly, some with their mouths open. I wasn't sure what to say, so I just improvised, telling them that I came from the other side of the world, that I enjoyed being in India, and other pleasantries. After it was all over I asked my friend Shankar how the schoolmaster had translated my remarks. Shankar evaded a direct answer, mumbling and changing the subject, but I finally got it out of him. The schoolmaster had apparently introduced me by saying, "We think this man, Robert, is a saint because he doesn't eat very much, he doesn't talk very much, and he doesn't do very much."

I was surprised and amused by my qualifications for sainthood, and for years afterward when someone back in America didn't know how to introduce me before a lecture I would tell them that my principal qualifications consisted of not eating very much, not talking very much, and not doing very much!

The children of the village soon learned that every evening at sunset I would go out for a walk. The sunsets were astonishingly beautiful; peacocks would fly into the trees to roost at night, and I would watch them arrive to herald the approaching end of day. Time slowed to a crawl and then ceased to concern me at all. Only the peacocks reminded me that another day had passed. As I walked down the road to survey the view from different spots, as many as two dozen children would soon be hanging from me. There seemed to be a hierarchy, probably by caste, that determined who had higher priority and therefore could get the closest to me. I had a youngster hanging from every finger, plus two or three grabbing onto my shirttail, two or three more on my belt loops. We advanced down the road in this way—what a strange entourage!

There was one small boy in Halasangi who, like me, suffered from an amputated leg; he had no artificial limb, however, and scraped along the red dust with his one good leg and a battered crutch held together with twine. After I had been in the village for a time, one day I took my leg off to show him that I too had a handicap. He watched with eyes as wide as saucers as I pulled my leg off, then he turned and ran. I feared that I would never see him again, but the next day he returned with a dozen of his young playmates, all of them now staring intently at my artificial leg as they had once been captivated by my white skin and blue eyes. They must have wondered what miracle this man from Mars would pull next, perhaps taking off an arm or unscrewing his head. One day my amputee brother brought a note to me, written by someone else. He had asked them to inquire if he could get a leg like mine for one hundred rupees. I was very sad to reply to him that mine had cost 5000 dollars or 165,000 rupees. He went away crestfallen with the information that he would be on his ragged crutch for the rest of his life.

The average age of an Indian at the turn of this century was only twenty years, but it had improved to forty-seven years when I was first there in the 1970s. Strangely, however, I found that most of the villagers looked younger than they actually were. A boy who appeared to be about fifteen was actually eighteen or twenty. The villagers seemed to remain in perpetual youth for three decades, and then they suddenly aged all at once.

There was another young man, probably twenty, who was shy, quiet, and blind in one eye. He walked several miles each day to come sit with me and share the sunset. Shankar told me the story of this young devotee: he was the son of a man who was caught thieving and subsequently was kicked out of the village. Without a community, the thief probably had to go to a city where he would be forced to live off the street. The villagers had decided not to dismiss the thief's young boy, however. He was allowed to work in the fields, but he was watched continually by suspicious eyes to see if he would follow in his father's footsteps. This son of the thief was working hard to earn the respect of the village, and perhaps he believed that I could somehow remove his social stigma and elevate his status. I often pondered his fate.

Nature has two ways of protecting itself. One is to produce a huge number of offspring and depend on chance to bring a few of these to maturity. One thinks of the dandelion producing thousands of seeds to fly away with the hope that one of them will produce a new plant. We can be joyful at the success of one of the thousands, but we rarely think of the many that perished along the way. The second way of nature is to produce a few offspring and take very good care of them and thus safeguard the species. This takes much care and intelligence but leaves less wreckage in its path.

India has been involved in the first manner of self-protection for all of its history and possesses a culture that obeys the harsh laws that accompany this attitude. An Indian family knows in what order it will die if there is famine. The youngest girl goes first, and on up the line of girls; then the youngest boy goes and on up the line of boys. Every Indian family knows that one must have twelve children in order to survive. Six of these will die before adulthood (the death rate of old India was something like 50 percent). Of the six remaining children, half will be girls and lost to the family by marriage. One of the remaining boys will be a monk or lead a religious life—the family's offering to the gods—which leaves two able-bodied males to care for the parents in their old age. This is the Indian way, and it is so deeply ingrained into the social fabric of this land that it cannot be changed quickly. Indira Gandhi was voted out of office in midcareer some years ago because she began playing politics with birth control and brought down the wrath of the Indian people on her head. No politician has dared touch the subject since.

What is a society to do when it thinks in terms of the dandelion seed and knows with certainty that its only safety lies in the largest possible number of offspring? There is no regulation of numbers and only limited supply of food and the necessities of life. So a social system was instituted to make sure that a small aristocracy of people would be assured of safety in case of disaster, and a way of life was obtained that would safeguard the race even if it cost the lives of many individuals. A hierarchy of value was set up wherein the top few were given safety and the rest allowed to survive if there was enough. Many animals function in this way in their instinctive aristocracy, and it is the law of nature as contrasted with the law of culture. I once heard it said that one can gauge the position of a society on the evolutionary scale simply by observing what it does with its elderly and its handicapped. If it has no time or means for its insecure members, it is a primitive society; if it cares for its disabled and elderly, it is a cultural entity. On this particular scale of values, India is far behind the Western cultures. I had never been aware before of the Christian virtue of compassion until I was in a non-Christian land. This seems such a contradiction; India is so sensitive to feeling matters but has little sense of compassion.

I was horrified early in my experience of India to discover that if I were to fall and break a leg on the street, no one would give me help. There is no 911 emergency telephone number, there are no ambulances to summon, no rescue squads as in the West. If one is incapacitated in India, one becomes a casualty ignored by the general flow of humankind. I did not realize until I went to India that charity is a Western virtue. In India, if you can contribute to society, then and only then are you worthy of food and keep; if you cannot contribute, you are left to die. Mother Teresa made an immense impact on India by challenging this concept, but she was certainly the exception.

This is so harsh a dictum that some safeguard had to be inaugurated to make life bearable and give some continuity. The caste system has provided this for centuries in India, though it is probably the most difficult aspect of Indian life for a Westerner to comprehend.

When the Aryan invasions of India took place (lighter-skinned people migrating into India from the north and west during early times), the caste system evolved to keep the new immigrants in power. The native Dravidian people had dark skin, so caste became a matter of skin color as well as cultural traditions. In India today, it is a general rule that the higher the caste, the lighter the color of a person's skin. The caste system regulates what occupation might be open to a person. The Brahmin is the highest caste and is traditionally a priest and teacher. The Kshatria is the next level down in the hierarchy and occupies the place of the warrior and political ruler. The Vaishna is the shopkeeper and artisan. The Shudra is the worker. Another group falls below any place in the caste system; these are the untouchables, who are looked upon as little more than animals.

India survives on its particular attitudes, which are so different from the West. There is starvation and illness for many but an intricate system for safeguarding a few. It is no different in character from the dandelion seeds except that the failures are so humanly apparent. It is a shock to a Westerner to walk the streets of an Indian city (the caste system reaches its worst dimension in urban settings) and see the millions of derelicts who are perishing so that a few might survive. I try to console myself with the thought of the dandelion seeds, but it is little comfort to me.

Western medicine and technology have interfered with the natural flow of Indian society by increasing the survival rate of all levels of people and dramatically reducing the death rate from epidemics such as cholera. The result is that the population of India is now rising by something approximating three million a month with the prospect of a billion people by the year 2000. This one-sided alteration of natural balance will have disastrous effect soon. Economists predict the loss of 300 million people by starvation the next time anything goes wrong with the social structure in India. It would take only a failure of the monsoon rains or a serious conflict between Muslim and Hindu to set this off.

When I face my Indian friends with this dilemma, they agree that some cataclysm is inevitable. By this time in the conversation I have generally lost my cool and say, "But it may well be you who dies!"

"Yes," is their matter-of-fact reply.

The caste problems and the overpopulation are beyond India's capacity to cope and certainly beyond my capacity to resolve. I had to learn to accept India for what it is, so I resolved to do what I could to make a difference on a small scale.

~

ONE DAY DURING MY STAY in Halasangi, Shankar hitched up the oxcart and prepared a picnic lunch, and off we went for two or three miles into the countryside. He stopped and took us over to a great mango tree. He didn't tell me what was going on, and by this time I was used to just following his lead. We settled down under the shade of this great, spreading tree. It was winter time so there was no fruit in season, but the leaves provided lovely shade. As we ate our lunch Shankar was even more quiet than usual. We sat there for a very long time and I would occasionally look over at him, but Shankar would say nothing. In America I can outwait almost anyone, as my introversion has its own power to wait with equanimity. Finally Shankar came out with a story.

"Robert, my father was a saint in this village. It is his tomb in which you sleep at night."

I gradually learned that Shankar's father used to come out regularly to this great mango tree to meditate. It was believed that a great yogi who was hundreds of years old lived near the tree, and it was known throughout the countryside that it was therefore a holy spot. One day when Shankar's father was a young man and meditating under the tree, the great yogi had appeared and had offered to serve as his teacher. Then they disappeared for three days of training. These days were almost entirely an ordeal, some kind of descent into hell, apparently, but after three days' journey, Shankar's father had returned enlightened.

I was fascinated by this story, though with my Western mind I took it with a grain of salt. Shankar would not tell me his father's name, and I was a bit suspicious that the whole tale was a fabrication, perhaps based on a local legend or on some Indian folklore. Nevertheless, I enjoyed Shankar's story and told him that it pleased me very much. Little more was said between us for the next two hours. Both of us were content to enjoy the day, and neither felt compelled to interrupt the peace with meaningless conversation. Eventually, as the sun was setting, Shankar announced that we had to be getting back to the village, so we climbed into the oxcart, and he took me back to what I now realized was my quarters in the shrine of a saint.

This story of the mango tree soon blended in my mind with the ebb and flow of images in dreamlike India, and I didn't think much more about it until weeks later. By this time I had returned to my guest house at the ashram in Pondicherry, nearly a thousand miles away from Halasangi. I was practicing the technique of active imagination, the art of dreaming while awake and taking part in the dream. To me it is a powerful tool, as are the yogas of India, but one that was devised especially for the minds of Westerners.

One morning, after enjoying a leisurely breakfast at the ashram dining hall, my mind unexpectedly recalled the story of the old yogi under the mango tree. I let the image enter my consciousness, without judging it or trying to control it in any way, and the mango tree grew and grew in my mind until it was a towering image. Then the scene shifted to me, and I could imagine myself meditating under the tree until a great yogi appeared. Convenient for me, he spoke English, and we began to have a conversation. (I want to underscore that in no way do I think this was an actual event. I did not magically transport myself back to Halasangi, and it was always clear that I was experiencing an imaginary vision in my room in Pondicherry.) After a brief conversation, the old yogi agreed to train me, and he took me off exactly as he had done with Shankar's father. He sat me down by a small stream and took my artificial leg away from me, leaving me absolutely helpless. He left me there for three days, during which time he devised everything imaginable to set off fear in me. I grew thirsty, but there was nothing to drink except water from the stream, which I was certain was contaminated. Eventually I cupped my hands and tasted the water, and it seemed to be all right. There were numerous other tests and tortures that I shudder to recall; during this active imagination exercise, my mind shuffled through these images rapidly like a deck of playing cards. Eventually, the old yogi came and took me to the old mango tree outside Halasangi. He gave me back my leg. Apparently I had successfully passed his tests, as I was feeling calm and intact once again. In fact, I was far better than I had been before the ordeal because this initiation had somehow left me stronger than I had been before. Then my vision ended.

It was such a vivid inner experience that it left me profoundly shaken, as though I had been through a real event. It is important to understand the level upon which this story was true; no great yogi ever came to me, but somehow the story spun itself out inside me and left a residue of wisdom. If one is careful enough to keep the levels straight, to remember that such visions are an inner experience, then active imagination applied in this way can be extremely powerful and helpful.

A few days after I had been working with these images, my friend Shankar came to visit me. I told him about my experience, covering my tracks carefully to say that this had happened in my imaginal world while sitting in Pondicherry. He immediately jumped up in glee.

"I knew the great yogi would come to you, Robert; that is why I took you to the great mango tree."

"Shankar, get the wax out of your ears. This did not really happen, but it was a wonderful kind of dream. It happened in my room, not in Halasangi."

He continued in his excitement, "Yes, the old yogi knew you were here and came to get you!"

"No, Shankar, this didn't happen under the great mango tree. It happened right here in my room. It was in my imagination!"

A funny duel began between us, as I tried to convince him that this event didn't really happen and he insisted with absolute certainty that it did occur. I am not a madman, and somehow the more we argued the more important it became to me to get across my certainty that this was an imaginal event. But he would have nothing to do with this differentiation of levels.

"It doesn't matter. It happened."

At that moment I began to understand the great depth of India's psyche, an insight that helped me to cope with that wonderful/terrible place. India values the imaginal and gives greater credence to that reality than to what we call the real facts of life. Our sound, scientifically proven realities are nothing but maya, a web of illusion, to a traditional Indian. In my estimation, my active imagination exercise had more to do with me and my inner state than with the mango tree sitting in a field near Halasangi, but for Shankar there was no separation of the two. From that day, I experienced a new way of seeing India, a way of feeling her interior power, and simultaneously I began to realize how great our loss is in the West. We think that the imaginal life is nothing at all, a waste of time, at best, and the ravings of psychotics, at worst. But I began to ponder: Did I dream of the yogi under the mango tree or did he dream of me?

～

AFTER NEARLY TWO WEEKS in Halasangi, I came down with some dreadful virus. I couldn't screen my food since it was delivered to me each day, and although I applied iodine drops to any water I drank, I suspected that this was an inadequate precaution. The water came from a fifty-foot pit where everyone in the village also bathed. I had discovered that this pit was home to a fiercely poisonous water snake. Shankar showed me how to make a big splash to scare the snake to the other side of the pool before submerging myself for a bath. At one point I naively asked why they didn't just kill the snake and be done with it, but Shankar patiently explained that the village would never kill the snake because he was guardian of the water; if any harm came to the snake, it would most certainly bring disaster down upon the villagers.

In any case, whether it was the water or the food, I soon found myself hacking and coughing. I loved Halasangi, but there was no way to protect my health there. When I fell increasingly ill, Shankar and his family made an even greater fuss over me, bringing me boiled rice water to consume three times a day. I realized, however, that to survive I would need to leave the village and return to the ashram. I made inquiries to Shankar about when it would be possible for my return.

Then, on the day before I was scheduled to leave Halasangi, Allamprabhu came to me for a talk. He began with the usual pleasantries, but soon he announced that if I was not going to be a holy man for the village, then I must accept a special gift. He had observed how solitary I was, and to help ease my loneliness, Allamprabhu and his wife had decided to conceive a child for me.

"If it is a boy, he will be your servant for life, and if it is a girl, she will be your wife."

I was so astonished by this "gift" that I could not even manage to thank my host. Instead, I quickly changed the subject and no more was said of the matter, but, unfortunately it did not end there.

When I traveled back to India the following year, Allamprabhu and his wife were, in fact, the parents of a new baby girl. It was explained that by traditional Indian custom, we could be married right then and there, or, if I preferred, the parents would raise this girl child and wait for our marriage when she turned sixteen. I selected the latter, thinking that I would possibly be dead by that time so it wouldn't be a problem.

To conclude this story I must jump ahead in time. During the ensuing years it became my habit to spend each winter in India, and though I stopped going to Halasangi, every year my friend Shankar would visit with me at the ashram in Pondicherry and bring news of the good health of my child bride. I had considerable time to weigh my options, which consisted of the following: (1) I could marry her, which would delight the entire family because then we would share all of our worldly riches; (2) I could give her to a younger brother of mine, which was no help since I have no brother; (3) I could find her a husband and produce a dowry; or, (4) I could sell her, like some water buffalo or other personal property.

Women still face a terrible form of oppression in India. Traditional India demands that a woman be seen only by one man other than her male blood relatives. Father, uncle, brothers, sons—all have easy access to her; but only one other man, her husband, may look upon her. In a strict household no male may look upon a woman except that woman's husband. Of course, there are many women on the street, and men can create extravagant fantasies through glimpsing through a sari only a shapely form or a bare midriff. But custom says men must not look and may *never* speak. All this is breaking down in the cities, but anything outside the old pattern is still considered taboo in rural India. There are many women working in public positions now, such as bank clerks and airline employees, but they still must navigate through the judgments of co-workers; even many modern women feel they must be short to the point of rudeness to any man—especially a foreigner—if they want to keep peace with their colleagues. I have been told that if a woman in a public place smiles at a man, her colleagues will not speak to her for a week. The serving girls at the ashram would parade through my room without knocking to bring water or clean the room, but no conversations were possible. I would give the headmistress of the house some money to distribute among them, but I might easily have ended up in jail if I had openly given any specific woman a gift.

With respect to my child bride, I felt as if I had somehow been caught in a trap, but that didn't lessen my sense of obligation. After evading the issue for several years, I decided to come to terms with this dilemma rather than wait to see what would happen when my bride would be sixteen. In that fateful year I packed an extra thousand dollars in travelers' checks to be applied to discharge my obligation. After I had been at the ashram in Pondicherry for a couple of weeks, Shankar, my prospective bride's uncle, came to talk to me. We were good friends, and I greatly admired his capacity for keeping his roots in old India but at the same time being aware of the modern world around him. He was very polite and very formal, but eventually he got around to asking about my marriage plans. Our discussion proceeded in classical Indian style in which one person says something polite, there is a long pause, then the other party says something and there is a longer pause. The conversation was going along in this manner, and we were probably about an hour into it when I finally managed to say that I was seventy years old and that there was no way a man of my age could marry a sixteen-year-old girl, it was simply against the customs of my land. He didn't see anything wrong with our age discrepancy; however he finally acknowledged that the girl really didn't want to marry me, either. She wanted to find an education (something impossible in the village unless some outside help appeared by magic), and her concern was to go to a preparatory school and then the University of Bijapur.

"If I will pay for her to go to school, would that discharge my duty?"

He was delighted. "Yes, Robert, I think that would be a very fine solution." Everyone seemed happy with the bargain. For the next several years I paid for my intended bride to go to school. Eventually she graduated from the University of Bijapur, where she was trained as a nurse. After her education I lost track of her, though I did hear that she eventually married an Indian man whom she met at school.

Through this muddle over my intended bride, I came to the realization that Indians—at least those following traditional Indian thought—dislike having anything perfectly clear or defined. I watched Indian people go to great effort to keep some issue from being directly defined, as if purposefully to leave room for error or confusion or uncertainty. To my Western mind it was frightening to find that nothing is ever clearly defined, made certain, or "nailed down," as we would say. It is presumed that time is not to be taken as exact. Shankar never wanted to discuss the impossibility of my marrying into his family. We had to approach the subject in the most indirect fashion and over several years.

I have come to see this indirectness not as a fault but as a basic human need, perhaps an archetype in the collective unconscious. I call it my Indeterminacy Principle, borrowing from Heisenberg's Uncertainty Principle. The Indeterminacy Principle refers to the reluctance of the unconscious to let anything be entirely clear, straight, or final. With this principle in mind, I understand a little better why a woman will upset the workings of a day's schedule or a man will introduce a mood to set the day into a bit of chaos. Victims of such blurring easily fly into a rage that the other has "gummed up the works," but they are rarely able to see their own unconscious serving this archetype. The goddess of indeterminacy must be served or she will intrude in her own way, and perhaps one can say that reality is not designed to accomplish a defined goal so much as it is made to serve the incomprehensible fact of what is. She, the goddess of indeterminacy, is certainly part of that reality of being. We must learn to accept and love what is rather than always wishing for something different.

I once heard a wonderful story that touches on this topic.

It seems that once there was a man from heaven sojourning on the face of the earth. He was walking along when he came across a yogi sitting by the roadside. The yogi had meditated for thirty years with such austerity that birds had built a nest in his hair and his right arm was encased in a beehive. The yogi sensed the presence of the enlightened one, and so he came out of his meditation and said, "Oh, man from heaven, please inquire for me how long before my liberation from this vale of tears."

The man from heaven agreed to do this, and the yogi went back to his meditation.

The enlightened one walked on and found a young man dancing under a banyan tree. He inquired of the young man, "Tell me, sir, what are you dancing for?"

"I am dancing for my liberation," the young man replied. "When you return to heaven, could you please ask how long before my liberation?"

The man from heaven agreed to do this.

Some years later the man from heaven returned to the face of the earth, and he went to discharge his duties. First, he went to the old yogi and said, "I have inquired in heaven, and you will be liberated in seven incarnations."

The old yogi, with the bird's nest in his hair and the beehive still on his arm, moaned loudly and said, "So long! How can I endure for seven more incarnations?"

The man from heaven said, "That is the voice of heaven," and then he walked on.

Next, he came across the young man still dancing under the banyan tree. The dancing man spotted the man from heaven, and without losing a step, he asked, "How long?"

The man from heaven said, "I have inquired of heaven, and you will be liberated in as many incarnations as this banyan tree has leaves."

The young man yelped with joy and said, "What, so soon?"

At that instant a voice was heard from heaven saying, "Young man, your liberation is this instant."

This story releases us from the rigid cause-and-effect world that rules so much of our human thought and delivers us over to that relative attitude that counts intention and feeling as more real than any mechanical view. The young man dancing for his liberation was more to the liking of the gods than the old man in his vice grip of asceticism. India delights in such stories, which give so much hope and encouragement to anyone suffering from a seemingly unbearable burden. This story can help remind us to dance.

14

My Beloved India:

Invoking Incarnations of God

Over the nineteen years after my first visit, India became my spiritual home. Each year I would arrange my lectures and appointments so that I could shut down my American household for the winter months and return to the ashram in Pondicherry. In time, numerous friends from around the world were meeting up with me there to see "Robert's beloved India."

India makes the most extraordinary relationships in the course of the most ordinary events. Anyone who stays in one place in India for more than a few days collects a rickshaw driver and one each of all the other carriers of the everyday necessities of life. My rickshaw driver in Pondicherry, Selvaraj, had a little English and a sense of time (not to be presumed in Indians), and he was young enough so that I didn't feel guilty at the moderately hard physical labor that his profession demands. One year he greeted me the first day I arrived in Pondicherry, and after that he haunted me everywhere I went. I needed him and finally just settled down to hiring him for half a day at a time.

The wife of Selvaraj died three years earlier, so this man and his ten-year-old son, Rama, made up one of the thin little families who lived on the street in front of my guest house. When I sought out Selvaraj to take me to the dining hall in the morning, I would often see the two of them wrapped up in their single blanket making a ragged bundle lying on the sidewalk. All of their possessions were within arm's reach and were covered by a plastic tarp no larger than their own dimensions. Birth, death, cooking, eating, worship—everything went on in that small space jealously guarded from the hundred other people who wanted to have that advantageous spot. The fact that Selvaraj belonged to me gave him some leverage in his ownership of that place. The rickshaw was owned by an entrepreneur who rented the three-wheeled device made of an old bicycle for twenty-five rupees per day. If I paid Selvaraj one hundred rupees a day, that left him a meager income, considering that the rupee was purchased for only three cents in U.S. currency. That was the value of the rupee during most of my time in India, and it later fell even lower in value.

I spent hour-long trips with Selvaraj as I went to the post office, the market, or restaurants. Soon I ran out of small change and set up an account with him. Most rickshaw drivers could not comprehend anything this complicated, but this fellow understood. I gave him one hundred rupees at a time and used it up over several trips a day. One evening he asked me for one thousand rupees for medicine; he would make up the money by rickshaw fees tomorrow and tomorrow and tomorrow. This instantly set off in me Shakespeare's famous lines, "Tomorrow and tomorrow and tomorrow creeps in its petty pace." Time is the legacy of every civilization and is a mystery to the learned no less than to the simplest rickshaw driver.

One night, as I was coming back from a dinner with friends in Pondicherry, Selvaraj got off his bicycle seat and walked me a short distance then unexpectedly collapsed on the pavement. What to do? I got him onto the rickshaw, but after that my mind was racing. Selvaraj had gradually become like family to me, and I couldn't leave him unattended. There were no ambulances or paramedics, so I ran down the street until I found another rickshaw driver to take care of him, and I put a fistful of money in this man's hand and told him to take Selvaraj to a private doctor. There are government medical clinics in India, but they are booked days in advance and mostly dispense a pill for any ailment.

I walked back to the ashram feeling heavy in my heart that I had nothing but my wallet to answer the crushing burden of my Indian friends. I remembered the only cruel barb that Shankar had ever delivered to me on a previous trip: "Robert, why is it that when your heart is touched you always reach for your wallet?"

It was days before I could formulate an answer, and then I only managed to respond, "Because that is the only language or power that I have in reply to the suffering and disaster of my beloved India."

Two days later Selvaraj appeared again at the gate of the ashram, much improved but still weak. He wanted to make sure he could have a trip I had scheduled for Sunday morning. It took all our combined languages and gestures to explain to him that he was too weak to make that long trip but that he was still "top man" and would make the trips "tomorrow." He got a friend to take me that Sunday, but Selvaraj was there to send us off and was still there when we got back to make sure it had all gone right.

⌒

YOGA IS A PIVOT POINT in Indian life. The word means simply "union" and derives from the same Indo-European root as our word *yoke,* to bind together or to make union of that which has suffered fragmentation. In their wonderfully practical way, Indians have devised four main branches of yoga, which fit neatly into Jung's system of typology. Of course it is the other way around, since yoga came long before Jung, who owes more to Indian philosophy than is commonly known.

Humankind divides itself up into four main psychological attributes, honored in many languages. The Greeks spoke of the elements of earth, air, fire, and water with the four accompanying temperaments. India similarly honors four yogas, and it is important to choose a yoga corresponding to one's own typology.

The only one of these four commonly known in the west is hatha yoga, the yoga of physical differentiation. One trains the physical body to do things that Westerners seldom realize as possible. Blood flow may be increased or decreased in a specific part of the body, temperature altered, blood pressure or heart rate changed, attention focused on a specific part of the body, control and differentiation achieved—all of which are uncommon experiences for us. This yoga brings the sensation function to a high pitch of differentiation and makes an art of one's physical body. This form of yoga was designed for sensation type people and is therefore more easily understood by most Westerners.

A person who is strongly intuitive is immediately at home in raja yoga, called the royal yoga since it is the most subtle. One meditates and "listens" as intently as possible, though not to any audible or specific information. When the listener finally hears the unhearable and experiences that which is beauty outside the realm of ordinary human consciousness, then he or she has attained enlightenment. Intuitives are delighted with this language and in it find a home for that quality in themselves that the Western world fails to honor.

Jnana yoga engages the thinking function. In this form of yoga you are instructed to reason and use intellectual focus until you have reasoned yourself out of the world of maya (illusion) and have escaped the errors that keep you ensnared in unreality. This strikes Westerners as rather high-flown language, but it only means that by intense concentration of intelligent thought you can pierce through neurotic behavior and stop the nonsense in your life. This cool, highly impersonal discipline is very good for the person who is ruled predominantly by thinking.

Bhakti yoga takes you to salvation or enlightenment by exercising the feeling function. You give devotion to a bhakti master—this may be an actual living person or a master of another age in history—and pour out devotion and love until everything but the living flame of love has been incinerated.

Some great Indian teachers have said that bhakti is the yoga best suited to Westerners. They pay Christianity a high compliment by saying that Christ was the greatest bhakti master who ever lived. Ramakrishna, last century, and Ramana Maharishi, this century, followed in that line. How many unremarkable Westerners are touched by this same quality and have no idea of the depth and profundity that has visited them? To see God and mistake it for a personal experience is a most painful matter. Probably the most painful experience for Westerners is their inclination to make a god or goddess of another person—only to find out that no person is capable of sustaining this great power. The term *honeymoon* originally meant sweet for a month. This is the usual duration of such a divine vision. I know of no more overwhelming problem for Westerners than the question of what to do with love that exceeds the personal capacity of the beloved. Bhakti yoga addresses this issue more directly than any other language I know.

~

BREAKFAST AT THE ASHRAM is simple with no variations: porridge, whole wheat bread, a banana, and a choice of milk, cocoa, or yogurt. Then off to the coconut man across the street for my morning drink of fresh green coconut juice. Arusakumar, the coconut man, is a master of his art at slicing off the top of a green coconut with his machete, inserting a straw, and giving it to his customer. I sit on a burlap sack of coconuts and watch this happy man ply his trade. He is perhaps the happiest man I have ever known, and this near-divine quality is highly contagious. He sings and laughs, and I am pleased to bask in his Garden of Eden atmosphere. One day an old English woman who has lived in the ashram for many years stopped and challenged me, "Why do you waste your time with this coconut man when you ought to be in the Samadhi (Sri Aurobindo's burial place) meditating?" This caught me unaware, and I was more direct in my reply than tactful. "Because I find more living spirituality here than anywhere else in Pondicherry." She had the grace not to dismiss my reply but went off saying she would think about it.

So I sit on my burlap sack and watch the wonderful/terrible procession of India go by. Saints and beggars, lepers, old women (an old woman without a husband or son to care for her is at the bottom of the precarious life of a beggar), young people with the New India stamped on their faces—the ebb and flow of humankind at its best and its worst.

⁓

ONE DAY I WAS on a very crowded Indian train, second-class carriage, and, as usual, it was hot and totally chaotic. All the seats were full—overfull, in fact—and there was no standing room left. I had managed to squeeze myself into the luggage rack up above the seats and sat there, doubled up, looking at India in its contortions of too-muchness.

A young man, blind, a beggar, squeezed his way down the aisle, singing old devotional songs of India. His thin, reedy voice made its way above all the din and carried a peacefulness I had never heard before. As he passed, I touched his head and drew his arm up so I could put a one-hundred-rupee note in his hand. He went on his sightless way, and I watched at the next station as he left my carriage (Indian trains have no passenger connection between cars) and got into the next one. Someone explained that he was on the train all day going from one car to the next at station stops.

How did he ever get back home again? Did he have a home? Where did he land at the end of his day? Who took care of him? My luggage rack was different after he had passed by.

⁓

ANOTHER TIME WHILE WALKING in the village I came across a small boy with a severe case of conjunctivitis, an eye infection that often leads to blindness. A friend who had come to India with me had some antibiotic ointment designed for use in the eye, and he gave this to the family. Without so much as one word in common between them, he got the idea across that the ointment was to be put under the eyelid four times a day. That worked well and soon the boy's eyes were much better.

After several days I could see that the boy with conjunctivitis was improving rapidly with the medicine. He began bringing his friends for some of the magic. I put a little mound of antibiotic cream on a cut and watched as a dozen youngsters took tiny smears from that one mound of ointment for some ailment of their own.

I ricochet between two worlds: youngsters dying of malnutrition, illness, infections running rampant, a world so insecure that one can vanish without a trace; the other side is magic telephone calls to America, antibiotics, my bottomless packet of travelers' checks, a Polaroid camera. It is a wonder we are not all split souls (the original meaning of the term *schizophrenic;* the ancients thought the soul resided in the phrenic muscle, which activates the process of breathing in the diaphragm, so a split diaphragm muscle meant a soul that was divided into two parts). But this can also be experienced as a breathtaking view of reality not available to any generation before our own.

~

A GRAY OLD MAN came to me on the street and asked me to give him some heaven. I hadn't thought this was in my power to bestow, and he saw my puzzled look. Only five rupees, he said. Five rupees—for heaven? Yes, only five rupees. I have never been indifferent to a bargain, and this sounded like the best one yet. So I gave him five rupees, and off he went. A half hour later the old man appeared again, staggering around and singing, hopelessly drunk, being guided home by three small village boys who were laughing and having a fine time with the old man. I chuckled to myself: Heaven anyone? Only five rupees!

~

ZAKIR, AN INDIAN who works at the ashram, is another fine example of the natural inner beauty of the Indian people. One day Zakir asked me in a wonderful, childlike way, "Robert, please take me somewhere I can be cold. I have never been cold." Zakir grew up in the Sri Aurobindo Ashram and was in his midthirties when we met. He idolizes America and drinks up every bit of information about the promised land that he can find. I provided him with a subscription to *Time* magazine, which quickly became his most treasured possession. He nearly memorized it each week.

It gets down to eighty-five degrees Fahrenheit once in a while in Pondicherry with very high humidity, but it can reach one hundred and twenty degrees there in the summer. I was touched by the purity of Zakir's request to feel cold, so I arranged a trip to KodiKanal, a hillside town in southern India that the British made famous for summer retreats. At an elevation of more than six thousand feet, it was a welcome relief from India's summer heat.

Late one afternoon Zakir and I headed off by taxi to a rail terminal, where we caught an express train. Once on board, we bribed the conductor to change our second-class tickets for first class, which moved us from six in a compartment with wooden let-down beds to four in a compartment with padded beds.

We arrived at our destination at 4 A.M. and through some miracle found a bus to take us directly to the town of KodiKanal. People seem to take the inefficiencies of travel in India in stride; there are even jokes about it. I recall one of them:

"The crowd is so dense at the Bombay commuter station that one man says to another, 'Honored Sir, will you be so kind as to take hand from pocket? It is my pocket.' The crowd is so dense at the Calcutta commuter station that one man says to another, 'Honored Sir, will you be so kind as to take hand from pocket? It is my hand.'"

Over time I became accustomed to delays and mix-ups, and I did my best to plan for them. Before leaving the ashram I had scheduled one night in an old British nineteenth-century hotel in KodiKanal. Zakir had never stayed in a hotel, however, and once we were there I had a difficult time getting him to relinquish his room, so we extended our stay for another five days. At only twenty-four dollars per room per night I was happy to provide this extravagance for my Indian friend. The temperature dropped to around fifty degrees at night and my friend had the thrill of being cold.

We hired a taxi to take us to Madurai, an ancient Indian city famous for its great temple. The temple ground is a walled compound about half a mile square with four great pyramidal towers at each of the cardinal points sculptured to represent a fair proportion of the four hundred million gods that comprise the Hindu religion. It was here that I learned with great force that the street is often more temple to me than the great prescribed temple buildings. I was emotionally touched by the building itself, but I began to thrill to the passage of humanity on the street. I sat for several hours watching elephants, beggars, holy people, children, cripples, lepers, mad people (there are no asylums in India), machines of all sorts spewing out pollution from their worn-out engines—things so ugly I was paralyzed, things so beautiful I was equally paralyzed.

Before returning to the ashram, we pushed on to Cape Coumarin, the southernmost tip of India, where one can watch the sun rise out of the Bay of Bengal and set into the Arabian Sea. Thousand of pilgrims come here, for it is a holy place. Fifty people will hire an old bus and travel a thousand miles, park as near the tip of land as they can, sleep in the bus, cook their meals out on the sidewalk, watch the sun set and then rise, and go back refreshed, thrilled, and blessed.

On the way back we took a train to Villapuram, enjoying another first-class berth. Berths are assigned only at the last moment by posting a sheet of paper on the outside of the car, so you must go down the row of twenty or more cars that make up the train, hunting for your name posted outside the car. This is India's total inefficiency at work. We arrived at the train only to find no postings. Finally, five minutes before the train was scheduled to depart, a sleepy conductor came along the row of cars, rubbed an overripe banana on the side of each car, and stuck the billing to the sticky residue. We managed to find our berths, though I marveled for one of many times at how India gets anything practical accomplished. The porter forgot to wake us when the train arrived at the Villapuram station at 3 A.M., but some intuition awoke my friend Zakir, and we scrambled off the train just in the nick of time.

The train moved off, leaving us on the siding, and we needed a taxi to take us the final twenty miles to Pondicherry. Eventually we found an old porter asleep in a corner. He was older than I, half my weight, and barefoot. After haggling over the price of carrying the bags, we walked a quarter of a mile, some of it over gravel, to the taxi stand. Another session of bargaining ensued. It is common to start at double the price, and a Westerner can get it down to one and a half times the usual price if he stays with it long enough. By this time, however, the night and the porter and the haggling added to my weariness, and suddenly I didn't care about the price of our taxi ride at all. Instead, I was overwhelmed by a rush of love for India that I could not control. Everything was beautiful, everything was as it should be, and heaven was irretrievably rescued from any geography or time frame. Happiness comes to us in the most unexpected ways. This moment reminded me that if you cannot find heaven here and now you will never find it anywhere else. Perhaps there is love only where there is nothing else.

On the drive to Pondicherry I watched the soft light of day come and wondered to myself what gentle magic abided in this wonderful/terrible place—India!

~

I HAVE SELDOM IN MY LIFE encountered people who seem unwounded psychologically, but I did find such people in traditional India. This astonished me—the directness, the at-easeness, and the lack of guilt. There is a childlike quality in their capacity to ask for what they want in an unself-conscious way. To be so free and uninhibited in Western culture generally means that someone is out of control. In traditional India, after relatedness is established between people, it is just assumed that you will share freely whatever you possess.

I came across a quote from V. S. Naipaul's *A Defect of Vision from India, A Wounded Civilization,* an observation on the Indian temperament as seen by a Western-trained Indian. It is a perceptive appraisal of the childlike quality that I love so much. Though Naipaul counts this as a fault, I am inclined to see it in the perspective of typology. Each specialization in typology costs an individual—or a culture—heavily in the loss of the opposite function.

America pays an enormous price for its high specialization in thinking and sensation. In the United States the telephones work, computers are easily available, the aircraft are safe and reliable. But the opposite faculty of feeling lies in disrepair. India specializes in feeling and intuition and pays a terrible price in its opposite faculties. Love and devotion and a wonderful feeling quality pervade the Indian atmosphere, but poverty is endemic and the physical structure of India is in a state of perpetual emergency.

Naipaul wrote:

> Meditation and stillness can be a form of therapy. But it may be that the true Hindu bliss—the losing of the self—is more easily accessible to Hindus. According to Dr. Sudhir Kakar, a psychotherapist at Jawaharlal Nehru University in New Delhi, who is himself Indian and has practiced both in Europe and in India, the Indian ego is "undeveloped"; the world of magic and animistic ways of thinking lie close to the surface, and the Indian grasp of reality is relatively tenuous. . . . Generally among Indians there seems to be a different relationship to outside reality, compared to one met with in the West. In India, it is closer to a certain stage of childhood when outer objects did not have a separate, independent existence but were intimately related to the self and its affective states. They were not something in their own right, but were good or bad, threatening or rewarding, helpful or cruel, all depending on the person's feelings of the moment.

This "underdeveloped" ego is created by the detailed social organization of Indian life and fits into that life. The mother functions as the external ego of the child for a much longer period than is customary in the West, and many of the ego functions concerned with reality are later transferred from mother to the family and other social institutions. Caste and clan are more than brotherhoods; they define the individual completely. The individual is never on his or her own: one is always fundamentally a member of one's group, with a complex apparatus of rules, rituals, taboos. Every detail of behavior is regulated—the bowels are to be cleared before breakfast and never after; the left hand and not the right is to be used in intimate sexual contact, and so on. Relationships are codified. And religion and religious practices—"magic and animistic ways of thinking"—lock everything into place. The need, then, for individual observation and judgment is reduced; something close to a purely instinctive life becomes possible.

The childlike perception of reality that results does not imply childishness; the life of Mahatma Gandhi proves this point. But it does suggest that Indians are immersed in their experiences in a way that Western people can seldom be. Seemingly, it is less easy for Indians to withdraw and analyze.

The myths of the Western world are filled with woundings of various kinds and heroic attempts to overcome those woundings. There also is a repeated theme of a fall from grace followed by feelings of guilt, as exemplified in our Garden of Eden story. Traditional India seems to be incapable of guilt. I have spent days pondering what it would be like to live without guilt, as it seems as if I was born feeling guilty. Of course, those people of India who are Westernized quickly lose this innocence. Anyone who can speak English in India has, to some extent, already eaten of the Garden of Eden apple and taken on guilt and subsequent neurosis. Undoubtedly, language shapes consciousness to a large degree. It provides a container for our thoughts, and I sometimes wonder if the English language itself, with its dualism and inadequate differentiation of feeling, inherently produces people who are neurotic.

Shankar, my first Indian friend, the young man who spent so much time with me in my early days at the ashram in Pondicherry and who took me to meet his family in tiny Halasangi, became more and more Westernized over the years, and eventually he actually came down with a compulsion neurosis. His is a tragic story, as today he lives on trains. He dashes around India getting off one train and getting on another. He always has some excuse—that he is delivering something or carrying out some errand for someone—but our mutual friends tell me that Shankar buys third-class tickets and sleeps on the hard wooden benches so as to continue to travel. It seems to be a kind of exile that he has put himself into. He adopted as much Westernization as he could and then became caught in a no-man's land between India and the West. His former life was spoiled forever, but he lacked the education and skills to adapt to modern life. At some point he forfeited the traditional Indian beauty and simplicity in his hunger for Western values.

Zakir gradually replaced Shankar as my traveling companion. We began a weekly ritual of traveling ten miles to the beach north of Pondicherry on Sunday mornings to watch the sun rise over the Indian Ocean. One Sunday I decided that I wanted to explore a bit and walked down the beach to a very primitive fishing village. It is a tiny village, perhaps five hundred people, clinging to the very edge of the ocean. This village is thoroughly rooted in the medieval world; it has no electricity, and, except for the fact that the fishing nets are made of nylon instead of coconut fiber, little has changed in a thousand years. Their boats, called catamarans, are made without any metal parts and consist simply of shaped wood sections sewn together with coconut fiber. The name *catamaran* has gone over the entire world now and denotes "double boat" in the Tamil language.

The involuntary fantasy always gripped my mind as I approached the village that this is what would survive if India's attempt to be a modern nation should collapse. Without electricity and fuel oil, the urban parts of India would collapse in a month. Such a collapse is not unlikely, but the small villages, entirely independent of fuel oil or electricity, could survive. Fish from the sea and the generous coconut trees would make a simple living for such a community.

On the way to the village we always went through the early morning traffic of the city streets, out through the suburbs, then through coconut groves and little hamlets, regressing in time a thousand years. We turned off the main road, glad to be rid of the trucks and noisy pollution-spewing vehicles of modern India, and descended the slight incline to the edge of the sea. I returned again and again to this village, and eventually I tried to strike up conversations with the fishermen. My friend Zakir disapproved of this and gave me a stern lecture on how it was not good to consort with low-caste people; apparently it not only lowered my dignity, it also compromised his social position.

I found this to be absurd, so I began hiring my rickshaw driver to take me to the village on my own. Soon the village children would anticipate my arrival and await me in a group of twenty to thirty. Some were scared of me and kept their distance, but others were fascinated to see what they might be able to get out of me. I always took gifts of some kind, such as marbles, balls, or candy. One day they got someone to write a note in English asking if I could please bring a cricket bat. I tracked one down, and it was received with yelps of delight. As my years in India went by, I ceased being a novelty and gradually became part of the scenery for these children. Many of the kids who are now teenagers have known me for most of their lives.

Half of India is under twenty-four years of age, so there are hosts of children everywhere. The coming of age in a fishing village consists of rowing a boat (really only a slightly hollowed-out log) through the surf. A boy may spend months struggling with the surf as he approaches manhood, finally taking his hollowed-out log through the heavy surf. This is a wonderful moment of triumph, for now he may have a wife and adult status and take his place in the village as an adult. How fine to have one's status and position so clearly and specifically defined!

Over time I became friends with one man in the fishing village named Babu, who was destined to become a fisherman like his father. At the time we met, Babu was twenty-eight years old. Each day, Babu would go out in his boat and bring home enough of a catch to earn about five rupees for the day's work. I once spent most of a day with him so I could get a sense of his life, and he even offered to take me out in the sea to set the nets. I examined his dark, leaky boat, felt the uncertain winds gusting against my skin, and decided that it was just too much for me. But I saw him off and waited until he returned from several miles at sea, bringing with him the two ends of a long dragnet, which the whole village then pulled in to the rhythm of chanting. A mile of rope and net is brought near the beach, boys swim out to close off the end of the net, and a wriggling mass of small fish is laid out on the beach. No fish is more than ten inches long, and a few are culled out as poisonous. Since I have always been one to identify with something or someone in trouble, my attention was caught by one small rejected fish wriggling on the sand just within reach of the uprush of each new wave. The fish wriggled an inch closer to the sea with each wave, and I was all but holding my breath at this drama and wishing with ridiculous involvement that the fish would make it to the sea. Just at the last wave, which would have made him sea-borne again, a gull swooped down and carried him off. Nature, fate, chance, destiny— all dissolved into an insoluble whirl in my mind.

At the end of the day, fishermen and the women of the village converged on the silvery pile of small fish on the beach and quickly sorted them into wicker baskets. Bidders arrived from the town, a bargain was struck, and ninety rupees exchanged hands. The sum of ninety rupees for a day's work of twenty men. The logistics are grim.

Once when I visited Babu, he showed me an amulet that he was wearing with terrible seriousness. He explained that the medicine man in the next fishing village north had put a spell on him to kill him. Babu had managed to buy an amulet strong enough to neutralize the spell, but it had cost two hundred rupees.

I watched Babu carefully the next visits and was relieved to find him well. But two weeks later a boy drowned in the surf, and this was construed as being the reflected spell that had been warded away from Babu. I could not find any argument to refute all of this.

One day I received a desperate letter from Babu telling me that the neighboring village—enemies since anybody could remember— had caught him asleep one night on the sand, had broken his leg, and had tried to cut off his foot. The foot could be saved and the bone would heal, but it was a close call. In the meantime, Babu had to sell his boat and net to pay for the doctor's fee.

It seemed doubtful that Babu would ever manage a boat again, at least not for some time, so I was pleased when he suggested another way he could earn a living. He proposed starting a school in the village. Two friends and I agreed to guarantee him fifty scholarships for students at ten rupees per student per month to get the project going. I saw this as a good investment for the village and a way to help Babu, his wife, and two children.

Before leaving to go back to America that year, I went out to visit the school and be honored as the godfather of the project. I was pleased with it all and thought I had brought this emergency to a good solution. But not so. While we were there, two of the boys fainted and fell off their stools! I found out they had not had anything to eat for three days and were too weak to sit. Now what to do? So I worked it out to get one hundred rupees a month to the families of the two boys—enough to keep them in food. But what about the rest of the village? Does the suffering of India have no limits?

The establishment of the school, coupled with my repeated visits, led to a day in which the village bestowed upon me a special honor. The following year I was allowed to witness a ceremony that is generally closed to Western eyes. It was revealed that one of the young men, a twenty-year-old named Ragu, whom I had known since he was the age of ten, was an ecstatic. This meant that, although he was a simple fisherman on most days, on days of religious ceremonies he became an intermediary to the gods.

Ragu had been hidden from me by the villagers for many years for fear that I would not approve of such things. The villagers watched and tested me in many ways before they would allow me so close to their private thoughts and ceremonies. Ragu quite literally lived with a foot in both realms, the earthly world and the Golden World. One of the highlights of his religious duties was a ceremony in which fish hooks were pushed through his flesh and positioned under the muscles and tendons of his back. He was then hitched up to an eight-foot wooden cart filled with a statue of the god and was led through the village pulling this cart. Fortunately, this ritual was performed in July when I was in America. Just hearing a description of it was shocking to me at first. I had seen Ragu with his shirt off while fishing, and there were no large or obvious scars on his back. I asked him directly about this ceremony, and he told me that he felt no pain because he was always in a trance when he spoke to the gods.

The year in which they revealed all of this to me I had hurt my own thigh during a fall, so when I was invited to witness a special ceremony, a puja, Ragu served as my crutch on one side and Babu on the other as we walked from the village to Babu's house. We sat down on the dirt floor.

Babu recited the long incantations and mantras, the god image was washed in coconut milk, oiled, washed with Ganges water, and bedecked with flowers. Ragu was given handfuls of neem leaves to eat. Neem is a bitter, bitter herb that desensitizes one to pain and also apparently has hallucinogenic properties. He stuffed handfuls of leaves in his mouth and managed to swallow them, and in only a few minutes he was entering an altered state. Ragu began to tremble and shake all over, then he started shouting out communications from the gods. Babu asked him to consult the gods on various matters important to the village for that day, and Ragu replied in a high-pitched voice that is the god's speech.

I pressured Babu later to tell me some of the conversation with the gods and only got the information that they had objected to the barbarian foreigner who had such bad manners as to sit on a chair for the puja instead of being in lotus position on the floor. Ragu explained that the foreigner was an uneducated person, and the god replied that I would be forgiven for such a display of vulgarity.

The gods asked that a cube of solidified camphor be put on Ragu's tongue and lighted as a sign of good faith for the uncomprehending foreigner. Babu did this, and I was horrified to see the lighted cube of camphor drawn into Ragu's mouth, making a terrible moment when the light was shining through his white teeth just before the flame disappeared into his mouth.

More conversation ensued that no one would translate for me. This went on for nearly an hour. Babu, serving as representative of the village, would ask for guidance on different things, and Ragu would sputter out an answer. After the ceremony, Ragu had no memory of what had happened. He became a simple fisherman again, a giddy, happy, unself-conscious kid.

I wondered about this display of fishhooks in flesh, camphor burning on the tongue, the bitterness of neem leaves, the loss of ordinary consciousness. Why? What purpose did this serve? To a Westerner it seemed a fantastic but useless display of occult power, at best, or a silly performance at worst. But soon I understood that the triumph of the spirit over flesh was exactly what primitive people need to counterbalance their earthy life. If wholeness is the great goal of human consciousness, then it would easily follow that earthbound people would need as dramatic a triumph of the spirit as they could find. I have been meditating ever since that probably we in the West, more detached from the earthiness of life than any people in history, need "earthing" as desperately as those people needed spiritualizing.

Following this puja, Ragu came to me the next day and wanted some money to make a pilgrimage. India has no concept of vacations; they make a pilgrimage instead and have the most wonderful fun and joy out of the mix of religious ceremony and country fair. All of my Indian friends quickly learned they could have one hundred rupees sometime during my visit to take them on a pilgrimage. Ragu, in asking for pilgrimage money, was the happy, smiling teenager again without a conscious trace of consorting with the gods the day before.

~

THE MAIL SERVICE IN INDIA can be a comedy of errors. I once took several letters to the post office and went through the procedure for getting them mailed. First I asked for postage for them after standing in line. The sleepy young man told me to have them weighed first. Another line, then a sleepy old man weighed them and told me that all but one was eleven rupees, the single one would be seventeen rupees. He had to weigh them all again when I asked which one was the seventeen-rupee one. Back to the first line again to purchase the sixteen stamps necessary for the five letters. Indian stamps have no glue on them, but generally there is a pot of glue on the table in the post office. The ceiling fan was strong enough to blow stamps away, so I had to cover the pile of stamps with one letter while I got enough glue on each stamp to make it stick. But someone had put sand in the glue pot, so it was very hard to get a sticky surface that would adhere to the letter. Add to that, a beggar had slipped past the guard at the doorway and was tugging at my elbow for some coins. Another one turned up and was eagerly waiting for a stamp to fly off in the wind so that he could make off with it. I got the stamps all glued in time but had used so much glue to offset the sand that the letters were sticking to one another. Time helped that. Then I went to a third long line, where the man canceled the stamps before my eyes to make sure that no post office employee would peel the stamps off the letters and resell them for new. Finally all the letters were properly stamped, canceled, and deposited, so I went off to meditate by a lotus pond. The impious thought would not leave my mind whether I ought to meditate on the inscrutable nature of the deity or on Laurel and Hardy.

THE FISHING VILLAGE THAT I VISIT each Sunday has no sense of hygiene, and I cannot consume food or drink from the village without severe danger of a dozen debilitating illnesses. One day I found the exact description of the dilemma of a Westerner and an Indian in this respect: my Indian friend was worrying about the caste of the person who was pouring a drink for me, while I was worrying about whether the water had been boiled or not. Contamination flies under many definitions! I finally found a way out by professing a great liking for a fresh green coconut cut open with a machete so I could drink the sweet milk. I like the tender meat also, but the machete they dig it out with has been on the ground only a moment before and is dirty with enough contamination to undo any Westerner. The villagers are often sick from typhoid, dysentery, and every amoeba, worm, and parasite known to humanity. So I profess no liking for the soft coconut meat, sometimes affectionately known as tropical ice cream.

⁓

ON EACH OF MY TRIPS to India I would take a Polaroid camera along in my suitcase. The villagers had great fun when I took a picture of them and handed it over while it was still developing. They would look at it, turn it over, hold it with excitement, and then burst out with shouts of joy as their picture gradually appeared. One old man was quite amazed when I showed him a photo and took great joy showing it to other members of his family. Then, after much chattering, I realized that he thought the photo was of someone else. The other family members were pointing at the photo and then at him; he shook his head vigorously in disbelief. He knew it was a photo of a man, but certainly not of him! I realized that he had probably never seen his own face clearly before. One year I thought it would be interesting to show my friends in the fishing village pictures of my house, some of the sights in San Diego, and shots of the Grand Canyon, but I was surprised to find that they had no interest in this. It could have been pictures of the surface of Mars, so far removed was my American life from their reality. Their only real interest was in seeing pictures of themselves.

⁓

ONE MORNING I ATE BREAKFAST before dawn and quietly made my way to the main gate of the ashram. It was two days before Christmas, a holiday that traditionally left me depressed at home but that was a happy day in India. My plan was to bicycle the length of the esplanade and watch the sun rise from the ocean before breakfast. However, when I reached the ashram's big iron gate, I found it closed and the padlock hanging in the center—locked, bolted, and unrelenting. It was unheard of for the main gate to be locked. I quickly went around the corner to a little gate that was only one person wide. "What happened?" No one knew; the order to lock the gate had been sent by a runner.

Feeling safer inside than out, I stayed in my room that day and tried to keep the darkness of India from creeping into me. India, the land of the tenderest love and devotion and gentleness in its character, becomes a horrifying demon when it chooses to rage and rush down the street in its dark mood. Sometime later I heard that the beloved governor general of Tamil Nadu (the state that contains Pondicherry) had died that morning and such a huge wave of remorse and loss had swept through the state that bands of young men appeared from nowhere to patrol the streets and to see that no one moved, no gate was opened, no business was conducted until the funeral was over. A year earlier the governor general had been desperately ill, and thirty young men had sat in a ring in the central park of Madras, poured gasoline on themselves, and set themselves afire in order to release their vital energy for the governor's healing. He had recovered; how could the gods have chosen otherwise after such an offering? But this morning he had died suddenly, and the only language left for Tamil Nadu was to set the whole state into silence even if that silence was manifested by gangs going through all the cities and towns breaking anything that was not tightly closed. A bus en route to Madras from Pondicherry was overturned and burned. Even the international airport at Madras was closed. The Catholic churches were closed, and I wondered what hierarchy of forces could silence a Catholic church the day before Christmas. Not a restaurant was open, not a shop, not so much as a front door was unbolted. A tacit understanding allowed one to walk on the street but not bicycle. By some strange power of hierarchy, the ashram dining hall remained open or it would have been a hungry two days. Christmas was, in effect, canceled.

A cremation took place the day after Christmas, and arrangements were made that buses and other forms of transportation were allowed in the direction of Madras for the cremation. A hundred thousand people made their way there, and it was a profound occasion of state. Christmas Day came and went with the streets characterized by the great locks grimly pronouncing silence.

～

I MADE NUMEROUS TRIPS beyond Pondicherry over the years—to Kashmir, Benares, Khajuraho, and other places. I loved Benares, and I think that if one could go to only one place in India, that should be the place, as it is truly a holy city. Hindus travel to Benares to die, and the smell of cremations in continually in the air. This sounds depressing, but I would sit peacefully by the holy Ganges River there for days at a time, and it was as if time had stopped.

One day I was inspired to travel to Calcutta, which is about one thousand miles north of Pondicherry. Despite my love for India, I can honestly report that Calcutta is the worst city in the world, filled with more poverty and desperation than any place I have ever visited. There are more than fifteen million people living there, with no sewage system and mile upon mile of filth and disease-ridden streets.

I had an Indian friend whose father lived on the outskirts of Calcutta, so I suggested that he go visit his father while I stayed on in the city to explore its sights on my own. By this time I had been coming to India for more than a decade, and I believed that I could handle anything that might occur and take good care of myself. So, after seeing my friend off at the Calcutta train station, I took a taxi to an old Indian hotel in the center of the city. My friend had recommended it, but after checking in I found that the room was a nightmare. The walls were paper thin, and it sounded like someone was dying on one side, while two people were fighting on the other side, shouting at each other in a language that I could not decipher. A loudspeaker located just below my window was broadcasting some political propaganda at top volume. Ordinarily I can hole up in a room and be content for a few days, but this setting seemed intolerable, so I decided to venture out on the street and search for more inviting accommodations.

I was in the oldest part of Calcutta, a location where one literally steps over corpses on the street. I had heard of this but never had seen it before in all my visits to India. Only in Benares, the holy city where Hindus go to die, had I seen such a public display of death, but there the corpses are cremated and received through religious ceremony. I managed to find a rickshaw driver to pull me around, but I had no luck in finding another hotel. Each street that we turned down seemed to be worse than the last, until I became inundated with the darkness and the agony of India. It became more than I could cope with, so I got out of the rickshaw to walk for a while. In the next block, a woman dressed in filthy, tattered clothes pushed a dead baby into my arms while begging for money. Next I encountered small children poking me with amputated arms and withered legs. I could not find a building that looked safe, and I began to lose my composure. I was one thousand miles from anyone I knew and felt myself falling into an abyss. It was worse than a panic attack; it was as if I had wandered into some corner of hell.

My courage was overtaxed. Calcutta wouldn't stop pounding on my senses. The Hindu name *Calcut* means "Kali's city," home of the female deity of destruction whose image is depicted in the most horrible ways imaginable. She often is portrayed with eighteen arms, each holding something revolting such as a skull or human entrails, each detail more horrible than the previous one. The city of Kali was living up to its name. When I was in the hospital as a boy, I had learned the point at which I would pass out from pain, but there was no comparable experience psychologically; it seemed as if I just kept falling down deeper and deeper into a dark spiral.

Then I remembered that there was something to do. I had once been told by a friend that in India you have the right to approach a stranger and ask that person to be the incarnation of God. It is a startling custom in Indian religious life where one may approach another person—man, woman, old, young, known, unknown—and ask that person such a profoundly religious question. This person may refuse the request, but generally it is considered a sacred duty to accept the role if he or she possibly can because it is an honor and such a profound experience. From that time on, the adored person will be treated like God and will be revered as if God were present in the form of that person. Strict rules apply for the protection of both persons concerned, and one may not make friends or a casual companion of this bhakti master. Only worship and reverence are appropriate in such a relationship; you must not ask for anything else from the person but that he or she serves as the incarnation of God for you.

Luckily, I had tucked away my knowledge of this custom somewhere in the back of my brain. I could see trees off in the distance, and I walked several more blocks until I reached a tiny park. Then I began desperately looking for someone I could approach and ask to be my incarnation of God. I spotted a middle-aged man; he was dressed in Indian fashion and was barefoot, but he had an air of dignity and calmness. I am amazed now at my boldness, but I was driven by desperation. I approached him.

"Sir, do you speak English?"

"Yes."

"Would you be the incarnation of God for me?"

"Yes," he replied, without losing his dignity at my extraordinary request.

It is a staggering thought that he would understand and accept this; all I had to do was ask the question. He pointed me to a bench, and for the next twenty minutes I poured out my woes, telling him who I was and how Calcutta had worn me down, that I felt as if I would soon disintegrate. He said not a word but listened patiently to me. I continued to lay out this burden that was too much for me to experience by myself, and gradually I began to feel calmer. It was as if the burden was halved in sharing it with him, and half of it I could cope with. He really didn't have to say a word, just listen to me, and that is what he did. Eventually I regained my wits; I wasn't happy, but I could function again. As soon as I could, I thanked him, at which point he stood up and bowed. I was afraid he was about to walk off and remain a total stranger forever, so I blurted out, "Please tell me something about yourself—who are you?"

He told me his name, which I cannot now recall. It was unpronounceable to me.

"Yes, thank you," I said, "but who are you in life, what is your work?"

"I am a Roman Catholic priest," he replied, plainly and directly.

I was speechless. Amid millions of people swarming in Calcutta I had tapped a Catholic priest on the shoulder and asked if he would be the incarnation of God for me. There are not that many Catholics in Calcutta and very few priests, yet I had somehow picked him out to hear my confession. Now I had nothing more to say. I thanked him and bowed, and he bowed back with quiet dignity, then he turned and walked away. I have never forgotten that man, and I suspect that he never forgot me.

I have often wondered if such an attitude—asking someone to be the incarnation of God—would answer the perplexing Western dilemma when one makes more of another person by way of romantic love than either can endure or bring into everyday relationship. Perhaps we Westerners have come into the presence of God and have only personal attitudes and concepts to use in this numinous experience. We could learn from India how to relate to the godhead of another human being instead of confusing such feelings with romance.

After this lifesaving encounter, I went back to my Calcutta hotel and ate a meal. My friend returned three days later, and he was very worried about me. I told him I had some difficulties but I was back on my feet again. So we traveled together back to Pondicherry.

⌣

BY ONE OF THE SLENDER THREADS that seem to take my life where I belong, during one of my visits to India I met a wonderful old Indian Brahmin poet. He is a Bengali named Simanta Chatterjee, and we became acquainted under a banyan tree, where so many important things have happened in Indian history. Our friendship began in the usual Indian way, with many long spaces and silences. He hid his true nature from me for more than a year but finally began showing me his poet side and extreme sensibility and refinement of thought.

Simanta was born in Calcutta into a famous Brahmin family, and he spent his childhood in the famous school founded by India's Nobel laureate, Rabindranath Tagore. Simanta lived through World War II and Indian independence. The partitioning of India and division into Hindu and Muslim states, the terrible migrations of displaced Hindus from East Pakistan, the revolt of the eastern section of Pakistan with the formation of Bangladesh—he has seen all of this in one lifetime. I contrasted this with my own life span: an only child, a broken family, hospital experiences in childhood, the Depression years, being a spectator of World War II, attending an American university, studying in Zurich, my struggle to find a place in the American way of life, my books, and then my discovery of India. Yet, despite such different sets of circumstance, we found that we had very much in common.

When I first met him, Simanta had two physical characteristics that contrasted vividly with his noble, graceful Brahmin form: two large tufts of straight black hair growing out of his ears, and a bandaged toe, which added a Huckleberry Finn touch to his regal nature.

When he finally trusted me with his innermost thoughts, Simanta gave forth a flood of his inner world. "Nobody has ever listened to me before!" he exclaimed. I often felt like a barbarian in his presence, but he needed a sensitive ear and that very need produced it in me.

One of his stories was particularly touching to me. When he was a small boy he had crossed the bridge over the Ganges River at Calcutta and had witnessed a scene at the end of the bridge that had haunted him ever since. A beggar, probably near the end of his life by starvation, had a morsel of food in his hand when another equally desperate soul swooped down on him, took the food from him, and left the beggar in a heap of despair. Sri Chatterjee was just at the age to comprehend the terror and despair of life, and he began to cry. There were two days of tears outwardly, then the tears went inside. He explained that he had been crying for the sixty years since, and he then looked directly at me and asked if I knew of anything to stop tears like that.

I told him that I knew no magic to stop the suffering of life, but now at least two people bore that burden and he no longer had to carry the solitary weight.

The highest of the castes in India are the Brahmins, the teachers and priests. Traditionally the Brahmins had little to do with society other than these two tasks. They were given many privileges so that they might put their whole attention on their teaching and priestly duties. Brahmins tend to be very light skinned and easily can be mistaken for Italian or Greek in feature. At one time they were honored and supported financially, but that is breaking down in modern India. Although superbly educated in Rabindranath Tagore's school and a gifted poet and writer, Simanta is entirely without any form of income in modern India. I have taken on the task of supporting him so that he can continue the noble, but impecunious, task of teaching. I have learned so much from him that it would not be possible to recompense him with any fee for what he does for me. He refuses any money for his services as part of his way of living, but asks for funds when he has some need. One day Simanta asked for some money for his rent.

"How much do you need?"

"Oh, I don't know; my landlady says I owe her quite a bit for the past year."

"Well, how much is your rent, and when did you pay it last?"

"My landlady never set an amount for the rent, and I paid her one thousand rupees sometime last year. She says I owe her some more now."

"Well, would one thousand rupees bring things up to something like a workable point?"

"I don't know, but we could try."

A thousand rupees changed hands, and the muddle subsided for a time. Simanta is one of the truly happy people I know.

Simanta taught me much of what I understand about India's history and philosophies. For example, India does not sharply separate ego and shadow as our Western culture does. India does not bar unpleasant human traits and experiences from everyday sight. There are no asylums, few hospitals as we are used to them, and almost no orphanages, and life in all its extremes washes over one every day. The shadow is represented in every corpse one passes on the street, every madman (they are considered to be possessed by God) who comes by, every gigantic hole that trips one up in the street while walking at night. Simanta has all of this ingrained into his basic character, and it shows in every cadence of his voice and gesture of his slender body.

Since he grew up under British rule, Simanta holds a strange mixture of resentment toward and idolization of the English language. India is so caste conscious that ambivalence toward anything British extends to language and a hundred other aspects of Indian life. Simanta has an insatiable hunger to be published in English, since this has been the symbol of success all of his life.

One day I asked Simanta if he had any needs that I could help with. His reply has set me to wondering ever since: "If I began thinking about needs, I would sink immediately to the bottom of the world. If I don't think, I get what I need." Is this true only for a Hindu living the life of a high-caste Brahmin with friends and devotees who love him, or might it apply to each and every one of us?

Simanta tried to teach me about his old world of Sanskrit scholarship, and often he waxed eloquent on some minute detail of Vedic philosophy, but on one occasion he launched off into a two-hour tale of the creation of the world. What an incredibly intricate story! It covered a thousand kalpas of years (one kalpa is a number with more zeros after it than I can comprehend). I can retell one small detail of the story.

"Lord Brahma caught the celestial overflow of Lord Vishnu's nightmare and began sweating profusely with the agitation of it. Though he tried to control his passion, he broke out into a most undignified sweat. The perspiration accumulated and suddenly coagulated into Lord Kama, the god of passion. This god is much like our Western Greek god, Eros. He carries a bow and arrows that inflict the madness of love upon every victim. It is right that the god who is the accumulation of Lord Brahma's passion should be the carrier of this quality. Lord Kama (you may read about his ways in any New Age bookshop anywhere in the world in the form of the Kama Sutra) takes a vivid place in the long story but that is not our subject in this brief telling. It is the fact that Lord Kama became so strong and was such a tyrant that all the other gods and goddesses quickly came to fear him, for none were immune to his arrows.

While they still had sufficient collective power to join together against this tyrant god (a few more days and they could not have withstood him even in their combined form), they banded together and lent Lord Shiva, the god of destruction, enough power so that with one mighty effort he incinerated Lord Kama with the glance of destruction, which has made the world tremble many times since. Lord Kama was gone, and in his place a light rain of the essence of love drifted down on the world to its great benefit.

"But the story may not end so gracefully as this. Mrs. Kama sued the gods for justice and put forth her claim that she had the right to bear children and could have them by none other than her lawful husband. The gods agreed this was a correct reading of the law, and they saw that something must be done in the name of justice. So they settled on the expediency of bringing back just enough of Lord Kama to perform his husbandly duties. His genitals were recreated, and this is why mankind ever since has been able to exercise reason and proportion in most aspects of life but Lord Kama still rules our sexual nature."

～

ONE DAY I MET an old snake charmer, younger than I but seemingly ancient. We have made a kind of relationship that would be possible only in India. He is a master of his art and can cast a spell over an audience with his two cobras and a mongoose. He flutes them up out of their baskets with his droning double flute and makes a dance that is equal parts horror and intrigue. He is a little man, standing only about as high as my third rib, but he carries a wonderful power in his art. I first visited him when his magic circle contained the two cobras, the mongoose, and his four-year-old son—all sitting in a divine/demonic grouping. I think I was most deeply touched by the absolute faith of the boy in his father's strength and safety. I basked in this trust and security for two years, often thinking of that wonderful scene. But one year when I returned, the old man came running to me when he saw me at a distance, put his arms around me, and wept. Finally he could tell me his distress: a new cobra had bitten and killed his son! We cried in each other's arms for a time and then parted to that bleak world of loneliness that takes over when one faces something that cannot be borne. Next year, there was no snake charmer to be found. I inquired and finally discovered that he was in the hospital with a damaged esophagus resulting from a magic trick that involved swallowing three golf-ball-sized rough stones and producing them again ten minutes later.

On a return visit I approached the banyan tree, site of so many excursions into the wonderful/terrible world of the snake charmer, with dread. What would I find? Wonderful! There was the old man with a big cobra, a mongoose, and an audience of foreigners in rapt admiration of his hypnotizing flute music. The cobra was swaying and the tethered mongoose cowering in apprehension at every movement of the cobra. A young girl was in attendance this time. The old man dropped his flute, came to shake my hand and apologize for being busy, and returned to his spell. When he was finished we had a great embrace, my six-foot-three frame and his four-foot-ten frame wrapping each other up in a wonderful reunion, and some order was restored in an inner corner of my being.

⁓

MANY LETTERS ARE PUT in my hands when I arrive in India each year. I reproduce two of them. They were created by professional letter writers who charge ten rupees for their translations and follow the forms of nineteenth-century English letter-writing manuals. One is from Arusakumar, the coconut vendor, and the other is from Ravi, a polio-stricken young man whom I have subsidized for several years. They are self-explanatory and are eloquent expressions of the suffering and tragedy of my beloved/terrifying India.

Pondicherry, India. 30,12,94
    Dear and respected Robert, Sir:
    Whereas, we are having one grievance, that we are residing in another's house and the landlord is now urging us

to vacate the premises. There is a house for sale nearby our present residence and we are intending to purchase the same, for which we need financial assistance from your kindself to the extent of seven thousand rupees.

The present house owner is now and then demanding to vacate the house and thereby disregarding us in public place amidst the neighbors. Hence, I could not know how to reply you as and when you are asking to come over to my residence for a visit.

My business is also not fair for the last six months.

My daughter is studying well with your grace.

In this context, I make this humble request that I may please be granted in one time the entire financial assistance of two years, which you now award to my daughter's education every month, and thereby enable me to purchase the above house for our dwelling purpose please Sir.

We have not asked for such bulk assistance in the past, but we are badly in need of money and we seek this assistance from your goodself.

Once again we appeal you Sir that we may please be extended this timely monetary help please, for which we shall be indebted until the end of our life time.

With best wishes and regards,

Yours affectionately

Arusakumar

Pondicherry, India. 24,12,94

My dear and affectionate elder Brother:

I, your grateful Ravi do write this letter.

My sincere salutations to you.

Be in good health and full of spirit with the Grace of the Lord.

Beloved brother, I am pulling out my life very hardly carrying huge loan burden. Brother, I took loan at the interest rate of fifty percent per year. I am paying four hundred rupees toward interest alone every month. I am peaceless in my life, which results in my ill health.

Your kindself has been pleased to give me two hundred and fifty rupees per month. If I am paid four thousand rupees at one time I shall be settling off three-fourths of my loan burden and having a peaceful life.

I assured the money lenders to discharge the loan this month (December 1994), if I will default, I will have to face great humiliation before them and run way out of my village.

I am deeply regretting for hurting your smooth heart frequently. Brother, there is no calm in my life even after my marriage.

We are leading a miserable life without any harmony in our life and our life is in unrest. My wife is threatening me now that she will end her life if I fail to discharge the loans due in the short future.

Please do extend this help as a last one and do save my life. I am once again beseeching your mercy to grant this timely assistance, for which I shall ever remain thankful to you Sir.

I am anxiously looking forward your fruitful reply Please Brother.

I shall not forget your so-far helps till my last breath.

I am praying the Almighty for providing you a healthy and wealthy life for ever.

Very affectionately yours,
    Ravi

~

IN ADDITION TO SIMANTA CHATTERJEE, a second Brahmin friend of mine in India is a priest at the temple of Chidambarram, fifty miles south of Pondicherry. He is a priest born into the temple, the son, grandson, great-grandson, great-great grandson of temple priests, and until he came to visit me several years ago in Pondicherry he had never set foot out of the temple grounds in his life. He is in his late twenties, married with a son and daughter, and he lives in a small ancient apartment within the temple grounds. He also is one of the happiest people I have ever known; he sings when he speaks his very limited English and dances more than walks when he moves. His priestly forebears have been doing the fire dance ceremonies for the Lord Nataraja, the dancing incarnation of Shiva, for longer than my mind can comprehend. Their lineage goes back into the ancient world. His name is Sundaramoorthydeekshitar. He knows little of the world but bases his entire life on the fire dance every evening at dusk. A hundred candles and lamps and as many bells are used in the dance of joy before the Lord Nataraja. I warn my visiting friends to come equipped with ear plugs, as all the priests who do the bell ringing are deaf from their occupation.

After several visits, Sundaramoorthy asked permission to take me and my friends into the sanctuary for the fire ceremony—on the condition that we wore no clothing above the waist or on our feet. Taking part in that ancient fire dance is one of the most profound religious experiences that India affords me, but it is Sundaramoorthy's happiness and unwoundedness that touches me most deeply. If one asked for an example of a well-educated, intelligent human being who has not been wounded by the modern illness of self-consciousness, one could not do better. He is a living embodiment of the proverb from a Hindu saint: "The highest form of worship is simply to be happy."

I HAVE MENTIONED MY PROBLEMS coming to terms with the caste system in India. In addition to the four primary castes, there is one group that exists outside caste, and that is the shame of India—the untouchables. An untouchable is not considered a human being and is usually treated little better than an animal. He or she is thought to be without a soul, the distinguishing characteristic of humanness.

I can name one untouchable whom I know reasonably well—me. Any foreigner is an untouchable and does not have the rights of any caste. My Indian friends give me honorary caste and sometimes put the proper identification on my forehead so that I can hold my head up in public. But I am an untouchable most of the time.

Despite the fact that I am an untouchable, there is one mitigating quality that makes life workable for me in India; I have a deep pocketbook. This goes far to make life bearable in a land where an untouchable has a miserable life. Mahatma Gandhi tried to raise the status of untouchables by referring to them as Harridans (children of God), but attitudes change ever so slowly.

⁓

DURING MY LAST VISIT to India in 1995, I had a strange but happy dream.

I have just joined a group of people who are having a contest to see who can bring up the first or largest fish from the ocean. I have come late and have only the shortest fishing pole. But I get the first fish, a big thick tuna that I fear will break the line or the pole. This is complicated by the fact that two young women are in the water trying to help me get the fish landed; but they are only adding their weight to the already overtaxed line and pole. Everything holds, and, by huge effort, I reel in the fish plus the two maidens and get them all safely on shore. There is much jubilation and festive celebration over all of this. End of dream.

I ponder this dream and wonder what on earth I have gotten hold of. Perhaps one of the greatest jokes of my life is that I first went to India to be spiritualized, and I came home humanized. I can end my description of India only with a saying that is offered by a host welcoming a guest into his or her house: "Will you honor my humble abode with the dust from your noble feet?"

15

Circle of Friends:

Lessons of the Transposed Heads

The wonderful Danish writer Isak Dinesen once suggested that there are three occasions for happiness in human life: when there is an excess of energy; during the cessation of pain; and when we possess the absolute certainty that we are doing the will of God. The first of these belongs mostly to youth, and the second is, by definition, brief. The third, however, is open to anyone at any and all times. To possess the absolute certainty that one is doing the will of God requires coming into relationship with the slender threads.

It puzzled me for many years that so many of the poorest of the poor whom I made friends with in India were happy when there seemed to be so little for them to be happy about. Over the years I learned that these people were in touch with a kind of happiness that is beyond the vagaries of fortune or possession. The will of God is theirs for the simple coin of faith, and nothing can take that away from even the lowliest beggar. No horror of the leper or despair of the abandoned can defeat the certainty that one is somehow carrying out the will of God, and, remarkably, this balm is still available to us all.

My whole life has been an attempt to find and follow the will of God, and at the same time it has been a passage into solitude; my sense is that, for me, the two have been inseparable. At some level I understood that this was my destiny from a very early age, but another part of me made a desperate rebellion against the solitude and thus set up the basic conflict of my life. When I was alone, I could not bear the loneliness of it. When I was with someone, a voice was constantly whispering in my ear that I ought to be alone.

Only in recent years have I reached a new capacity. Now I can be alone for long stretches of time and yet not be inspired to do anything to remove the aloneness; I can stand the solitude of being with God. What a strange and marvelous goal to reach! Why does it take so many years to learn something so simple? In a similar way, I can enjoy companionship with my friends or even lecture and take part in large communities without having it spoiled by the insistent voice in me gathering me off into my solitude.

I am repelled by most of what I have read or heard on the subject of serving God, but one passage has stayed with me as a quiet solace: Thomas Merton once wrote that any man who is obliged to bear the solitude of God should not be asked to do much else in life. He implied that it was so difficult a job that the true servant of God often has little energy or strength for anything else. Maybe this is slightly overblown, but in general I agree, and Merton's suggestion seems to be borne out in my life. Each of us seems to have different degrees of the Golden World available to us, but I know that we all must have at least a taste of it.

I have learned to accept the necessity of solitude, but that does not impair my friendships. It was, once again, a dream that told me the next progression of my life. Soon after my last trip to India I had an extraordinary dream:

A few friends of mine, perhaps a dozen, are on the top of a great mountain. We are standing at the pinnacle of the highest peak in sight, far above timberline. It is exceedingly, breathtakingly beautiful. The air is clear, the sunshine bright and golden, and the vista is breathtaking. You can look around for 360 degrees and see snow-covered peaks on every side. The entire scene is thrilling, exhilarating, magnificent.

My friends and I are all awestruck by this setting, when, to my astonishment, I notice that all the mountains in sight, with the exception of the one we are standing on, are melting. Like burning candles, they are gradually losing their shape, becoming liquid, and draining back down into the sea. Despite my recognition of this, I am still inordinately happy. I possess the knowledge that the mountain on which we stand is also going to melt and dissolve away quite soon. But I also know with absolute certainty, as if I have heard the voice of God, that everything is exactly as it should be.

No words are spoken in my dream, but a thought comes to me: "There is one act of volition remaining in your life, and only one. You may do it or not do it, as you wish."

I immediately know that this action is the will of God, and so I must do it. The final action is to draw my friends together in a small circle, put our arms around one another's shoulders, and lean inward so that our heads make a slightly smaller circle. I must make this circle as perfectly symmetric as possible. We joyfully form the circle and stand there together waiting for the melting of our mountain, but I am not frightened; I am absolutely joyous. The dream ends with our circle waiting for the mountain to dissolve away, as it is the end of the world.

Like all dreams, this one has apparent meaning and yet also is mysterious and puzzling. Often dreams fail to tell us on what level they are pertinent. They may be foretelling an outer event, or they may be describing an interior psychic event. The situation depicted in the dream also may be general in nature, such as a comment on society or on the time in which we live. The time dimension in dreams is maddeningly imprecise. Our dreams do not follow linear clock time, so I must ask myself: Is this event something that has happened, that is about to happen, or that is a prediction of something far off in the future?

Once when I lectured with the great Jungian analyst Marie-Louise von Franz many years ago, she spoke about death dreams, and that is what I believe visited me here. One of the characteristics of an impending death is the perfection of the dream, when everything is just right, or some perfect order has been established. Often this is an indication that the dreamer is near the end of earthly life, as though the dream is saying there is no longer a need to stay around because the work is done. This dream is obviously about the end of *a* world, though I don't believe that it means the planet Earth is about to melt. I have no intention of making a placard and going out on a street corner to shout, "Repent, the world is coming to an end!" There are people who do exactly that in response to a dream or vision, but I feel that this would be interpreting the dream on the wrong level. I presume this dream means one of two things. It could be a simple message announcing my physical death. I am in good health and nothing is apparently wrong with me, but I am already one year older than the average life span of the American male, so I have surpassed the statistical average. Or, could it mean the end of an era in my life, a change in direction or vocation?

Carl Jung once wrote that we should accomplish our death, a statement that has great meaning for me. I recently overheard a conversation in which a woman who was dying was listing all the things she and her husband were going to do as soon as she got out of that hospital bed. "We will go sailing, and then we will take that trip to the Bahamas that we always dreamed about," she said, going on with many other things that had remained unlived up to that point. This woman actually died in the middle of a sentence like this. I was greatly saddened by this death because it revealed so much unfinished business in the woman's life. My ideal is to die in a state of equilibrium, a point where there is nothing churning in me or demanding attention, no unfinished business.

The Hindus say that it is unfinished business that leads to reincarnation. Although I don't entirely subscribe to the idea of reincarnation, I do believe that unlived life is a terrible burden that our children inherit. Many people end up saddled with the unlived lives of their parents, trying to make up for all the things their parents never did. Ideally, all of the contents of our interior being should either be experienced or sacrificed by the time of our death; this is what it means to accomplish our death. Of course, none of us can experience all of our potential, but we can draw energy out of the unlived aspects of our being.

I regret the general attitude in our society that we should keep our lives completely full—forever thinking up new horizons—right up to the end. I don't think that is what old age is for. In the collective American consciousness we are taught to cling to youthfulness, warding off gray hair and wrinkles. An unlived portion of life can be sacrificed—that is, transformed by making it sacred. For example, if I harbored an unfulfilled wish to be an Olympic runner, that wish clearly could not be fulfilled in my life. But by working consciously with that desire, I could at least rechannel the energy into something possible to me. I would start by recognizing the fact that my dream of being a great runner has never and will never be fulfilled. Then I would allow a period of time to grieve the loss. Then, and this is the key, I would create some ritual to mark the passing of this unlived potential.

Here is another example. Some time ago I found a silly resentment in me concerning the fact that most of my friends had been to Hawaii and I had never been there. Whenever someone talked about a trip to Hawaii, I felt that I had missed out on something desirable. Of course, I had been to India and other places much more exotic than Hawaii, but still this somehow bothered me. A couple of years after becoming conscious of this wish, I accepted a lecturing trip to Hawaii and got it out of my system. But suppose that lecture opportunity had not presented itself? I could still have created a meaningful ritual to sacrifice this unlived potential. A psychological response would have been to use active imagination to explore what this Hawaii issue was really about for me—to confront my own unconscious wish.

Sacrifice is an important concept for anyone interested in leading a religious life, but most people today seems to think that sacrifice means giving something up, such as giving up candy at Lent. This is how shallow our religious sense has become. Sacrifice really involves the art of drawing energy from one level and reinvesting it at another level to produce a higher form of consciousness.

Human existence seems to be for the express purpose of advancing consciousness. We do this by building up one level of consciousness and then sacrificing it to a higher level of consciousness. In time we master that new level of consciousness and then we must in turn sacrifice it to a still higher level. All of us have the experience of being confronted with something that simply will not work with our familiar way of doing things. The innocent consciousness of the child must eventually give way to adult consciousness. A young person at the age of twenty-one must step into his or her own life; this person is no longer a teenager who can properly live in his or her parents' house and let them do the laundry. The energy invested in an old way of being must be pulled out of the old pattern and reinvested in a new pattern.

We go through several distinct passages like this. Each of us must sacrifice childhood to enter adolescence, then adolescence must be sacrificed for early adulthood; in the marriage vows two people must sacrifice their individual desires for a new, higher purpose—the marriage; and parents must in many ways sacrifice their selfish desires in order to serve the needs of their children. Women experience a major transition at menopause, and if they can consciously realize this change as a sacrifice performed in a sacred manner, they gain a new maturity and a higher form of consciousness. The same applies to men: if they can get through a midlife crisis by sacrificing their youth in a meaningful way, then they can go on to a rich old age, but if they cannot make this sacrifice properly, then you will find instead an aging adolescent driving a sports car and chasing after his youth. Few things are more pathetic.

Sacrifice is an interior event, but it seems to be greatly aided by external ceremonies. The ancients would take their best ox and cut its throat to mark a sacrifice, or they would kill a goat or a bird. I abhor the killing of animals, but I understand why ceremony is such an important aspect of sacrifice. Today we have available to us other ways of accomplishing the same thing. It is possible and necessary to create our own meaningful rituals and ceremonies. I often prescribe this for people who have lost touch with traditional religious teachings: make up your own ceremony. "What shall I do?" they ask, and I say that it will be fresh and powerful if it comes directly from your own psyche. I've seen people discover or invent profoundly meaningful rituals to help carry them through a needed sacrifice.

One of the finest ceremonies I have observed came from a young friend of mine. This fellow had a dream that he was at a Saturday night party where everything was going wrong. The food was inedible, no one would talk to him, and he was feeling absolutely miserable. We talked this dream over, and he went home and worked on it. He came back the next week and said he realized that Saturday night consciousness had died for him, by which he meant the American ideal of Saturday night as the time to party, get drunk, and have mindless fun with the gang. Usually this Saturday night syndrome is not as much fun as it is said to be, but I watch most young people trying to wring some personal satisfaction out of it anyway. People know they have a God-given right to some feelings of ecstasy, so they are driven to more and more excessive behaviors to get that Saturday night high. The very word *Saturday* comes to us from the Latin *saturnalia,* which means an occasion of unrestrained or orgiastic revelry, and the festival of the god Saturn, a Dionysian deity, was celebrated with feasting in ancient Rome.

My friend researched all of this and decided that a sacrifice was called for; he decided to sacrifice the Saturday night syndrome. He hunted around his house for something that would represent this syndrome and decided to go out and buy a Big Mac hamburger. He then took a shovel, went out to the backyard, and buried this symbol of the "fast life" and instant gratification. He did this ceremony with great seriousness to mark a change in his lifestyle. Saturday night was never quite the same for this young man again. He was able to reinvest the energy that had been tied up in the old pattern and thereby move on to the next level of consciousness. This was a wonderfully creative, meaningful, tailor-made ritual not found in any book.

It is in a similar fashion that we should approach those unlived aspects of our life before death. That which is unlived should be examined, made conscious, and then transformed.

Learning the value of meaningful sacrifice is not the same as denying pleasure or practicing asceticism. There is a wonderful saying from the Judaic tradition suggesting that every legitimate joy you deny yourself on earth will be denied you in heaven. This speaks to the false spirituality of asceticism. Trading in one thing to get something better is not a spiritual act at all; in fact, it is highly egocentric. You shouldn't make a sacrifice in hopes of getting something back from God. I see many people who pray to God to make things go the way they like or who tithe to a church to achieve social standing or some other worldly goal. This is not sacrifice at all. Properly, a sacrifice should be suffered simply because it is necessary for the transformation of consciousness—to get beyond the wishes of your ego, not to satisfy those wishes in some backhanded way.

So, getting back to my dream of the circle of friends, it may be suggesting the death of an old perspective or a form of consciousness. The circle may indicate a meaningful ritual for marking this transformation.

I recently had another dream that seems to speak to the same issue. Here is the dream:

> I sit down at my desk to write. I am using a fountain pen, and I discover that the pen no longer uses ink but instead is filled with water.

Taken together, these two dreams could be suggesting the end of my writing career, or, alternatively, they could suggest that my work should be performed with no trace—that is to say, without any ego involvement. This is a primary goal in the Buddhist tradition—to carry out worldly acts with total presence, appreciating the fullness of each moment, acting with "no trace" and without asking "what's in it for me?" Most of the great religious works of art, including the cathedrals, the stained glass, the illuminated manuscripts, were never signed by their creators. Probably both ways of viewing the dream are true.

In the Western tradition there is a delightful medieval story called "M'Lady and the Tumbler" that is instructive.

There once was a monastery that was famous throughout the land for its beautiful tapestries, its fine illuminated manuscripts, its paintings, its weavings, its choir, and its philosophical writings. Everyone who lived at this monastery was expert in some high art, except for one little fellow. This monk felt terribly inadequate because he couldn't do anything with such high art. This feeling went so deep in him that finally one day he said to himself, "I will give to M'Lady, the holy Virgin Mary, what I can, for that is all I have." He had been a circus performer before coming to the monastery, and he was a tumbler.

Several days later, when all the other monks were up in the chapel participating in the high mass, the little monk went down into the crypt. He was such a nobody in the monastery that no one ever missed him or knew where he was. He found himself entirely alone in the crypt and began to perform his circus tumbling act before the statue of the Virgin.

This went on for some time, until one day another monk came down to the crypt to fetch candles and witnessed this strange scene. He was scandalized and immediately ran to the abbot. "Your Holiness, do you know what is going on in the crypt during high mass?" The abbot had some perception, and he told the monk that they would meet the following day and go down to the crypt to witness this scene.

The next day during the high mass, the abbot and the informer left the sanctuary and went down to the crypt to see what was going on. Sure enough, there was the little monk doing his tumbling act before the statue of the Virgin. The informer was by this time shaking with outrage, but the abbot held him back and continued to watch. When the tumbling was over, M'Lady the Holy Virgin came down off the pedestal, held out her hand, and blessed the small monk for what he had done.

The abbot turned to the informer and said, "More real worship goes on here than takes place upstairs."

It is told that the tumbler later became the next abbot of the monastery, ushering in a golden age.

This story helps me to understand that if I write with a fountain pen containing only water, that is enough. While the human, practical side of me has a hard time relating to this dream, I have grown rather fond of that simple yet elegant image: writing with the ink that leaves no trace. It speaks to me of performing every act as a sacrifice.

Whatever the purpose of my recent death dreams, their effect has been to leave me intensely happy and satisfied for months, and this is a gift that I do not take lightly. My visions and my dreams tell me that death is a happy experience, and I am convinced of that. There was a time when the biggest fear in death for me was the loss of my friends, but now that I have had the circle of friends dream, even this prospect has lost its sting. These dreams seem to be saying that not only is death a natural occurrence, it is a valuable and meaningful experience in which I am linked with those people who are dearest to me. What a happy thought!

~

I HAVE TALKED THROUGHOUT THIS BOOK of slender threads and the need to balance heaven and earth, but I must admit that my capacity to hold the splendor and the glory of that experience has varied enormously at different times throughout my life. It's tempting to talk about golden light and ineffable glory when one is thinking of heaven, but this is literalizing the Golden World too much. I can say that gradually the two worlds—the Golden World and the earthly world—have come to coincide in me. I will argue against those who talk of heaven as the next world. It is more accurate to say that we all are in heaven right now, and we are all in hell right now. The difference in our experience has to do with each person's capacity of perception.

At present, my friends have become the strongest expression to me of the Golden World. In the circle of friends dream, as the mountains are dissolving away, I am instructed to put my hands on the shoulders of my friends and make a circle. You will recall that this is the second time it has been revealed that the form of a circle would save or transform me. In the dream of the snake and the three Buddhas, the huge, archetypal dream that I once told Dr. Jung, I was running desperately from a giant snake; it was my making a circle for the snake with my arm that led to transformation. In this more recent dream, as I face the end of the world it becomes clear to me that making a circle with my friends is the will of God. I have one act of volition open to me; I can choose to accept or reject the will of God. I know that I must affirm it. I am sobered by the Catholic doctrine that one has free will only to do—or not do—the will of God. This seems small choice in life, but the subject is so vast that it overwhelms every other consideration.

In a larger sense, this is the business of any artist—and we all are artists of life—to give form to the will of God. Everyone needs to ask how he or she can make a container to hold the splendor of God within life. It is up to each of us to create this form. No matter how poor a household I visited during my years in India, there always was a small corner that was designated as a holy place; even those people who lived on the street and had few possessions always had a tiny altar to honor the gods and to remind them that this is our earthly task.

I once asked my learned Brahmin friend in India, Simanta Chatterjee, if he had ever been in the presence of an enlightened man. He refused to answer.

"This is an issue of life and death for me, Simanta, and I must know," I insisted.

Again, I was greeted only with silence, but I was like a bulldog who wouldn't let go.

"Does it exist only in the collective unconscious? Does it ever exist on the face of the earth? Have you ever been in the presence of an enlightened being?"

Finally he responded, "Once."

I nearly stood straight up. "Who was this person?" I asked.

"You," he said, and I was so shocked that we never talked about the subject ever again.

I don't share this exchange as proof of my wisdom; on the contrary, it is an act of humility. What I think Simanta was trying to tell me is that every one of us is an enlightened being. It is not necessary to go dashing across the world to sit at the feet of Sri Aurobindo, Sai Baba, or anyone else. To do so is to miss the point entirely. Enlightenment is simply being, the act or fact of being a human with consciousness that you are following the will of God. Nearly everyone gets a taste of this through romantic love. When you love someone, some part of you knows that the other person is just an ordinary human being, but in your heart you know something else is also true—the beloved puts us in contact with heaven. What the sages and prophets tell us is that this experience doesn't have to be located in just one person. Now, approaching my seventy-sixth year, I go walking down a street and I am sometimes bowled over by the beauty of some person or some simple thing. I have to stop and catch my breath. This comes with a ripeness of consciousness, a growing capacity to see the Golden World frequently.

Not long ago I had another fascinating dream:

I am backstage at a concert hall in ordinary dress. Suddenly someone opens a door onto the stage and thrusts me through it. I find myself on a brightly lit stage with an organ console ready for a concert. Music is on the stand, and a huge audience of people is applauding for me. Everything is set for a concert, but I don't know what to do. Thoughts race through my mind: I am not prepared to play; should I announce to the people that it is a big misunderstanding? The atmosphere is full of expectation. I walk to the music rack of the organ and see that it is filled with compositions I have played at various times in my life. But I have not practiced! Perhaps I could bluff my way through it. Then suddenly I know what to do. I sit down at the organ console, but I do not touch the keys. There is no audible sound, but I look at the music score and hear the music, and the audience hears it, too. I play the whole concert in this manner, never touching a key. At the beginning of the concert the audience is hearing the music because I hear it, but by the end I realize that they hear the music as if direct from heaven, and they no longer need me as intermediary. The concert ends; I bow and walk off stage.

This seems to be one more in a series of death dreams. As the dream suggests, I am ready to leave the stage. I do not fear death, as I see it as being akin to a dewdrop falling back into the sea. Unlike most people, I have identified with the sea rather than the dewdrop for most of my life. In India the word for death is *liberation,* and a funeral there is a celebration. More then anything else, this dream tells me that it is in the most subtle, undisplayed way that the divine music may be presented.

~

DURING MY LAST TRIP to India I witnessed a remarkable funeral of a man who was one of my rickshaw drivers in Pondicherry. I awoke early one morning to hear a great wailing down on the street and the sound of a single drum beating a slow rhythm. I looked over the edge and saw a knot of rickshaw drivers gathered around the bit of sidewalk "owned" by the driver who was lying there dead. He had died in the night, without warning, and his family was making the most dreadful wailing. Never have I been faced with the paradox of India more directly than in hearing this wail of despair and the funeral preparations which are the joyful departure of a soul and the celebration of his liberation. I walked by, shy, trying to think what would be good manners and what would be evasion and coming up with my best/worst English understatement.

When I came back from breakfast, the funeral arrangements were being organized and the body was on a bier made of coconut palm leaves piled high with flowers. The rickshaw community of that street is close-knit and mostly family related; they were all there, each doing his or her part of the funeral arrangements. They saw me coming and drew me into the family circle, asking for money to get the things they needed and for me to take pictures of the dead one so they could keep him in their shrine forever. Every Hindu house has a shrine; it may be an elaborate room in a wealthy house never used except for a puja or a few square inches of the six square feet of sidewalk that was this man's home. So I dropped my shyness and was drawn into the endless flood of tradition and ceremony that constitutes an Indian funeral.

Several drummers came and alternated their brazen noise as relatives and friends danced the funeral dances. Even the two orphans were dancing the strange explosive steps that seem to fling any part of the body that can be extended out into space, to be balanced by another part of the body convulsively moving in the opposite direction. The lepers and elephantiasis victims on the street were doing their version of this ecstatic wild dance. Only the widow refrained from the dance, and she kept up her screaming wail and rending of her garments. The heads of the widow and orphans had been shaved, and a special caste mark had been put on the foreheads and chests of the two children.

One of the strangest customs for this Westerner to absorb prompted me to ask, "But why have they put sunglasses on the dead man?"

"Oh, Sahib, it is very bright in heaven and he could not see his way without sunglasses," I was told. I had to go lean on a wall for a while to contemplate the questions in my mind: Will someone think to put sunglasses on me when I die? Will it be that bright? Isn't the idea silly? No, it is *not* silly! How do they know? Where does ceremony stop and fact begin? Who can know? I had to wrench myself away from the wall and get busy with something else to keep from drowning in an abyss of unanswerable questions.

The widow was shorn of all her ornaments (perhaps a dollar's worth of finger rings, toe rings, a cheap necklace), for she may never wear any ornament again as a widow; she may never marry again, may never again wear any cloth but white, and is doomed to what is nicknamed the "White Death" in India. It was not all that long ago when she would have been put on her husband's funeral pyre and burned with him.

The drums and the dancing went on all day long. It was the liberation day for the man, and everyone except the widow was celebrating the joy of it. Even the two orphans were dancing, though tomorrow would begin the uncertainty of their lives. But I had to lean on a wall again to ask, What certainty had they to lose? The next famine or epidemic would take them over the edge of certainty; their father's death was but the disguise of the hand of fate.

At 5 P.M. the body (sunglasses now replaced with two coins) was lifted onto a wooden bier and was carried off to the burning ground. I had gathered enough intelligence to tell both my number one and number two rickshaw drivers they had no more duties that day and should take their friend to the burning ground. As they left to walk the dead (liberated) man to the burning ghat, I felt unbearably lonely and out of it all. Here I was in my luxury and with the safety of a thick wallet, but I had nothing of the safety or community of those people. Who was the deprived one? Who was the lucky one? Who belonged to whom? Since that emotion-charged experience, which I recounted many times to friends after returning home to the United States, I have had more than one offer to put the sunglasses on my body at the appropriate time, which pleases me immensely.

~

OLD AGE HAS BEEN the best time in my life, a reality that no one ever predicted or told me about. Without question, these are the happiest days, and I feel slightly guilty about that happiness. For most of my life I was so weighed down with meaninglessness and loneliness that the contrast now is remarkable. One reason for this happiness may be that I am more likely to follow the will of God because I have so much less energy to resist it. I don't have the surfeit of energy that Isak Dinesen says is the first occasion of happiness. It also is possible that an introvert like me has the psychic structure to be more at home during the second half of life. As physical activity decreases, one is forced to drift into the inner world in old age, and this is a territory in which the introvert is likely to feel quite at home. I am aware each year of my energy decreasing, I speak more slowly these days, and I simply lack the energy to do everything I might like to do in a day. This slowing down may be quite frightening to extroverts, who thrive on the stimulation of the external world.

As I reflect on the present time being the end of an era, it is difficult for me to imagine what the next millennium will bring. On a psychological level, I see signs of what could herald a major change in the collective unconscious. The symbol of "up" that has been dominant in nearly all recorded history seems to be changing. In common sense, nearly everyone in modern society believes that up is good. We all want to have an "up" day, we believe that heaven is "up there," the abode of the "man upstairs." Similarly, if you are getting anywhere in life it is always up, such as climbing the corporate ladder, ascending to the heights of popularity. But I have a sense that this attachment to up may be changing in the next century.

Virtually all the good dreams I hear from patients lately seem to be "down" dreams. Downward can also be a holy move, a desirable direction. For example, I encounter dreams in which someone enters a cave, goes down a mine shaft, falls down a well, or in some other way moves downward. One man I saw recently had a dream in which he was walking on the street when a downpour began and he was washed by the deluge into a sewer—an image that is about as down as you can get. When he finally landed he was in a holy place, and the Virgin Mary was there. I wonder if only a modern consciousness would carry such imagery. This may be a turning to the opposite, by which down becomes desirable. If this is true—it's too soon to tell—then we have a lot to learn about downward movement.

Until the industrial revolution most people lived close to the earth, submerged in the earthy side of life. People lived off the land, they walked to wherever they were going if they traveled at all, they pulled water up out of the earth in buckets. Since people were bound to the earth, the holy movement needed to make them whole was upward movement of thought and abstraction. This upward movement was built into our language and customs. The place up away from the earth became equated with good; cities competed to see who could have the tallest skyscraper, nations competed to see who could go the farthest into space. For decades now, people have looked for artificial ways to "get high" and escape the earthy bounds of their lives. But what if we have escaped so much from the earth that our psychic need is now reversed? We hardly ever set foot on soil these days. People must discipline themselves to run just for exercise. It is conceivable that what is required to round out a modern person, to help make us whole, is to incorporate the downward, earthy movement of things. This will require an entirely new ethos and mythology. New symbols may be stirring in the collective unconscious to reverse the movement that has been predominant for thousands of years.

There seems to be a wave of nostalgia for earthy things; the American collective unconscious seems to be in love with old-fashioned qualities. For example, I see people who don't need to bake returning to home-baked bread just so they can have the pleasure of dough in their hands. Urban people increasingly collect antiques and go on "primitive" vacations. Kids purchase jeans that have already been worn down or torn at the knees. I have even heard that one of the most famous New York fashion designers hired technicians to make the gates squeak at his newly constructed ranch house in the Rocky Mountains. This nostalgia for the earthy seems to be a growing hunger for Westerners who are too far removed from the earth. When I was traveling to India each year I would take with me a suitcase full of modern gadgets for my village friends there and bring back a suitcase full of old jewelry, gems, statues, and other items for my friends in America.

The rise of the feminine in our culture also may be an important step in this turn to the downward. Though the lineage of the ancient goddess religions is, for the most part, lost to us, we do know that they were much more grounded in matter and the earth. I was once at a conference when a woman confronted me at the lunch break and out of the blue said, "I understand, Mr. Johnson, that you have spoken against the ordination of women priests!"

I'm not sure where she got her information, but I thought for a moment and then replied, "Now that you mention it, I'm not sure I am in favor of women priests, but I would certainly support women priestesses."

"What would a woman priestess do?" she inquired.

"Well, I'm not sure, because that lineage has been destroyed by the patriarchy," I said, "but I have a sense that their ceremonies would take place in a crypt at midnight."

This reply reflects my belief that the feminine, earthy element must be different from the masculine, sky god quality that dominated Western thinking for centuries. Wholeness requires that we develop both aspects.

Here is yet another dream from my recent series of death dreams:

> I am in San Francisco at a great nineteenth-century hotel. It is aristocratic, dignified, and beautiful. Every detail is wonderfully tended to. A woman is with me in the dream, and she is clearly my woman. I'm not sure if she is my wife or if the hostess of the party has assigned her to me or what, but I have a clear feeling that she belongs to me. She is in her twenties and most beautiful. She is dressed in a subdued way, with no ornamentation. The cut of her gray velvet evening gown clings to her body with perfection. This woman never says a word in the dream, though she is awake and alert. We are in a small public room with a few other people, when an earthquake begins. At times the quake is so violent that the room is turned on its side. No one in the room is hurt, however, and after the quake subsides not even a vase is out of place. We all know that the rest of San Francisco—everything outside our building—has been completely leveled. We go down the stairs and out into the street. Nobody is frightened, but someone has a portable radio and they hear that Cal Tech has announced that the earthquake was a 12 on the Richter scale. We all are in awe of this. Until recently the Richter scale stopped at 10, so this means it was a

record-breaking quake. A few minutes pass, and then someone says that they have reconsidered, and it was really a 12.5 earthquake. End of dream.

When I awoke from this dream I was feeling fine, though I was a bit shocked. Although the city was destroyed, my little circle of gracefulness and aristocracy was fine. I am fascinated by the numbers 12 and 12.5 in this dream. Christ has long been associated with the number thirteen, as there were twelve apostles with him at the Last Supper. The number thirteen has been thought to be unlucky because it is so good no one can hold up to it. If we were coming close to the number thirteen it could mean the end of the world or the second coming, but again, when seen in the context of my series of dreams, I tend to think this is yet another signal of my impending death and/or a transformation.

I often wonder about what the remainder of this desperate century will bring, and I have come to the conclusion that God is out of the box. That sounds like a joke, but I mean it in all seriousness. Long ago God lived in the tabernacle, and only a priest had the key. Not only were we locked out, but God was locked in. There was safety in this arrangement. Then, somehow, the box became broken in the twentieth century, and God got out. Very few of us seem to know what to do with this desperate fact: God is loose! God is out and is now appearing everywhere. I would love to read a history book written a hundred years in the future to see what we will do with this new power. It has wonderful possibilities and dreadful consequences if it goes wrong.

～

ONE OF THE MYTHS from India that I find particularly touching and profound is the story of Sita, Shreedaman, and Nanda, an unlikely trio. It is not a happy story, but it is a deeply moving one, concerning desire, human folly, relatedness, and purpose in life. I will bring my personal story to its conclusion with this mythic story, which is called "The Transposed Heads." I am indebted to Thomas Mann for his retelling of this Hindu gem.

From the outset it is important to keep in mind that this is an interior story. Of course, it has exterior repercussions, but our story relates to the double animus in a woman (or the double anima in a man). Animus and anima, feminine and masculine forms of soul, were used by Dr. Jung to describe the personification of the masculine in a woman's unconscious and the personification of the feminine in a man's unconscious. All of us carry within us an internal soul image, an image that pulls us toward the Golden World. The problem is that in the West so many people have lost their connection to the divine world that they project this holy image exclusively upon another human being who cannot bear its weight. We call this romantic love.

What is this double soul image that is so deeply etched into the expectations of every man and woman? Every woman has built into her a double expectation or set of ideals of what a man should be. Similarly, every man carries within himself a set of images of what the ideal woman should be. Our story concerns these expectations within a woman, but a similar process takes place in every man. When a young girl is sixteen it may be the local football star who will set off her inner soul image—a big, strong guy who is a Saturday afternoon hero. Slowly, throughout a young woman's life, the animus may migrate through other stages and end up with a cultural hero, a lofty masculine ideal. But no woman—and no man—escapes being torn between ideals and expectations of the opposite sex, as our story will clearly demonstrate.

The less conscious this inner expectation is, the more totally it may come to dominate us, creating all kinds of havoc and suffering. Many people in Western culture get into a pattern of trying to marry one of these soul images, since we hunger so greatly to possess it. Inevitably, we become disillusioned, as over time it becomes clear that our human companion reflects only partial aspects of what is so deeply desired. People then have an affair or get divorced and marry someone else who constellates other aspects of their ideal. Eventually that projection, too, begins to wear thin. This is a terribly painful pattern, leaving much wreckage in its wake. The worst of this projection of a divine image on another human being is that it obscures a true human love, which, though less compelling, is far more stable and valuable than any projection could possibly be. It is my hope that the more we know of these dynamics, the more we can be free of them. So, let's turn to our story.

"The Transposed Heads" is the story of Sita, but it begins with two blood brothers: Shreedaman and Nanda. In India, this relatedness of blood brothers does not mean that they are biological brothers but rather that they have sworn lifelong friendship and have sealed this pact with the exchange of blood. There is no word in the Western language that does justice to this form of relationship; it is presumed that blood brothers will take care of each other, serving as companions to each other and safeguarding each other for the rest of their lives. If you are sick, lost, or facing misfortune, your blood brother will be called.

Shreedaman is a Brahmin, the caste of priests and teachers in India. He is so intelligent that he has a big, wonderful head atop a slight body. When you look at Shreedaman, you get the sense that his body must be tired of carrying around such a big head. In fact, he possesses the stature of a bent cucumber. Shreedaman is thinking all the time, as is the custom for Brahmins.

Shreedaman's blood brother, Nanda, is from a lower caste, and, accordingly, his body is all thick, strong, and muscle bound. He has a low brow, and he works as a goatherder. Nanda wakes up in the morning with high energy and works all day without ever becoming tired. He is the epitome of physical strength, but he possesses not much in the head. The unique thing about Nanda is that he has a lucky calf mark pattern in the hairs of his chest. It is a special configuration.

In this pair of blood brothers—a pair of opposites if ever there was one—Shreedaman provides all the sense and Nanda provides all the strength. They spend as much time together as they possibly can, and they need each other. One lives on muscle and the other on intelligence (here it is important to keep in mind that our story refers to two inner forces). If Shreedaman has an errand somewhere, then Nanda will find an excuse to tag along, and vice versa. They are like two halves of a single organism.

So one day Shreedaman is called upon to travel on some Brahmin business, and Nanda discovers simultaneously that he, too, must go to a meeting at very nearly the same location. Off they go together, departing early in the morning. Shreedaman is already tired before the day is scarcely begun, so Nanda carries all their belongings. They never quibble about this; it is just accepted that one has the muscle and the other possesses the brains.

Along the way, Shreedaman talks and talks, quoting the Upanishads and other learned books; he puts forth articulate interpretations of Hindu theology, going on and on. Nanda isn't much interested and doesn't understand most of what is said, but he enjoys just hearing Shreedaman talk. Nanda takes it upon himself to make sure that his companion doesn't wear out too badly.

It is noontime, and since the two have a lunch with them and it is growing increasingly hot, they decide to rest under a tree next to a tributary of the Ganges River. They sit down on the banks of the stream and enjoy their lunch. After eating, both men become a bit drowsy in the heat of midday. They are about to doze off when Nanda, the one who has ears for the doings of the outside world, hears something unusual. He looks about him and then whispers, "Shreedaman, wake up! It is incredible. It is not supposed to be, but a young woman is just around the bend, and she is walking down to the river to perform her daily absolutions. She surely believes that she is unseen."

One of the worst things in India is for a strange man to see or watch a young maiden undress. Shreedaman looks around the corner and spies her. Then he whispers to Nanda, "You are not supposed to look. Simply close your eyes."

Nanda says back, "But you're watching!"

"Yes, but we are not supposed to," Shreedaman says, still gazing intently.

"We must avert our eyes," Nanda insists. "It is the law." But venturing into the rudiments of theology, Nanda says, "You're always telling me that we must accept the misfortunes and hard knocks of life; well, surely we are meant to accept the nice things, too," and he continues watching.

Some part of Shreedaman knows that he should immediately stop what he is doing, but strangely he cannot think of an answer to Nanda, so the two young men continue to watch.

Sita, for it is she who has gracefully glided down to the river, is the loveliest creature imaginable. She has long, flowing black hair, a gentle curving neck, great round breasts shaped like ripe melons, a slender waist. It is Sita—doe-eyed, sloe-eyed, dove-eyed, partridge-eyed, almond-eyed, lotus-eyed—the loveliest of all the maidens.

The two young men watch spellbound as Sita disrobes herself and walks with the grace of youth and the dignity of heaven. She steps down into the water and performs her noonday absolutions, then returns to dry her body in the sun, dress, and walk back to the pathway.

The two observers are struck with silence. Nanda breaks the silence by telling Shreedaman that he has seen Sita before—more than that, he once held her in his arms! This is unthinkable in Hindu custom but is somewhat explained as Nanda's story goes on. There is a custom in old India that on the shortest day of the year the strongest youth takes the most beautiful maiden from another village and performs the ceremony of "The Enticement of the Sun." This consists of the youth tossing the maiden into the air as far as he can manage. This is an enticement to the sun to cease its withdrawal and return to make another season. If this ceremony is not performed, the sun might forget its worldly duty and continue declining, which would bring time and life to a stop. Nanda explains to Shreedaman that Nanda and Sita had been chosen for this ceremony several years earlier.

Shreedaman and Nanda were almost never quiet, but when it came time to gather up their things and continue on their journey, they were strangely silent. Presently, they had to part ways, so they said good-bye and agreed to meet back at the same place by the river three days later. Off they went to their business meetings, and they soon became lonely for each other.

Three days later, Nanda returns to the appointed meeting place. He is always the first to arrive. He has not waited long, however, when he sees Shreedaman coming down the road. Even from a distance it is clear that Shreedaman is in a terrible mood; he drags his tired body along in the dust, and his big head, which is simply too much for that frail body to hold up, sadly flops from side to side. This is not the first time that Nanda has seen this, so he shouts out to his blood brother, "Shreedaman, you look like a monkey who has just fallen from a tree. What is the matter?"

"It is too terrible," Shreedaman replies. "Please just make a funeral pyre for me. Set it to burning immediately so that I can cool my misery in the flames!"

Nanda is accustomed to such poetic utterances from the mind of his Brahmin friend, so he does not take him seriously.

"Shreedaman, what has happened to you. Are you ill?"

"Nanda, I tell you, just light the funeral pyre."

"Shreedaman, what is the matter?"

"Just light the funeral pyre, like I said."

At this, Nanda agrees to gather wood and prepare a funeral pyre, but he admonishes his friend, "I warn you, if you climb into the flames I will accompany you. I cannot conceive of living in this world without my beloved friend."

This startles Shreedaman enough to gain his attention, and his story begins slowly to unfold. "It is simply too much, Nanda, I can't stand it. I have fallen in love with Sita, and I can't live without her. Just get the funeral pyre going."

"Oh, that is all it is," replies Nanda. "There is an easier way of coping with that than a funeral pyre. If you like Sita that much, I will go play intermediary, court her, and win her for your wife."

When courting in traditional India, it has long been the custom that a man never goes on his own behalf. To do so would be a terrible breach of custom. The proper approach is to send an intermediary, preferably someone who can sing well and who knows how to perform as a desirable suitor. All the preliminaries of courtship are carried out by this intermediary.

"What's the point?" asks Shreedaman. "She would never have me."

"How can you think that?" says Nanda. "You are a Brahmin and the most eligible bachelor in the land. You are handsome, you have a good reputation, lots of money. I'm sure her parents would jump at you in a minute."

In due course, Nanda convinces Shreedaman of the possibilities of this courtship. Nanda then goes off to do all the courtship formalities, and Sita's parents refuse them all, as is good manners during the first several weeks. This is proof of the young woman's virtue. It is not until Shreedaman's parents approach them that Sita's parents agree and the long formalities of courtship begin. An astrologer is hired, who puts the two charts together, then gives his approval. One parent takes a gift to the second set of parents, then the astrologer is brought forth, and, if all goes well, a date is set for the wedding. An Indian wedding is five days and five nights of ceremony and celebration. Garlands of flowers are placed around the heads of the bride and groom, and they are led around the village in triumph.

Ideally, a bride and groom should never see each other until the end of the wedding, or it is a terrible breach of custom. At the end of the fifth day, the groom meets the bride, and they walk together seven times around the camphor fire. Only then do the attendants take the abundant flowers away from the face of both bride and groom, and they look at each other for the first time. But in this story, the bride saw her husband for the first time while the husband saw his bride for the *second* time. This bodes ill fortune and foretells a dark time ahead.

Shreedaman is delighted with Sita, and he hides the fact that he already knows her beautiful face. Nanda is delighted to see his friend Shreedaman so happy. Sita, too, is happy. Nanda and Shreedaman have been together for most of their lives, and Shreedaman cannot even think of leaving his friend, so all three depart the marriage celebration together and set up a household.

It pains me to tell what happens next. After several weeks of happiness, Sita somehow loses custody of her eyes. Her eyes keep drifting to peruse the fine, muscle-bound body of Nanda, most particularly that lucky calf mark on his chest hair. Her husband, Shreedaman, talks all day of virtue and great wisdom, and she loves him deeply, but still Sita cannot keep her eyes off Nanda.

Some might say that you could expect such a disaster considering the fact that the laws of marriage were broken from the very beginning. Shreedaman had seen Sita prior to the fifth day of the marriage celebration. It isn't long before relations begin getting very tense among the three parties in the household. Shreedaman is so intensely involved in his intellectual pursuits that he does not notice how acutely unhappy Nanda has become. And soon the guilt-stricken Nanda will not even look at his blood brother. A tornado of energy begins to build.

As anyone knows, if things are going badly, the first thing to do is to tell the neighbors and family how well things are going. Everyone in the village is told how fine things are in the new household. In fact, the trio decides to reveal to Sita's parents that a baby is on the way, for, indeed, Sita has become pregnant. They set out to the house of Sita's parents with Shreedaman and Sita sitting in the back of the dromedary cart and Nanda in the driver's seat.

Now, when you are lost on the inside, it doesn't take long before you become equally lost on the outside. Soon Nanda takes a wrong turn, and by nightfall they are off on a little road that comes to a stop in the middle of the forest. It is getting dark, and there is nothing more to do. They spend a miserable night in the forest, bitten by mosquitoes and bugs and beset by lack of sleep. Sita is unhappy. Shreedaman is unhappy. Nanda is unhappy. No one ventures to say a word, but when dawn comes up they can see that they are stranded near a temple. It is a temple dedicated to Kali, the personified nightmare of Lord Vishnu. She is the most horrible of the many gods and goddesses in India. She has snakes for hair, fangs like a canine, eighteen arms—all holding something terrible—and she wears human intestines and skulls for necklaces.

Shreedaman announces, "Before we backtrack, give me five minutes to say my prayers to the goddess Kali." He goes into the temple, and by this time Shreedaman is so in despair that for once in his life he is speechless. He realizes that he was the one who set all this trouble into motion by not averting his eyes from Sita at the river. Shreedaman confesses to Kali, "There is only one thing left for me to do in this world, and that is to add my blood in sacrifice to the goddess." Pulling out the knife that he wears on his belt, he severs his own head with one swift blow.

It is a terrible scene. Shreedaman is lying there, blood gushing forth from his severed neck, the goddess Kali surveying the carnage. Meanwhile, Sita and Nanda remain seated outside in the cart, both suffering from acute embarrassment over their mutual attraction. They don't dare look at each other.

Finally, Sita grows tired of waiting and declares, "That husband of mine! He has probably gone into a trance state and will be in there until noon meditating and thinking nothing about us. Nanda, go in and get him!"

Nanda goes into the temple and beholds the terrible sight of his beloved Shreedaman lying there with blood coursing from the severed head. Nanda, who was never given to thought, snatches the knife from Shreedaman's hand and cuts off his own head. If Shreedaman has poured forth his blood before the goddess, it is enough for Nanda to do the same.

Sita continues to wait outside. She waits and waits and waits, until she loses her temper again. "Those two boys are probably sitting in there talking and forgetting about me entirely!" She jumps out of the cart and goes into the Kali temple, where she sees the most horrible sight imaginable. Her widowhood flashes before her, and not only does she witness Shreedaman's body, she also sees her beloved Nanda lying in a pool of blood. There is nothing in the world to give her solace or comfort. She goes out to clear her eyes and reenters to make sure she has seen correctly. Then she staggers out of the Kali temple, grasps a vine hanging down from a banyan tree, ties it around her neck, and is about to hang herself. At that instant, the voice of Kali comes out from the temple.

"Sita!"

She freezes, for the goddess has spoken. The goddess gets up from her throne and walks out of the temple to address Sita. "Do you know why all of this has happened? It is completely your fault.

I put judgment upon you for the worst possible punishment, and that is that you may not die; you must live."

The men were at fault for being voyeurs, but Sita was at fault for wishing to change her husband's character or physical appearance. All three were engaged in a consciousness much too narrow for the magnitude of their relationship.

Sita falls to her knees, washing the feet of Kali with her tears and imploring the goddess to hear her pleas. Then she thinks of a ploy that might soften the heart of even the terrible stone goddess. "There is another life to take into consideration," Sita says, "for I am bearing a child. Please, can't you repair all of this?"

Kali is so touched by this that she replies, "I think that you are truly sorry in a genuine way. Go into the temple and put the heads back on the two young men. If you do it quickly enough, and with genuine contrition, then they will live and you will be forgiven for your sins. But, mind you, be sure to get the heads on facing the right direction or the men will be the laughingstock of their village."

So Sita, hardly believing, goes into the Kali temple and picks up a grisly head and places it onto a body. It comes back to life! Having seen a miracle once, she takes up the other bloody head and puts it on the other body, and it too comes to life! In a few minutes, three people stagger out of the darkness of the Kali temple, delirious with life as is possible only when one has faced death. They are laughing and singing as never before. They dance and dance and dance. Guilt has been assuaged and life restored. They are safe and together, and everyone is happy.

But now the greatest shock ensues. Shreedaman says to Nanda, "Take your hands off my wife!"

"What are you talking about?" replies Nanda.

They set to quarreling, and it takes some time before they realize what has happened: Sita has put Shreedaman's head on Nanda's body and Nanda's head on Shreedaman's body! When Sita sees what she has done she feels considerable guilt, but then she laughs delightedly, for now she has the best of all worlds, a fine head atop an equally fine body. Then all three fall completely silent.

Shreedaman's head with Nanda's body says, "I tell you, that is my wife! Get your hands off her."

And Nanda's head with Shreedaman's body replies, "Well, who slept with her on the wedding night—you or me?"

"But who said the marriage vows?" asks Shreedaman's head with Nanda's body.

"Well, who's the father of the child within her?" replies Nanda's head with Shreedaman's body.

They argue back and forth like this until they came to a complete stalemate. India knows what to do when you run into an insoluble problem—find the nearest holy man and put the matter to him, accepting his word as absolute law. So they all get in the dromedary cart, and off they go to find a holy man. The journey takes three days, but they find a holy man beside the Ganges River. It seems that at some earlier time Nanda had approached this very holy man and had poured out his anguish that he was simply a bunch of muscles; he had told the holy man that he longed to be more spiritual, and the holy man had given him a set of exercises to help spiritualize himself. The holy man sees Nanda's head with Shreedaman's body approaching and cries out, "Oh, you see the yoga has worked! See how slender your body has become. See how ascetic you are now!"

But Nanda with Shreedaman's body is not at all pleased by this, so the holy man inquires if something else is wrong. They pour out the dreadful story, and in the end the holy man is holding his head in pain. "You have given me such a headache," he tells the trio. "Go away and come back in three days, as I must meditate upon this matter."

They return at the end of three days, and the holy man says, "It has cost me all of the meditative power I have, but the answer is quite clear: the head is dominant over the body. So Shreedaman's head, even with Nanda's body, is the rightful husband of Sita. The couple must go home. Nanda with Shreedaman's body, you stay here with me and do your asceticism. You once asked me for a spiritual life, and now you have the proper body to do it."

So Shreedaman with Nanda's body and Sita go home to reestablish their lives. Things go well for a while. Sita is happy, as she now has a husband with a good head and a good body. In time, however, things begin to change. The head is so dominant over the human organism that soon Sita can see that Shreedaman's head is shrinking down Nanda's beautiful body. In only a few short weeks it is looking just like Shreedaman's body again, and Sita is in despair to find that she is back where she had started.

Soon after that, Sita's baby is born, a son who is named Samadhi. In the moments after birth Sita is in terror. It is well known in India that if a mother is thinking of a man other than her husband at the time of conception, the child will be born blind. So Sita holds up the baby as soon as possible and is relieved to see that he is not blind. But still Sita cannot control herself; she is intent upon going back to the river where the holy man lives to see Nanda with Shreedaman's body. She has to find out if he has transformed his body back into Nanda's beautiful body with the lucky calf mark on the chest.

So early one morning Sita hitches up the dromedary cart and sets out with her baby son, Samadhi, in her arms. Shreedaman-with-Nanda's-body-grown-increasingly-Shreedaman-like awakes at dawn and knows immediately where his wife has gone. He borrows a dromedary cart and follows his wife. He arrives a day later than Sita and peers into the hut, only to find Sita in the arms of Nanda-with-Shreedaman's-body-grown-increasingly-Nanda-like. Lest my readers be distressed at this, I must point out that it is Shreedaman's body who is embracing Sita, so no dharma is being destroyed by this apparent breaking of the law.

Shreedaman-with-Nanda's-body-grown-increasingly-Shreedaman-like realizes he has come to the end of his life, and he quietly walks down to the Ganges River, where he sits down to meditate. Soon Sita and Nanda-with-Shreedaman's-body-grown-increasingly-Nanda-like awake, and, without a word, the three of them join in a circle, a circle of friends that is reminiscent of the time that they danced together before the Kali temple. They stand in absolute silence and realize that they have come to the end of their human resources. There is no place else to go. They stand mute for a long time and watch the sun rise. Each understands that nothing that causes another pain is worth the having; nothing that diminishes another is of any value; nothing that is won at the expense of another is workable; no happiness that causes another loss is worthy.

Finally, Sita breaks the silence and instructs Nanda-with-Shree-daman's-body-grown-increasingly-Nanda-like to go gather wood for a funeral pyre. This is a relief to him, and he does exactly as she instructs. The funeral pyre is built, and Sita, the loveliest of all young women, Sita of the black hair, the moon face, the slender neck, the great round breasts—doe-eyed, sloe-eyed, dove-eyed, partridge-eyed, almond-eyed, lotus-eyed Sita—ascends the funeral pyre and sits down upon it. Then Shreedaman-with-Nanda's-body-grown-increasingly-Shreedaman-like joins her on the funeral pyre and sits at her right hand, and Nanda-with-Shreedaman's-body-grown-increasingly-Nanda-like joins them at Sita's left hand.

Samadhi lights the funeral pyre, and so concentrated are these three individuals that not one sound issues forth from them. The funeral pyre burns for twenty-four hours, as is the custom, and a Dom, from the caste of funeral attendants, sweeps the ashes into the Ganges River.

Samadhi, the boy left by Sita, is given to a temple widow to be raised until the age of twelve; at that time he is to be turned over to the Brahmins for instruction. It is told that by the age of twenty-one Samadhi was incredibly wise and had a beautiful body, including a fine Brahmin's head, sleek muscles, and an unmistakable lucky calf mark on the hairs of his chest. So fine was Samadhi that the king of Benares employed him to be the court reader for the palace, and he led a long and illustrious life.

THE STORY "THE TRANSPOSED HEADS" instructs us on the dangers of projecting the soul image, called the animus in a woman or the anima in a man, into the human world. We try everything in the world, except the right thing, to possess this divine image. The story

tells us that the solution is to gather up these split images, along with the ego, and put them on a funeral pyre. This must not be taken literally. It is a prescription, not for suicide but rather for the burning up of one's animus or anima illusions.

In our story, a young boy survives; his name is Samadhi, which in Sanskrit means peace, joy, and tranquillity. He has the best characteristics of the three main characters—the grace of Sita, the Brahmin head of Shreedaman, and the fine inexhaustible body of Nanda. That is the experience of samadhi. Samadhi is the sum total of the three—the ego plus both sides of the soul image—incorporated into a fourth to provide a new unity of consciousness.

If you can consent to the funeral pyre in the proper way, then the duality that makes such a shambles of both our inner and outer lives can be brought to a unity. Some part of Shreedaman, the Brahmin, knew immediately that a funeral pyre was called for when he first gazed upon Sita. Connecting with the divine image called for a sacrifice, and this might have provided a solution early on, but no youth ever seems to realize this truth.

A false way of dealing with the struggle is depicted midway in our story, when the two young men cut their own heads off. This is akin to giving up the struggle. It only leads to more confusion and suffering. Transposing of heads is a false transformation, a clever trick to get both of a pair of opposites. Only a true synthesis can bridge these apparently irreducible opposites in our nature.

It is only later, when the funeral pyre can properly be built, that the unitive experience is possible. A funeral pyre is necessary for burning up the old form of consciousness. As long as you think in terms of this one or that one, then you are still caught up in the world of duality. But if you can stand to live in paradox long enough, then a transformation takes place and a new consciousness is born—a child called Samadhi. This occurs when one has stopped trying to maneuver external reality so that it will work out as the ego desires. One turns authority over to something greater than oneself; the ego is sacrificed to the Self, the earthly world serves the heavenly world, and one learns, at last, to trust the slender threads.